T0330410

Islamic Banking and Finance in the European Union

STUDIES IN ISLAMIC FINANCE, ACCOUNTING AND GOVERNANCE

Series Editor: Mervyn K. Lewis, *Professor of Banking and Finance, South Australia and Fellow, Academy of the Social Sciences, Australia*

There is a considerable and growing interest both in Muslim countries and in the West surrounding Islamic finance and the Islamic position on accounting and governance. This important new series is designed to enhance understanding of these disciplines and shape the development of thinking about the theory and practice of Islamic finance, accounting and governance.

Edited by one of the leading writers in the field, the series aims to bring together both Muslim and non-Muslim authors and to present a distinctive East–West perspective on these topics. Rigorous and authoritative, it will provide a focal point for new studies that seek to analyse, interpret and resolve issues in finance, accounting and governance with reference to the methodology of Islam.

Islamic Banking and Finance in the European Union

A Challenge

Edited by

M. Fahim Khan

Chairman, Riphah Centre of Islamic Business, Riphah International University, Islamabad, Pakistan

Mario Porzio

Professor of Banking Law, University of Naples 'Federico II', Italy

STUDIES IN ISLAMIC FINANCE, ACCOUNTING AND GOVERNANCE

Edward Elgar

Cheltenham, UK • Northampton, MA, USA

Published by
Edward Elgar Publishing Limited
The Lypiatts
15 Lansdown Road
Cheltenham
Glos GL50 2JA
UK

Edward Elgar Publishing, Inc.
William Pratt House
9 Dewey Court
Northampton
Massachusetts 01060
USA

A catalogue record for this book
is available from the British Library

Library of Congress Control Number: 2009938427

Mixed Sources
Product group from well-managed
forests and other controlled sources
www.fsc.org Cert no. SA-COC-1565
© 1996 Forest Stewardship Council
FSC

ISBN 978 1 84980 017 4

Printed and bound by MPG Books Group, UK

Contents

Contributors

Pietro Abbadessa, 'Cattolica del Sacro Cuore' University of Milano, Italy.

Christophe Arnaud, Comité des établissements de crédit et des entreprises d'investissement, (CECEI), Banque de France.

Valentino Cattelan, University of Siena, Italy.

Celia de Anca, Center for Diversity in Global Management IE Business School, Spain.

Luigi Donato, Bank of Italy.

Johannes Engels, BaFin, Germany.

Maria Alessandra Freni, Bank of Italy.

Gabriella Gimigliano, University of Siena, Italy.

M. Fahim Khan, Riphah Centre of Islamic Business, Riphah International University, Islamabad, Pakistan.

Elisabetta Montanaro, University of Siena, Italy.

Gian Maria Piccinelli, Second University of Napoli, Italy.

Claudio Porzio, Parthenope University of Napoli, Italy.

Mario Porzio, University of Naples 'Federico II', Italy.

Gennaro Rotondo, Second University of Napoli, Italy.

Umberto Santarelli, University of Pisa, Italy.

Vittorio Santoro, University of Siena, Italy.

Frank E. Vogel, Harvard Law School, USA.

Rodney Wilson, University of Durham, UK.

Preface

This book is a multidisciplinary volume, comprising of four parts. After a short introduction by the editors, outlining the *theme* of the book, Santarelli, a skilful scholar of legal history, deals with the common origin of Islamic and Western traditions in commercial and banking transactions, in a period in which Italian merchants and their organizations had been at the forefront of the post-medieval renaissance in trade and law (Part I).

In Part II Gian Maria Piccinelli, Frank Vogel, Muhammad Fahim Khan and the young Valentino Cattelan present the main features of Islamic banking. They raise several doubts and different questions on the future development of Islamic banking in European Union. What will the next challenges be? Will the European banking framework be a suitable context for the development of Islamic financial intermediaries? Some questions have been answered in Part III and some others in Part IV.

Part III deals with the challenges of the authorisation of Islamic banking in the European context. The first two chapters adhere to an economic approach (Claudio Porzio and Elisabetta Montanaro) and consider the profit- and loss-sharing mechanism but in different ways. The authors give a detailed analysis of Islamic banking activities, paying attention to either the profit-sharing approach and the main objectives of prudential regulation based on minimum capital requirements (Montanaro), or the profit- and loss-sharing mechanism and the current evolution of financial intermediary theory and supervision regulation (Porzio).

In the same Part, when De Anca makes a comparison between responsible investment and Islamic investment, she thinks that 'Although their history, subject matter, sources of funds, or management might differ, the responsible investment movement and the Islamic investment movement are both responses to a desire by investors to live their financial lives according to their own values'. The desire that De Anca refers to is further developed by Gimigliano, who considers whether the religious/ethical roots of Islamic banking operations might evoke different approaches from EU and US regulators. Rotondo also considers the religious/ethical root of Islamic banking as a competitive advantage in comparison with Western banks.

Part IV contains responses from four European countries (the United Kingdom, France, Germany and Italy) because the European framework has not widely enforced a full harmonization of banking and financial rules. Most of the chapters deal with the European Banking Code, according to Directive 2006/48 EC, but Part IV also follows the most recent development in European law, namely the up-to-date payment institutions (Directive 2007/64 EC).

We have invited scholars and officers from national authorities to contribute to this volume. The reader will forgive us for giving slightly more emphasis to the Italian results: this represents an acknowledgement of the great interest constantly showed by the Italian academic community since the beginning of this experience.

Muhammad Fahim Khan and Mario Porzio

Acknowledgements

The editors wish to thank the Department of *Diritto comune patrimonia-le* at the Law School of University of Naples 'Federico II' for its kind cooperation since the workshop on 'Islamic banking and the European banking law' held in 2005 and the Editrice Giuffrè (Milano), which published the proceedings in 2006.

A special mention must be made of the Islamic Research and Training Institute (IRTI), to which we gratefully acknowledge the financial support provided for the present publication.

All are grateful for the patient editing by Dr Gabriella Gimigliano, who has taken care of the manuscript since the beginning of the initiative.

Introduction

M. Fahim Khan and Mario Porzio

When the Prophet Muhammad began His war to defend poor debtors from the insatiable demands of their lenders, the Christian Church had already condemned *usurae*: any kind of interest claimed on a loan. However, since the twelfth and thirteenth centuries, economic development created pressure to remove the prohibition, and merchants – especially Italian merchants – thought up many kinds of contract to make profits from their money outside the confines of the church laws (Chapter 1). Almost the same thing happened in the Muslim world, too (Chapter 3).

In more modern times, when the needs of growing capitalism prevailed, theologians from the reformed churches (Lutheran and mostly Calvinist) felt that interest on loans was legitimate and, at the same time, in Western Europe civil law had become sharply distinct from religious rules (Castro, 2007; also Chapter 5). So the 'war' of the Christian Church ended in defeat, and the Napoleonic civil code of 1804 definitely allowed paying out interest for any type of cash loan. This code was widespread and was especially enforced in Egypt by the French army; although obviously, during the time of colonization, the European laws were valid in every country colonized.

In the frame of decolonization, the prohibition of *riba* was again under discussion in most Islamic-profile countries and the first formal attempt to put the concept of Islamic banking in practice is often reported to have taken place in Egypt – an historical joke – around 1963, when a savings bank was opened in a small town, Mit Ghamr. There is, however, evidence that suggests the basic principles and practices of some of the recent forms of Islamic finance date back to the early part of the seventh century (Euromoney Report, 1997, www.euromoney.com).

We shall call an 'Islamic bank' a financial institution which, complying with *Qur'an* and *Sunna* precepts, neither gives nor requires any interest (Chapters 2 and 3) and also chooses its investments according to ethical criteria.

Islamic banking appeared as a global reality in the early 1970s when Islamic financial institutions popped up in Geneva, Luxembourg, Dubai and Jeddah. Since then this phenomenon has showed an unprecedented growth over the global scene. Now the institutions dealing with Islamic finance exist in more than 50 countries. The total number of such institutions is more than 275 of which 54 are reported in Europe.[1] These institutions are estimated to be handling funds somewhere around $500 billion growing at a rate of more than 15 percent per annum. The emergence of these institutions is helping to bring out funds into the banking channels which were previously avoided on the grounds of the religious injunctions against interest-based banking. It is this phenomenon of capturing the money which has previously bypassed the formal financial channels that is causing the Islamic banking and finance industry to show unprecedented growth.

The historical developments which were briefly summed up at the beginning of this introduction have tried to explain why *Qur'an* proscriptions against lending with interest are not a problem in Europe. In fact, now, Western banks do not often pay interest on deposits, especially in the case of current accounts (Chapters 10 and 14).

Generally, the operations of Islamic banks are often very similar to common European banking or finance operations (Chapter 2). Islamic banking is far from problematic; indeed recently, many European bank and investment institutions have made their financial instruments compliant with Muslims' needs (Chapter 8).

Many issues may arise when an Islamic bank attempts to carry out its business in a European Union country. This is the main concern of this book.

It is not easy to say whether and how an Islamic bank may operate in European countries because of the high number of European States and market rules. It explains why single State authorities do not give the same answer to this question (we have asked French, German, British and Italian authorities).[2] However, we can try to draw some conclusions from the papers in this book (see Chapters 11–15).

First, we have to look at European Union legislation. In European countries the business of receiving deposits or other repayable funds from the public is not free, and the European Commission and the European Parliament have laid down two kinds of institutions entitled to operate in financial markets.

1.   Credit institutions (or banks). Under the European Banking Code, a credit institution is defined as 'an undertaking whose business is to receive deposits or other repayable funds from the public and to grant credit for its own account' (art. 4, Directive 2006/48 EC). Indeed, according to ancient western traditions, the obligation (duty) to 'repay the funds received' and to 'grant credit for its own account' makes

banks different from other financial intermediaries: banks bear the risk of investment of the repayable funds and their clients are always entitled to have back the funds granted.
2. Investment firms. An investment firm is defined as 'any legal person whose regular occupation or business is the provision of investment services for third parties on a professional basis' (article 4, Directive 2004/39 EC). In other words, investment firms behave as brokers and dealers in the transferable securities market.

Recently, the European Union has passed a new directive providing rules on payment institutions. A payment institution is a financial intermediary different from banks and investment firms, and been defined as 'a legal person that has been granted an authorisation (. . .) to provide and execute payment services' (Directive 2007/64 EC). But banks preserve their competitive advantages because they are authorized to perform payment and investment services under the same rules, exactly like payment institutions and investment firms.

Credit institutions and investment firms may not set up and perform their business unless they have been authorized by the national authority empowered by domestic law and, once authorized in relation to the listed activities, they are subject to the prudential supervision of a competent authority (art. 6, Directive 2006/48 EC; art. 5, Directive 2004/39 EC). The domestic authority must grant the authorization when statutory requirements are met but, as regards both of them, it refrains from granting the authorization when the management of the business, the links between the credit institution and other natural or legal persons or the suitability of shareholders or members do not fulfil a 'sound and prudent' assessment (art. 12, Directive 2000/46 and article 10, Directive 2004/39 EC).

Once authorized by the home state regulator, credit institutions and investment firms are enabled to establish their branches and to provide cross-border services in all EC Member States (the host States); they are entitled to perform the authorized activities complying with only their home statutory rules. It is the so-called principle of mutual recognition of authorization and of prudential supervision systems: the European passport.

Starting from 31 December 2007, banking activities and also, in some respects, investment firm activities have to comply with Basel 2 provisions (International Convergence of Capital Measurement and Capital Standards, Comprehensive Version, June 2006).

The principles mentioned above concern financial institutions having both their registered office and head office in the same EC country (article 11, Directive 2006/48 and article 5, Directive 2004/39 EC). While the

EC framework has not enacted any precise proscriptions on the credit institutions and the investment firms having their head office outside the European Community, it does prevent Member States from laying down any statutory regimes more favourable than those accorded to European financial institutions. Nevertheless the EU Commission carefully controls the authorizations granted to non-EU institutions and, in accordance with the directives, the Commission is allowed to reach an arrangement with third countries on the business of financial intermediaries.

Looking at the European definitions there is no doubt that Islamic banks are not banks, but if we look at every single European jurisdiction, the answer appears more doubtful and extremely complex (Chapter 14).

Although EC directives try to bring about the harmonization process of domestic legislation, even the definition of credit institutions (or banks) is not the same in each Member State. Especially in UK, German and French jurisdictions even the definition of 'bank' does not meet the European definition of 'credit institution', and their respective terms of reference are broader than the European definition (in this book, Part IV; also Cranston, 2004). Furthermore, the authorization of banking does not include the same services in all jurisdictions, and therefore in some countries the difference between bank and investment firm is hard to perceive. Moreover, the enforcement of the EU rules is very different in single European States. For example, looking at the Italian experience, the Bank of Italy, as home State regulator, frequently refers to 'sound and prudent' management rules to refuse the authorization, adding up to interesting polemics (recently, Oddo and Pons 2005).[3]

In the legal framework outlined above, a distinction may be drawn among the following hypothetical situations:

1. An Islamic bank, having its head office outside the European Community, carries out its business in the European Community Area (with or without a branch). Certainly, it needs authorization to establish its business either as a credit institution or as an investment firm from the competent authority, but we cannot easily foresee if the authorization will be granted. It depends on home Member State law and the enforcement action.
2. An Islamic bank either keeps a 'participation' or takes a 'qualifying holding'. In both of these it may have an interest either in European credit institutions or investment firms. In this case, it needs a specific authorization and the refusal of authorization can be justified not only because the 'sound and prudent' management may be at risk but also because the third country's regulations may prevent the exercise of the

supervisory function of the authority of the EC Member State (article 12, Directive 2006/48; art. 10, Directive 2004/39 EC).

3. A bank located in an EC Member State asks for authorization to take up business complying with Islamic prescriptions. In a lot of European countries, the statutory framework allows this institution to be authorized either as the bank or as the investment firm (see, in this book, Engels, Arnaud and Wilson). However, it raises two kinds of doubts:

    (a) Whether the authorized Islamic institutions were able to get a European passport and, therefore, to exercise the right of establishment and the freedom to provide services throughout the European Community: the answer depends, again, on the definition of bank set out in every jurisdiction.
    (b) How the prudential rules of Basel 2 might be enforced, allowing for the remarkable balance-sheet outline of the Islamic banks. This is the most noticeable issue (Chapter 7).

Besides the controversial issues dealing with banking and investment firm authorization, the 'sound and prudent' management control, namely the enforcement of Basel 2 rules to the Islamic banks, is an equally important issue.

There are, however, some infrastructural developments taking place in the context of the Islamic financial industry. These infrastructural developments, initiated and run collectively by countries with a substantial presence of Islamic banking and finance, aim at providing credibility and support to the Islamic banking and finance industry at the global level. The most important of these developments, perhaps, is the establishment of a body known as the Islamic Financial Services Board (IFSB) which is governed by the Central Bank Governors of countries where Islamic banking exists. The membership of the Board also includes the IMF, the World Bank and the Bank for International Settlements.

To help the regulators and supervising bodies in providing a level playing field to Islamic banks without compromising on the efficiency and ethical standards already in vogue in the national and global financial markets, the IFSB is rigorously reviewing international standards and developing standards for Islamic banks in the following areas:

*   Capital adequacy
*   Risk management
*   Corporate governance
*   Transparency and market discipline.

The Board is also in the process of developing prudential and supervising standards in these areas for the purpose of promoting best practice for the industry at the national as well as global level. These standards are meant to complement the guidelines issued by bodies such as the Basel Committee on Banking Supervision and the International Organization of Securities Commission. Besides the establishment of the Islamic Financial Services Board, the following important infrastructural developments are also worth mentioning:

1. The establishment of the International Islamic Financial Market. One of the most important elements of risk management in Islamic banks is related to liquidity management. The problem of liquidity management arises because of the fact that most available conventional instruments for liquidity management are interest-based and therefore cannot be used by Islamic banks. The absence of an Islamic money market and an Islamic inter-bank market is, therefore, a serious hurdle in the way of liquidity management. The development of the International Islamic Financial Market in Bahrain which will provide a secondary market with Islamic instruments will provide a good opportunity to Islamic banks for liquidity management.
2. The Accounting and Auditing Organization for Islamic Financial Institutions (AAOIFI), based in Bahrain, plays an important role in integrating and harmonizing the accounting and auditing practices.
3. The Islamic Rating Agency (IRA) is another infrastructural institution which gives credibility to Islamic financial institutions.

A FINAL REMARK

There is no doubt as to the positive effects of the increasing business and number of Islamic banks in the European Community on the global economic integration and on the growth of financial services on offer to Muslim people in Europe.

However, we want to underline, as many scholars have stressed, a relevant feature of Islamic bank management (see Chapter 5) that relates to the governance issue and ethical control over the Islamic banking business. Certainly, a large number of *Shari'ah* prohibitions do not agree with Western culture, but, in general, it is very important that the relevant ethics and issues of social responsibility must be taken care of, for good governance of these institutions.

The idea of ethical accountability is being increasingly emphasized within the hub US and European business and financial cultures (Buonocore,

2004; Chapter 8, this volume); referring to emerging ethical funds and ethical banks (Becchetti and Paganetto, 2003; also Chapter 9) and also to the campaigns waged worldwide against the non-ethical behaviour of banks and business entrepreneurs (Centro Nuovo Modello di Sviluppo, 2002). Such campaigns are expected to increase from the Islamic banking and finance industry bearing in mind the ethics and moral fibre of the culture that these institutions refer to as the *raison d'être* of their existence.

NOTES

1. This includes fully-fledged Islamic financial institutions as well as the conventional banks and institutions operating Islamic windows or conducting Islamic financial transactions. Source: Institute of Islamic Banking and Insurance, London. Website: http://www.islamic-banking.com/ibanking/ifi_list.php
2. It is known that there is an interesting economic, management and legal literature in the field (Porzio, 2009), but there are very few specialized studies about the issues of Islamic banking in the European legal framework.
3. At the time of writing, only the Financial Services Authority (UK) has granted authorization to an Islamic bank.

REFERENCES

Becchetti, L. and L. Paganetto (2003), *Finanza etica. Commercio equo e solidale*, Bari: Donzelli.

Buonocore, V. (2004), 'L'etica degli affari ed impresa etica', *Giurisprudenza Commerciale*, **I**, 181–92.

Castro, F. (2007), *Il Modello Islamico*, G.M. Piccinelli (ed.), Turin: Giappichelli.

Cranston, R. (2004), *Principles of Banking Law*, Oxford: Oxford University Press.

Centro Nuovo Modello di Sviluppo (2002), *Guida al risparmio consapevole*, Pisa: Centro Nuovo Modello di Sviluppo.

Oddo, G. and G. Pons (2005), *L'intrigo. Banche e risparmio nell'era Fazio*, Milan: Feltrinelli.

Porzio, C. (2009), *Banca e Finanza Islamica*, Rome: Bancaria Editrice.

PART I

Historical background

1. From the poor to the merchant

Umberto Santarelli

INTRODUCTION

When one considers the comparison between Islamic banking and European banking law, it is impossible to ignore the range of different issues which arise from the complex historical context. Indeed, the precedent in itself does not make any difference, but in every legal tradition, the origins (historical or more recent as they may be) can never been forgotten without making hermeneutical and misleading mistakes.

Going back to the origins, it is possible to trace the rationale and function (and, consequently, a coherent system of rules) of Islamic banking institutions in Europe today, whose binding rule is, according to their statutes, the proscription of usury. Indeed, such a rule seems to prevent Islamic banking institutions from performing banking activities in those legal contexts such as the European framework which seem to have released themselves not only from complying with, but even from remembering, such an ancient legal proscription.

This chapter tries to verify whether the existing legal system is consistent with the proscription regarding usury; namely, reformulating the question so as to ask whether such a proscription belongs to the genetic heritage of our (European) legal order. It might represent the preliminary issue and, if the right solution is found, the following substantial problems can be addressed in the correct way. Dealing with substantial issues entails ascertaining the uniformity of the Western legal framework with the proscription of usury, as posited above.

THE ORIGINS OF USURY

Usury has ancient origins, being rooted in a cultural experience – a real and spiritual experience – which cannot be set aside. For the civilization to which we belong, the history of this experience begins with the exodus from Egypt towards the Promised Land. Ever since then, the Israelites have seen this point as the beginning of their own identity. This is a very well known story.

The agreement which Yahweh made with His People in the desert stated clearly that

> If you lend money to one of your poor neighbours among my People, you shall not act like an extorter towards him by demanding interest from him. If you take your neighbour's cloak as a pledge, you shall return it to him before sunset. For this cloak is the only covering he has for his body. What else has he to sleep in? If he cries out to me, I will hear him; for I am compassionate. (Exodus, XXII, 24–6)

When the meaning of such a rule was reflected on, it was stated that 'You shall not demand interest from your countrymen on a loan of money or of food or of anything else on which interest is usually demanded. You may demand interest from a foreigner, but not from your Countryman' (Deuteronomy, XXIII, 19–20).

According to the Old Testament approach, those precepts, which were at the same time ethical and legal rules, draw a very precise picture of a community of poor people involved in the extremely arduous experience of the exodus. In such a context, the protection of poor people and their survival were understood to be needs, and the most severe sanctions were imposed as a deterrent and to punish every breach of the prohibition of usury.

From the beginning, the extreme state of poverty of the weak party in the contract seemed to be strictly connected with the prohibition of usury. This was the essential reason for providing the same legal measure. Not even in living conditions like those of the exodus, would the question of the merchant's position have made sense; the merchant's position did not exist. As a matter of fact, there were two homogeneous situations, therefore both of them had to match the only legal solution, which was in itself perfectly homogeneous and very severely sanctioned against (Santarelli 1998, p. 154).

After many centuries, in a historical context where *mercatura* performed a far from ancillary role which could be very risky but, at the same time, extremely profitable (for example, the caravan trade), the *Qur'an* did not forget Moses' ancient lesson. In fact, the *Qur'an* confirmed the tradition of strongly condemning a number of customs which were very common in the pre-Islamic merchants' societies such as those of Mecca and Medina at the time of the Prophet Muhammad.

The act of giving alms to Fellow Countrymen (such as were entitled to receive alms), as well as to the Poor and to the Wayfarer, was laid down as a condition for redemption 'for those who desire Allah's pleasure' [*Qur'an*, XXX, 38–9]. Hence, the *qur'anic* text maintained the general rules on the protection of Fellow Countrymen and of the Poor, and followed on the prohibition (a strictly unexceptionable prohibition) of usury as a profit, which did not find any justification apart from the undue intended enrichment – an evident infringement of the law – at the expense of the extremely weak part of the contract. Profit becomes usury whenever the reward is an unjust enrichment due to the performance of the party who claimed it (for example, when the party of the contract has made 'no further' act to legitimate the reward) (Piccinelli 1996, p. 17).

THE OLD TESTAMENT

The legal order established in the Old Testament tradition was in force throughout the Mediterranean civilization, wherever the conditions of life which had shaped it remained unchanged. The Roman legal context gives us the most precise and forceful confirmation: it – not by chance – established the *mutuum*[1] as a contract with which '*re contrahitur obligatio*' and, as a result, fungible things (*res:* gold, oil, corn, money) are given by one man to another, so as to become his but on the condition that an equal quantity of the same kind shall be restored. Therefore, the same quantity of interchangeable *res* performed a double function: setting up (*datio*) and fulfilling the obligation (*restitutio*). If the payment of both principal and interest was promised, it was to be considered a contract strictly connected with the *mutuum* as regards its performing legal function, but distinct from it in structural terms. The *mutuum* was in itself a free of charge contract, whose nature confirms that in Roman agricultural society it was no more than a legal act, likely to govern a relationship based on the rules of amicable solidarity and which compelled the task (*officium*) to satisfy the other's needs.

THE NEW TESTAMENT

The New Testament sources, consistent with the novelty of the Christian message compared with the Old Testament tradition, utterly changed the approach from how it appears in the only book dealing with the *mutuum*. The New Testament books did not intend to lay down any new rules on such a contract, as 'even sinners lend to sinners, and get back the same amount' (Luke, VI, 34), but the same books considered obligatory a completely new and different form of behaviour, 'lend expecting nothing back' (Luke, VI, 35). The New Testament refers to hope, but no legal proscription can be laid down on hope; hope never entails getting back the funds given as *mutuum* because this kind of behaviour is carried out by sinners and their accomplices (Santarelli 1989, pp. 847–53).

Considering the surprising aspect of this novelty, legal scholars refrained from drawing any conclusions on Luke's pages where he spoke of the *mutuum*. They did nothing more than, on one side, confirm in principle the ancient rule of *mutuum* as a contract without a valuable consideration and, on the other hand, deem that such a rule was to be enforced on the matter of *mutuum* (Santarelli 1998). The above-mentioned conclusion (it sounds an almost obvious one) will play a useful role later, when it will become necessary to lay down some new provisions in compliance with the essential priorities of trades.

Around the end of antiquity and the beginning of the Middle Ages there was no reason to change the legal framework of the contractual relationships mentioned above. The occasional statutory activities, which were carried out by both secular and Church power, never questioned the main features of the framework whenever, throughout the centuries, an attempt was made to rule on the different usury practices in order to fix a ceiling price on interest rates and to sanction conduct which appeared most reprehensible.

Some special rules were provided on trade activities, especially on maritime relationships: the Roman *fenus nauticum*[2] is such a case. Arangio Ruiz pointed out that this kind of agreement became widespread in the Roman legal experience but it never really belonged to the Roman culture: not only was it barely tolerated by the jurisprudence without being studied in the main treaties, but the judicial rules to apply were difficult to establish (Arangio Ruiz 1966, p. 306).[3]

Finally, it does not seem far from the truth to declare that there is no interruption between two centuries of *mutuum* regulations for the (more or less efficient) protection of the weak party of the contract. Protection was felt to be an ethically binding measure in those communities where merchants' activities were kept outside the table of values at the basis of the legal order.

AFTER THE MIDDLE AGES

Something new came about during the second millennium of the Christian era as a structural effect of the 'urban revolution' when, around the thirteenth century, the birth or the rebirth of towns and cities throughout Europe took a fresh turn in the history of European civilization, ultimately affecting the whole world (Cipolla 1974, p. 163).

In such a context, the new merchant classes imposed their own interests and were able to establish their supremacy. It followed that merchant law began to grow, being able both to distance itself from the ancient legal culture and to become an autonomous system (Santarelli 1998, pp. 57–64). This effect resulted also from the consideration, which was shared by the new legal doctrine, according to which the rules allowed traders and craftsmen to improve their jobs.[4]

In the new society, poverty did not disappear, although it was no longer its only characteristic. The poor had to be carefully defended (including from the 'insatiable demands' of the loan sharks), but the legal order of the merchants' society did not have to move only in this direction. In fact, money in the safe hands of the traders was able to produce new money without damaging third parties.

Therefore, the ancient, venerable prohibition was neither to be broken nor sidestepped (as is often stated and all too readily believed). At the same time, it could not be extended to govern contexts and relationships which could not be expected to tolerate it, when the (quite useless) enforcement of such a rule would ultimately bring about damage and significant paralysis, without benefiting the poor people who would be hard to find here.

In a mercantile society, the growing problem involved the process of redefining and reclassifying every commercial relationship in order to maintain the ancient prohibition of usury, whose effectiveness nobody questioned. That result could be reached without widening the prohibition's effects to those contexts in which the enforcement of the prohibition was not justified by the protection of the rights of the poor. Any enforcement would have been useless and would have produced irreparable damage.

Jurists were deeply involved in the process of understanding. First and foremost were the canonists, who were particularly competent. They found the historical and logical clue when they asked themselves with surprising presence of mind if a trader was a weak person.[5] If the answer was 'no' (no other answer could be imagined), it was possible to reach the conclusion that the prohibition of usury must not be applied to the mercantile juristic acts when the premise of fact, which had always represented its justification, could not be found.

This is not the forum for a more detailed analysis of the complex process through which the legal experience of the late mediaeval mercantile society was able to redraw the limits for enforcing the prohibition of usury (on such a rule nobody dared question the 'natural' limits of the protection of the poor). However, we can refer to two pertinent features. The 'new' legal solutions, matching the 'new' needs imposed by the *aequitas mercatoria*, were worked out through the rethinking of the construction of mercantile contracts. Furthermore, such a process was very consistent with the constant interpretation (the interpretation was certainly unanimous, but

– clearly – also mitigated and excessive) (Santarelli 1998, p. 165) of Luke's pages, according to which the prohibition of usury could be applied to the *mutuum* contract. If it were true, the 'new' question had very precise points: it was sufficient that the mercantile contract could not be construed as *mutuum* in order to obtain the non-application of the prohibition.

Of course, such a diagnostic procedure was meant to be simply applied to the (not secondary) interpretative ground, since the result of excluding the prohibition of usury from the law of mercantile contracts found its basis in the absence of the weak party to the contract (traditionally identified as the poor), who, as such, needed the special protection of their rights.

It must be made clear that, throughout history, it was never the intention to either break or sidestep the prohibition, which was never questioned: the issue was about the non-extension of the application of the constraint to a hitherto unknown context (the context of trading activities), in which the prohibition of usury would not have had its traditional justification.

The first type of contract to be examined was the contract made between the client and the bank to which the client entrusted his own funds. It was obviously a *mutuum*, and if it was considered as *mutuum*, it would entail the enforcement of the absolute and unexceptionable law on contracts without a valuable consideration. However, such a rule could not in fact be justified (no justification could be found in the interpretation *ad litteram* of Luke's (VI, 35), Gospel message) and, above all, the poor would have been bereft of protection. Therefore, the construction of a different contract, the 'irregular deposit' (Santarelli 1990, pp. 67–198), is the conclusion of a process which it is not necessary or possible to summarise here. This construction has survived to modern times: art. 1782 of the Italian Civil Code still covers it providing that, despite its *ex lege* denominations, the same rules provided on the *mutuum* will be enforced in this special deposit. The reasons provided in the late mediaeval mercantile society to support the above-mentioned construction can no longer be found; therefore, it is the 'extra' effects of the regulations which are still extant.

The second type of contract whose construction needs to be considered was the financing of others' trading activities. Such a contract had its origins in the distant past. One recalls the Roman *fenus nauticum*[6] as mentioned briefly above, and also the Islamic tradition which had not so very different contractual practices.

One may reflect on those events, neither negligible nor rare, which united the merchants – all of whom were 'Mediterranean' though different. Their origins and cultures were apparently heterogeneous, but they came together for trade, operating with this type of contract.

Clearly, we do not need to describe the *commenda*[7] (or whatever was defined as *commenda* in the different places and times where it was used) (Santarelli 1998, pp. 146–51, 171–87). Also in such a contract, though in a less obvious and straightforward way than in the contract which was to be constructed as 'irregular deposits', there might be a *causa mutui* (and this feature may be concurrent or even perhaps prominent). If this had happened, the absolute rule for the contract without valuable consideration would also have to be applied to such a contract (faithful to the consolidated interpretation of Luke's precept) and, accordingly, would have made the contract unfeasible. Yet, in this case the rule for contracts without valuable consideration could not benefit the poor, who were not involved in such transactions. Once again, it was necessary to interpret the contract in a different way. The different construction did not depend on rhetorical devices but on the absence of the poor to whom legal protection need be addressed, hence construction as a contract with a valuable consideration could never have made the contract unfair.

Yet such an interpretative process was not easy. In the *Naviganti* Decree (Decretal, V, 19,19 (= c. *Naviganti. X. De usuris*)) Gregorio IX, a remarkable jurist and legislator, described with great precision the *commenda*'s contractual fact in law, although He could not consider it other than as a *mutuum* in which there was a precise quantity of money lent.[8] Therefore, in the case of a contract without valuable consideration He had to state that a financier or *stans* was to be considered as one who lent at usury.

After some centuries, a non-jurist like Tommaso d'Aquino, carrying out a very sharp analysis of the economic characteristics of *commenda*, assumed that the relationship arising from such a contract seemed to perform the function of a partnership contract.[9] Therefore, an economic analysis made it possible to carry out a construction which seemed to be less coherent (as can be inferred from the reference to any types of partnership ('*quaedam societas*'), but was certainly able to stress those features of *commenda* which could not objectively be traced back to the *causa mutui*. The construction as *societas* (partnership), which was correct, as well as the construction as *mutuum* suggested in the *Naviganti* Decree, made it possible to form a contract with a valuable consideration and such a construction was essential to make the contract feasible for trading activities.

This solution was to prevail. Interpreting the Gregorian Decree, the Scholars, who were never able to express a formal dissent from the Pope's legislative choice (even though it was a disabling choice), assumed that when the contract was constructed as *mutuum*, the nature of the contract with a valuable consideration would have implied its interpretation as a usury relationship. The same conclusion could not have been reached when the same contract was constructed as a partnership. This construction rightly allowed the *Naviganti* Decree to become a classic example of *lex non recepta*.

In this case, the solution has survived longer than the reasons which initially necessitated it. It is still extant and has an effect on modern codified frameworks, even though it was created to allow a contract with a valuable consideration be consistent with the law – a contract in which the absence of the poor in need of protection made it possible to not apply even the 'holy' and unquestionable prohibition of usury. The Italian case is far from being the only example.

In a *società in accomandita* (limited partnership) whose label (*nomen iuris*) makes its origins clear, the *accomandanti* or *stantes* (limited partners) are excluded from the economic activity performed in common and, at the same time, they are liable for their own capital share. If the rule of refraining from economic activity was broken, there would follow a strict sanction, precisely as *stantes* (limited partners) would have had no more limited liability for partnership duties and would have been liable for present, past and future partnership obligations. Therefore, they would have been in the same position of *tractatores* (active partners) only as for duties.

We may wonder if such a regime of liability makes it possible to construct a relationship among stakeholders definable as a company (the regulations of a company imply the common performance of economic activity, as established under art. 2247 of the Italian Civil Code) while the limited partners can perform economic activity only '*in forza di una procura speciale per singoli affair*' (by a special proxy dealing with single acts) conferred by active partners (art. 2247 Italian Civil Code). So, it would be useful to look into the real difference (not on the formal difference, namely construction as a company) between the limited partnership and the profit-sharing agreement (Santarelli 2001, p. 207).

One thing is clear: now, within our codified framework, the current legal construction recognises a *causa societatis* both in irregular deposits and in limited partnership although the activity of financing an undertaking belongs to someone else. This conclusion can be explained, taking into consideration the need — a 'mediaeval' need – to allow financing activity with a valuable consideration.

CONCLUSION

Perhaps what seems to be, at first sight, a very difficult matching of legal systems which belong to two different and extremely distant civilisations appears, in the end, to be a comparison (far from unfeasible) to be carried out on homogeneous grounds. It is called, as Riccardo Orestano has shown, a 'complex' of the legal experience (Orestano 1987, p. 370): this way of reasoning neither denies nor forgets the internal differences and, therefore, suggests that the differences do not contradict the radical and essential unity of the whole.

The shape of our framework, which we are tempted to call 'modern' and 'European', can be recognized only if we look to the past, as it certainly did not come into being with the non-existent 'omnipotence' of the post-Enlightenment codifying 'genius'. In our legal system, the construction of the main banking operations – on the 'assets side', taking repayable funds from the public, and on the 'liabilities side', the financing of the industry system – seems to be clearly influenced by some needs connected with the 'natural limits' of usury prohibition enforcement, an age-old prohibition against which a late Middle-Ages mercantile society had to measure itself at the outset.

In different ways, but for the same reason, the main protagonists in that experience, which seems far off but is still able to represent the foundation of the existing legal order, were all the merchants trading in the Mediterranean area. They had to maintain a difficult balance with a system of ethical and legal values which was written in different, but not contradictory, terms in the books which contained the wisdom (*sapientia*) that everybody considered as revealed truth. Theirs was a long journey.

Nowadays, the descendants of those traders are meeting once again around the same sea. It would be an unforgivable mistake if they did not realise that they had already met, and if they believed they had to start from scratch to look for completely new solutions. The journey ahead is still long, and comprises none too easy steps: however, admitting their evident common origins will make the journey much less difficult if all involved seriously wish to undertake it.

NOTES

1. The *mutuum* contract might be translated as a loan for consumption, even though they do not have the same legal regime.
2. The Romans called *fenus nauticum* a type of loan in which the capital and its interest were repayable only at the final return docking of the ship, therefore the interest rates were high. We might say that the *fenus nauticum* corresponds to the bottomry loan of modern times.
3. Arangio Ruiz wrote (1966, p. 306) 'accolto in Roma per ragioni pratiche, vi rimase come un corpo estraneo, piuttosto tollerato dalla giurisprudenza anziché assoggettato al rigore della sua disciplina: nelle opere sistematiche (. . .) non trovò posto, e non si sa bene in quali forme si svolgesse la tutela giudiziaria'.
4. '*Statuta per quae providetur ipsis mercatoribus et artibus ut melius mercatura et artes exerceantur, pertinent ad statum civitatis et bonum publicum*' (Santarelli 1998 p. 60).
5. '*An mercator sit miserabilis persona*' (Piergiovanni 2005, pp. 617–34).
6. See above, note 3.
7. On the definition of *commenda*, see, in this book, Chapters 2 and 3.

8.   He wrote: '*certam mutuans pecuniae quantitatem*'.
9.   '*Per modum societatis cuiusdam*' (De Aquino, qu. LXXVIII, 2: Santarelli 1998, p. 180).

REFERENCES

Arangio Ruiz, V. (1966), *Istituzioni di diritto romano*, Naples: Jovene.
Cipolla, Carlo M. (1974), *Storia economica dell'Europa preindustriale*, Bologna: Il Mulino
De Aquino, T., *Summa Theol.*, IIa IIae, qu. LXXVIII, 2.
Orestano, R. (1987), *Introduzione allo studio del diritto romano*, Bologna: Il Mulino.
Piccinelli, Gian M. (1996), *Banche Islamiche in contesto non islamico*, Rome: Istituto per l'Oriente.
Piergiovanni, V. (1992), *Il Mercante e il Diritto canonico medievale*, in *Monumenta Iuris Canonici*, Serie C: Subsidia, (9), 619–29.
Santarelli, U. (1989), '"Senza nulla sperare" (lc., VI, 35). Storia di un'occasione perduta', in *Studi in memoria di Giovanni Ambrosetti*, Milan: Rubettino.
Santarelli, U. (1990), *La categoria dei contratti irregolari – Lezioni di storia del diritto*, Turin: Giappichelli.
Santarelli, U. (1998), *Mercanti e società tra mercanti*, Turin: Giappichelli.
Santarelli, U. (2001), 'Di certe aporie (passate presenti e future) del sistema societario', in D. Maffei (ed.), *A. Ennio Cortese*, (3), Rome: Il Cigno.

PART II

Islamic banking business

2. The provision and management of savings: the client–partner model

Gian Maria Piccinelli

INTRODUCTION

The ethical–religious character assumed today by Islamic banks, in the intent of preserving consistency with the divine precept prohibiting any kind of usury, is itself part of a common historical heritage; early Western depositories and, later on, banks were born from the same cultural hummus. The latter institutions appear only in more recent times to have 'forgotten' the ethical aspects connected to lending and, consequently, to the so-called irregular deposits.

With reference to Islam, the fundamental and constant dialectic between ethics and market had already emerged with clarity in pre-capitalist times: the historical context in which the relation between *qur'anic* prohibition of usury and the financial demands of medieval trade surfaces is that of the city of Mecca, flourishing as one of the most prosperous trade centres at the time of the Prophet, showing indeed an indisputable understanding of such demands. This specific dialectic emerges as peculiar also to the other social contexts in which the other monotheistic religions were founded and began to spread.

According to the historical accounts developed, and commonly acknowledged, by the monotheistic faiths, the first interference of divine origin into the economic field occurred at the time of the genesis, or, better, when our progenitors were removed from Eden and were prescribed to 'earn bread by the sweat of their brow', from which the duty of making profit from labour descends. From this event a (moral) question emerges concerning the method of profit-making and responsibility in the use of material goods. It is the same issue of method underlying following interventions in Exodus (XXII, 24–6) and Deuteronomy (XXIII, 19–20), in which the 'norm' prohibiting usury is determined, at a time of historical transition and suffering for the Jewish people in the flight from Egypt. In such a moment God gives pre-eminence to the logic of sharing and solidarity towards the weak and the poor. It does not appear plausible, in my view, that God may want to impose a general prohibition of wealth accumulation. The logic of solidarity completes, rather than contradicts, the logic of profit deriving from daily labour.

In conformity with the Old Testament, the *Qur'an* constantly sets usury (*riba*) against almsgiving (*sadaqa*); merely lucrative activity against solidarity; individual profit against social wellbeing. God stands with the weak in his Community and asks the wealthy to share their prosperity, establishing the obligatory duty (*zakat*) aiding orphans, widowed women, pilgrims, slaves to be redeemed, all those who commit their lives to promoting and defending the Faith.

The further (and definitive) opposition between usury and trade, as established in the second *sura* of the *Qur'an*, is particularly significant within our analysis; in the context of the Meccan market, the act of trading comes to symbolize the making of a profit by 'the sweat of the brow', and therefore in a licit manner. It is, however, in the full passage of the *sura* that the social function of free human economy, in Islam, fully emerges: 'Those who devour usury will not stand differently from one whom the Evil one by his touch Hath driven to madness. That is because they say: Trade is just like usury; whereas Allah permitteth trading (al-bay') and forbiddeth usury (al-riba)' (*Qur'an* II, 275).

Through a conjunct reading of this passage and of verse 280 of the same *sura*, laying down an invitation to leniency towards the debtor who is in trouble by remitting his debt, and thus calling for a general attitude of munificence (God uses a word with the same root as that of 'almsgiving'!), the original principles of solidarity and sharing re-emerge, not only making the prohibition of usury absolute in the case of a poor debtor, but also implying, in the specific *qur'anic* terminology, a hypothesis of debt remission.[1]

In Islam, as in the Jewish tradition, the general prevalence of *nomos* on *ethos* has not allowed legal scholars to delve into the symbolic value of usury prohibition and of the possibly implied invitation to debt remission, which would then appear as a natural appendix.

The juridical meaning of *riba* – usury – is thus consolidated in Islam, comprising in itself any kind of profit not justified by man's work, and any imbalance caused by predominance, abuse or risk occurring in trade relations. However, the debate on the actual limits of the prohibition has never ceased and practice has quickly developed autonomously, albeit in respect of the *qur'anic* precept.

The gap between theory and practice, in this specific area, emerges in the historical experience of the elaboration of a series of 'fictions' (*hiyal*) through which, following the indications of the juridical doctrine itself, it was possible to work around the strict divine prohibition. At the same time, however, a significant strengthening of associative relations between traders developed (based mostly on family relations); such partnerships worked as suitable devices for the circulation of capital with a uniform distribution of the risks involved in commercial operations at the time.

In Europe, with the progressive disappearance of the pre-capitalist concept of money as something distinct from commodity – and thus not tradable like all other goods – profit/interest owed to the creditor within a material relation of 'trade' (even if within the licit limits according to practice and to the law) comes to be recognized as a virtuous mechanism for economic growth and the development of commerce.

In Islam, on the other hand, prior to the nineteenth century – the period of codification and birth of nation states – there was no theorization of autonomous rules and regulations with respect to religious *jus commune*, whereas this autonomous character of state law has mostly meant a slavish adjustment to the civil and commercial normative models of colonial western powers. For this reason, in the latter part of the twentieth century, modern Muslim doctrine has pursued the design of an Islamic economy newly founded on a more attentive reading of the prohibition of usury (*riba*), imagining the possibility of building a 'valid alternative' (in a Muslim perspective) to the social projects founded on capitalist liberalism and on socialist statalism – an alternative founded, among other things, on the abolition of the pecuniary interest system, substituting it with a system based on profit- and risk-sharing.

Ancient associative contracts were thus recovered. This type of contract was (consciously or unconsciously) common to all traders in the Mediterranean *koiné*, itself active and in force already prior to the time of the Prophet Muhammad. These contractual instruments – such as the *mudaraba*, which already in the fifth to sixth centuries AD showed great affinity with coeval usury activity – were adopted by the Prophet, a skilled trader himself, and continue to be used by Muslims after him. The *mudaraba* is quite close to the *commenda* and such development progresses in modern European corporate law; here, however, a progressive separation takes place, with the bank reaching, at the end, complete neutrality with respect to the risks involved its clients' transactions.

On the other hand, the ideological perspective founding the Islamic bank system has deliberately included and operatively re-affirmed the client–partner model, and it has developed, around this central core, increasing competitive ability through the elaboration of specific financial products in compliance with values, principles and ethical–juridical precepts of Islam.

Here, the true challenge faced by this conference appears to emerge: that of sewing past and present through the reading and critical analysis of an 'other' experience of the bank system. The topicality of such a system, for us Europeans, does not reside only in the news of the constitution of the first Islamic institution inside a member country in the EU – the Islamic Bank of Britain – or in the emission of Islamic bonds (*sukuk*) in a German Länder. It is, rather, the ethical challenge revolving around the modern meaning of the prohibition of *riba*, re-inscribed in the light of the fundamental values of solidarity and cooperation, justice and fairness in the social and economic realms. Such values should be the bases of financial and entrepreneurial activities, both private and public; a goal pursued, also in the West, by various bank initiatives, such as ethical banks, microcredit and renewed strength in cooperative credit. This reality and a (historical) convergence has been necessarily included and underlined in the following comparative analyses.

FROM THEORY TO PRACTICE

About forty years on from the first experiment of a 'bank without interest' in Egypt (it would indeed be interesting to compare such an experiment with the rural banks and cooperative credit banks of the European tradition), the Islamic bank system has clearly based itself on the adoption of an associative relation between bank and client, thus representing an ethically licit alternative to the arithmetical calculus of interest both in giving and in taking.

Being the subject that contributes the capital to the bank, the client cannot be alien to the company, but instead becomes a 'partner', taking on the risks connected to such a position and, at the same time, gaining the right to receive possible benefits (profits) from the bank's economic activity, according to the typical pattern of profit–loss sharing which has demanded a quick and complex trial of innovative operational instruments, as well as the regulation of conventional tools.

The fundamental element in an Islamic bank is not so much the absence of interest in giving and taking (although this is a strongly distinctive aspect when compared with the Western bank experience), but rather – in theory at least – the implementation of the partnership scheme of sharing between bank and client in most transactions, both active and passive.

As emphasized above, participation in financial risk legitimizes the profit both parties gain from the use of capital, and allows human activity to prevail on the gainful automatisms of capital. In theory, this frees the contractual relation of aleatory vexing and speculative elements, guaranteeing the highest possible equality for the two parties of the contract.

It is in such a conceptual framework that the recovery of traditional types of capital and labour association must be analysed (such as *mudaraba* or *qirad*), or more typically corporate (such as *musharaka*), in which the profit shared among the partners is always the result of the activity of the enterprise, implemented with the contribution of both parties.

The profit–loss sharing model is applied to both transactions of funds and savings management, as well as to unitization. More recently, this system was extended to insurance companies, with the aim of overcoming the limits imposed by the ban on aleatory contracts (*gharar*): a system similar to traditional mutual insurance was created using *takaful* – literally 'solidarity' – contracts, in which the element of solidarity prevails on the speculative-aleatory factor.

In the Muslim tradition, the model for business is the *mudaraba*, or *qirad*, a capital and labour trade similar to limited partnership (with reference to the structure), and to joint-ventures (with reference to the effect). In the *mudaraba*, the capitalist (*rabb al-mal*) entrusts his capital (*ra's al-mal*) to an agent (*'amil or mudarib*), to be managed and employed in generally determined trade operations. The agent agrees to return the capital when the transaction is complete, along with whatever profit had been agreed upon, while keeping the remaining amount of profit as compensation for his work. The financial risk is entirely assumed by the capitalist, while the agent is not charged with any refund in case the deal fails for a cause not attributable to him.

The combination of the elements of *qard* (loan), *wakala* (mandate) and *sharika* contracts (in which *intuitus personae* prevails) is the principal reason for the success this institution has attained throughout history.

The double classification of bank deposits in the Islamic banks is a procedure in which the potential shared management of the same deposits through the *mudaraba* as a *profit–loss sharing* tool is taken into consideration.

On the one hand, we find call accounts, for which there is no participatory structure and therefore no form of profit nor, generally, any charge. Deposit accounts (*al-hisab al-jari*) and savings accounts (*hisab al-tawfir*) are classified as call accounts. The bank may use the deposit funds (on the basis of a *wakala* – a mandate by the client) and guarantees the repayment of the entire amount of money at any given moment. Although there is no compensation conventionally agreed upon, at the end of every financial year and at the bank's discretion, the clients who have opened large accounts may be rewarded through a payment in kind (*hadiyya, ikramiyya*), through small donations (*hiba*) in money, or with certain 'privileged' conditions in the access to credit (*tamwil*) for the sponsorship of small projects, or for instalment purchases of durable or instrumental goods. The Islamic bank account is not different in its structure from the non-Islamic one, except for the absence of a remuneration based on interest. This is why, much more rigidly than in other systems, clients may take out money and write out cheques only within the limits of their account or of the overdraft agreed upon. The same happens with the use of debit cards and ATM cards, while credit cards are not popular yet, due to the difficulty of accessing the international circuits based on interest-operation accounts.

The transactions involving savings accounts, on the other hand, are usually recorded on a nominal passbook (*daftar*) registered in the depositor's or the beneficiary's name. In this latter category we find investment accounts (*hisabat al-istithmar*), with a sharing structure based on *mudaraba*, which are proportionally profitable, depending on the profits the bank makes from the related funds. Another option is that of mixed savings and investment accounts. In general, these are time deposits, the typology of which may vary significantly; they may be designed for a specific investment project, or re-used by the bank for its ordinary financial activity, including investing in common *mudaraba* or *musharaka* deposits managed by the bank. In this case, it may be necessary for the depositor to sign a mandate to the bank, specifying the operations his funds may be used for. Without a specific mandate, the bank either uses the funds freely, or establishes different, specific investment funds. This specific condition is designed to guarantee a broader transparency to the management, allowing both the client and the *Shari'ah* Control Councils – or other control bodies inside or outside the banks – a strong control of the ethical–religious aspect of transactions.

Theoretically, the consequence of the general implementation of the participatory principle and the consequent idea of risk permeating the entire activity of the Islamic bank, is that no form of guarantee on the deposit is allowed, and the lack of an explicit obligation of reimbursement of the funds collected from the public may represent one of the main elements of 'incompatibility' with the European bank discipline. In this respect, a distinction is due between the protection of cost-free deposits and that relative to participation deposits. Only the latter can actually suffer losses potentially deriving from a negative sign in the bank operations balance and only if the bank's capital and reserves are insufficient for covering the losses.

With the introduction of profit–loss sharing, the distinction between deposit funds and capital belonging to the bank – directly burdened by management expenses and potential liabilities – is not erased. Under this profile Islamic banks maintain the same structure as non-Islamic credit institutions, reimbursing the deposits through capital and reserves whenever necessary. This structure is obligatory due to the fact that, notwithstanding the abolition of the capital remuneration system based on interest and the introduction of the profit-sharing mechanism, Islamic and non-Islamic banks are equally subjected to the general bank legislation in force in the legal order to which they belong and, particularly, to liquidity and reserve regulations. Moreover, a protection, albeit limited, of participation accounts is realized through diversification of investments and related risks. It is also clear that such a model may be implemented only among individuals accepting the risks connected to the activity of the institution.

One of the main problems for the Islamic banks is liquidity management, especially over the long period. In this respect, a difference must be emphasized in the function of deposits in the two systems. In most Islamic countries, the bank deposit mainly attends to the function of capitalization of savings and the guarantee of their maintenance. In Western countries, on the other hand, the bank deposit constitutes, or has constituted up until very recently, a mixed tool of investment and short-term savings. The main difficulty Islamic banks face, namely the prohibition of interest, turns into the impossibility of accessing the inter-bank market and of investing in short-term and low-risk conventional bonds, such as government bonds, with secure profit and ready liquidity.

In some Islamic countries the problem has been solved by issuing specific forms of Islamic bonds – Islamic titles emitted by government and other public administrations through the securitization (of sales and leasing transactions) of public goods. The problem of liquidity management in the short period has been reduced thanks to the increase in Islamic mutual funds, which today represent the main provision and investment means for Islamic banks: a licit alternative instrument to conventional obligations, which, as debit and interest funds, are not acceptable according to the *Shari'ah*.

On an international level, the variety of Islamic funds is quite large. About 150 Islamic funds are currently active on the national and/or international level. The general trend for such funds – over 60 per cent of the total funds – is the investment in stocks on the international, regional and national markets. This is also due to the preference for the equity investment in the light of the *qur'anic* system of *riba* and the traditional inclination towards risk-sharing forms of investment.

A number of criteria for the identification of companies operating in compliance with the Islamic precept were progressively developed. Such companies are periodically collected in national and international directories. In Malaysia, for example, the audit activity is carried out by the *Shari'ah* Control Council, part of the Securities Commission, which in turn controls stock market operations. A similar directory is used in India, commissioned here by private groups (Parsoli IBF-Net Equity). Up to 2001, an experiment in an Islamic Stock Exchange was accessible on the Internet at the IslamiQ Fund website, one of the major Islamic companies for online trading.

Since 1999 the West also has seen the emergence of stock directories containing stocks considered to be 'compatible' and listed on the international markets: the Dow Jones Islamic Market and FTSE Global Islamic Index. As the first global benchmark of investment performance for *Shari'ah* compliant equities, after 2005 the Dow Jones Islamic Market Index family expanded to include the components of 65 country-level benchmark indexes, at the beginning of 2009.

The Dow Jones Islamic Fund, created for Islamic equity funds in 2000, selects 'compatible' companies among those listed in the Dow Jones Global Equity. The criteria according to which stocks are considered compatible according to the *Shari'ah* may be summed up as follows:

1. The main activities carried out by the company in question must not be involved in any of the following fields:

    ● swine breeding and swine food production;
    ● alcohol beverage production;
    ● conventional financial services (banks, insurance companies, etc.);
    ● entertainment (gambling, betting, pornography, cinema, music, etc.);
    ● according to some, production and transformation of tobacco, or activities connected to military defence and weapon production or commerce.

2. The company balance must prove that:

    ● the total liabilities are not larger that 33 per cent of the total assets;
    ● profit from bank interests is no higher than 5 per cent of total assets and must be used for social and charitable causes;
    ● collectable credits must not exceed 45 per cent of the total assets.

With respect to the latter condition, it must be emphasized that the ratios are calculated on a venture capital basis, so that any hypothesis of interest loan is impossible in the ordinary activity.

Since 1997, the provision of Islamic investment funds has increased by an annual average of 20.5 per cent reaching a total of 1.4 trillion USD at the end of 2008 after a peak of 5 trillion USD in the first half of 2001 (*Global Investor*, June 2009). After the crisis following 9/11, a recovery is now taking place, in connection with the diversification of savings and investment services offered by Islamic institutions.

Another typology of investment funds is represented by those funds whose securities represent transactions involving material goods or assets, resulting mainly from securitization of *musharaka* and *mudaraba* contracts, or of contracts for asset financing through *ijara*/leasing, *murabaha*, *salam* and *istisna'*. *Murabaha* funds are very common, especially in connection to real estate transactions, as are the more recent *ijara* funds, or Islamic leasing, which have grown remarkably since 2002. Each of these transactions must be certified *halal* – considered licit according to the *Shari'ah*.

The Islamic mutual fund generally has a *mudaraba* structure, in which the client (*rabb al-mal*) entrusts a specialized operator (*mudarib*) with his capital (*ra's al-mal*); the operator receives a fixed part of the profit coming from the fund management. The investor is not eligible for a fixed gain, but is entitled to a *pro quota* share of profit and loss on the fund. Investment funds and accounts with the same expiry are run together as one fund, the profit of which is owned by the bank as legal tender. The profit coming from each group of funds and accounts is therefore calculated on a daily basis using the same method as that applied to the Western models of mutual and participation funds.

The conditions governing each Islamic participation account are registered in a *mudaraba* contract between the bank and each depositor participating in the fund, according to the following criteria:

- the bank agrees to keep the profit of the participation account in one single mass which will remain distinct from the bank's management profit and other profit deriving from other participation accounts with different expiry dates;
- mutual account funds will be invested according to Islamic criteria, approved and under the surveillance of the *Shari'ah* Control Council of the bank;
- management costs of an account will be charged to the bank;
- the bank receives a fixed percentage (for example 20 per cent) of the profit deriving from the investment of the fund as compensation for the administration services provided in connection to the fund.

In countries where the *mudaraba* contract is not considered a common transaction and its discipline cannot be covered by Islamic law (even through local Islamic conventions), Islamic mutual funds are governed through a trust agreement between the bank, as depository of the account, and the depositor, as beneficiary. The contract must include all obligatory provisions of the *mudaraba*, including the mandatory segregation of the depositor's funds from those of the bank. At the expiry date, the fund is liquidated and the profits deriving from the cession of equities are split among the subscribers.

Islamic banks have set up various types of interest-free bonds, intended for different transactions, the aim of which is to attract Muslim people's savings, offering clients a wide variety of options to choose from. Among such options are the so-called *takaful* certificates, which offer an 'insurance' type protection – a 'mutual insurance' following the Islamic solidarity principles – in case of death, illness or other negative events regarding the life or health of fund participants. For example, in case of death, the heirs receive the total sum that the deceased would have deposited up until the expiry date, and in addition the profit earned based on the sum that was actually deposited. *Takaful* companies, specialized in the management of such funds, are widening the range of insurance services offered, including both the civil responsibility and the credit insurance sectors.

The certificates representing participation in the mutual funds may be registered or bearer shares; the same certificates are necessarily registered shares if a *takaful* fund is associated to a *mudaraba* one. The management company in charge of the fund is responsible for the correct administration of the investment and the funds, in compliance with the principles of Islamic law and the decisions of the *Shari'ah* Control Council, with the obligation to refund the depositors in case of any financial loss due to negligence or to violation of the *mudaraba* contract. Administration expenses are charged to the *mudaraba* fund and are detracted from operating profits. Each participant's share is represented by the *mudaraba* units subscribed to, of which the initial value and number purchased with the first instalment are specified on the certificate. Profits deriving from the investment fund increase the value of the units owned by participants and are distributed according to the clauses indicated in the contract.

We must now mention the structure of so called Islamic bonds, or *sukuk*. The term *sukuk* means bond, participation certificate, and indicates tools similar to asset-backed securities. These are generally rather liquid bonds, three or six months in duration, and not marketable like bonds that can access the secondary market. Their role shows many similarities with classic obligations and, as a matter of fact, governments may resort to this type of tool too.

Malaysia was the first state to use *sukuk* – named Government Islamic Issues – based on *qard hasan* (interest-free charitable loan) offered by the citizen to the State signing of one or more bonds. The latter pays the former, at the expiry date, through a *hiba* or donation, representing the more or less fixed productivity of the bond.

Sukuk are more useful if they can be traded on the secondary market, thus becoming almost completely liquid. Certain peculiar characteristics may be underlined with regards to the trading capacity of the bonds on the Islamic financial market:

1. They cannot represent a debt (in Islam debt-selling is forbidden), as conventional bonds can; they must instead represent a property of a specific asset. Such a bond is obtained through the securization of the asset, the property of which is divided into equally valued units and incorporated in the *sukuk* certificates. The value of the *sukuk* thus remains connected to the value of the underlying asset.
2. They are issued in zero coupon and coupon versions, but the productivity is linked to the profit of the underlying asset and not to the interest rate. The performance is usually obtained by making the asset itself productive, in the ways analysed above: *ijara* or leasing, *murabaha* or profit sale, *salam* and *istisna'*.

The AAOIFI (Accounting & Auditing Organization for Islamic Financial Institutions) has so far issued standards for fourteen types of *sukuk*, the most widely spread of which in 2004 was the *ijara sukuk*, which, as the name itself indicates, is linked to assets granted in leasing through a specific account. This way, bonds are asset-based; they are tradable and provide a fixed performance exactly like our obligations (which, however, unlike *sukuk* bonds, represent debit bonds, not property rights). The *mudarib* – the management agency in charge of the transaction – administers the bonds and the underlying assets; this position, as we shall see, could rather unproblematically be covered by a conventional intermediary.

A current example comes from Germany, in the Saxon-Anhalt region, where 100 million USD were issued in *sukuk al-ijara* in 2005. The underlying asset is constituted by buildings owned by the German Ministry of Finance, sold to the Special Purpose Vehicle-*mudaraba*, manager of the transaction, for one hundred years. The SPV has re-let the buildings under a leasing contract to the Ministry for five years, at the end of which period it will decide whether or not to renew the lease. The following are the fundamental data:

●   the transaction rating has been AAA for Finch and AA for Standard & Poor's;

- the benchmark was set to one basis point above six-months Euribor;
- the SPV was registered in the Netherlands, so that the *sukuk* could be made competitive with conventional bonds, since the municipal tax in Germany would be imposed on the *sukuk* and not on the conventional bond;
- the lead manager for the transaction is Citigroup, which has worked (in co-lead) with the Kuwait Finance House, while the *Shari'ah* Board of the City Islamic Investment Bank has been in charge of auditing and certifying that the transaction is compliant with the Islamic precepts;
- the *sukuk* is listed on the Luxemburg stock exchange.

Other types of *murabaha*-, *salam*- and *istisna'*-based *sukuk* work in the same way.

The tradability of *murabaha*-based *sukuk*, however, is highly questioned on the basis of the fact that, once the asset is sold – immediately after the purchase – the property is transferred to the client and the *sukuk* comes to represent nothing else than a debt owed to the client. This is precisely the reason why the Malaysian *bay bi-thamam ajjil* (*murabaha*-based) *sukuk*, a 500 million *ringgit* (132 million USD) operation structured by the IFC (International Financial Corporation, a private branch of the International Monetary Fund), was not listed on any other Islamic market.

Also the *sukuk* linked to *salam* and *istisna'* transactions are not considered fully tradable, because the underlying assets are not determined at the moment of emission; however, in order to increase market liquidity, the *Shari'ah* councils usually accept an underlying asset corresponding to 51 per cent of the bond value, in order for the bond to be tradable on the secondary market. Every increase in bond value will then be attributable only to the increase in the asset value and not to the liquid part of the bond.

Such a limit is also set for equity fund shares, so that these can also be tradable. *Musharaka sukuk* deriving from the transformation of company assets into (property) bonds are particularly interesting. They are especially useful in the case of a project financing requiring very large monetary resources. If the company activity is to be put into operation and its assets are still largely liquid, the stock tradability is blocked until liquidity is transformed into material assets, following the proportions required.

Sukuk are therefore expanding surprisingly also among conventional clients, probably because of the higher guarantees such tools offer being connected to material assets.

Since 2003 the *sukuk* market increased from 5.7 billion USD to 43.2 billion USD in 2007 with a decline of about 40 per cent in the following year due to the global financial crisis. The first global corporate *sukuk*, the Tabreed Trust Certificate, was launched in 2004 by the IIFM (International Islamic Financial Market), holding a value of 100 million USD. The volume of transactions in 2005 amounted to 12 billion USD and 27.2 billion USD in 2006 (*Euromoney*, January 2008). This indeed paves the way for an involvement on the part of companies in the Islamic financial market, as well as for a further expansion of such a market, fuelled by the appeal it is starting to have on conventional investors.

CURRENT DEVELOPMENTS AND CONCLUSIONS

The ongoing expansion of the Islamic financial market is undoubtedly connected to its appeal to Muslim investors, deriving both from the ethical–religious conformity of its banking and financial practice, and from the possibility of contributing to the support, the recovery and the affirmation of Islamic principles in the contemporary economic context. The expansion of the Islamic bank industry is still very closely connected, however, to funds and shares coming from member states of the Gulf Cooperation Council, with a consequent strong influence on the theoretical and operational models applied.

More recently, financial companies operating in conformity with the principles of Islamic Banking have started operating in the USA and Europe. In February 2004 the Islamic Bank of Britain was founded. Such a presence in the West, though not yet significant in terms of quantity, is producing management operating models that are distinct and autonomous from the original models, in an attempt to achieve a stronger credibility at both the local and the international levels. This, I believe, could have positive consequences for those institutions operating outside the West.

In this respect, three specific matters must be taken into consideration: (1) the question of liquidity; (2) the elaboration of regulations facilitating the external control on these institutions by the central banks, while each following its own essential peculiarities; (3) the development of uniform procedures of internal control by the *Shari'ah* Control Councils (equivalent, in their functions, to ethical committees, but applying the ethical–judicial rules of the Muslim law). These issues are all closely related.

The first two issues also underlie the access of Islamic banks to a special inter-bank market that may solve the connate liquidity problems and, as a consequence, allow for a better allocation of the investment portfolio with the aim of obtaining a larger transparency of the standards of accounting and of the internal financial strategies.

Clear rules and reliable external control procedures, in compliance with the standards currently required by the national and EU regulations, may represent a solution to the international credibility crisis that, especially in the West, has weighed on Islamic finance from the beginning of the 1990s, following the bankruptcy of BCCI (Bank of Credit and Commerce International, 1991–1992) and even more so after 9/11. The effects of this process are fundamental in the long run and at the international level, as a reaction to the widespread suspicion of involvement in the financing of Islamic militant integralist movements.

Such submission to an institutional vigilance must be accompanied by an increased capacity to converge and harmonize the rules applied to the Islamic system and to carry out an internal control of the ethical–judicial compliance (with the *Shari'ah*) of bank activity. So far, except for a few cases (the Dallah al-Baraka Group in Jedda and the Central *Shari'ah* Advisory Board of the Islamic Development Bank), a large number of *Shari'ah* Boards produce sometimes diverging counselling (*fatawa*), which, especially as regards the smaller institutions, are subject to the risk of being 'polluted' by the desire of attracting clients. Moreover, the dominance of the ethical–ideological profile, aiming at consolidating sections of the market, does not appear to be accompanied by an adequate level of effective protection and transparency. Much still needs to be done in this direction. The future of Islamic banks, especially in the West, will largely depend on the overcoming of the exotic label, the 'Islamic label', which currently characterizes them as 'alternative' to conventional banks. This is a fundamental step in order to verify their actual 'competitive' capacity on the financial markets. It is certainly difficult to imagine that Islamic banks may operate without the 'Islamic' label and that they may attend to a substantially different public from the Muslim one; this must not, however, influence the common comprehensibility of their practice and the theory that underlies it. Moreover, the current discipline in privacy protection does not allow the survey of personal data regarding religious faith.

Albeit that the normative and technical differences between the two bank systems are manifest, a clear analogy is emerging between Islamic banks and those banks which, in the Italian order and in Western systems, pursue a privileged relationship with their associates and the local community: institutions such as cooperative credit banks, in which 'the wide distribution of shares among the clients has represented an effective means of customer retention' and 'an important element of economic democracy'.

The success itself of popular banks, which have increased their quota of the market notwithstanding the deep changes that have taken place in the Italian banking system, demonstrates how the cooperative model has been capable of responding to the challenges of the new market – growing, but also linking the privileged relation with partners with very high standards of operational efficiency.

In a wider convergence scope, the Islamic institutions will certainly be able to make their contribution, with their long-term experience, to the international movement of ethical banks and microcredit, in 'financial engineering' and a stronger ability to allocate resources. Islamic banks could benefit, under a normative and organizational perspective, from the strong experience accumulated by cooperative banks in the Italian and European markets and they could re-affirm the liveliness of a model that seemed to be no longer taken into consideration in the legislature reforms of the 1990s in Italy and Europe.

An objective difficulty derives from the necessary adjustment of the structures and contracts. How can the profit–loss sharing principle – in respect to depositor protection – be applied while also considering the (if only theoretical) possibility that the deposited capital is proportionally diminished in the case of loss on the part of the bank? Or, how can a complete accounting separation be carried out in the case of an Islamic service, which would then have to represent an actual Chinese wall in respect to the other activities, 'polluted' by the implementation of interest rates?

There are institutions in Italy and Europe that have rather lightly proposed – and currently still do – certain products as consistent with Islam; given the fall in interest rates at the European level, such products can be subscribed to 'without interest' and, often, without charge (such as the so-called 'zero-credit' accounts): although there is some consistency under a merely external profile, the roles of the contract and the bank structure are still tied to criteria that are ethically and judicially illegitimate according to the *Shari'ah*.

I would like to conclude with an emphasis on how the European and international future of Islamic banks (in the quality of ethically oriented institutions) mainly depends on the homogenization of current standards of transparency, operative vigilance and control (in conformity to *Shari'ah* law). I therefore wish to express my sincere hope that areas of cooperation between the two bank systems emerge, regarding all operational specificities, allowing for a re-evaluation of common values.

NOTE

1. As Bausani intentionally emphasizes in its translation of the *Qur'an* by exposing the extreme meaning underlying the 'generosity' of the creditor.

BIBLIOGRAPHY

Akram Khan, M. (2003), *Islamic Economics and Finance: A Glossary*, London: Routledge.

Amereller, F. (1995), *Hintergründe des Islamic Banking*, Berlin: Duncker & Humblot.

Ansari-pour, M.A. (1996), 'The Illegality of Taking Interest from Muslim Countries', *Arab Law Quarterly*, **XI** (3), 281–4.

Anwar, M. (2003), 'Islamicity of Banking and Modes of Islamic Banking', *Arab Law Quarterly*, **18** (1), 291–308.

Azmi, I.M. and Engku Ali, Engku R.A. (2007), 'Legal Impediments to the Collateralization of Intellectual Property in the Malaysian Dual Banking System', *Asian Journal of Comparative Law*, **2** (1), 1–34.

Bekkin, R. (2007), 'Islamic Insurance: National Features and Legal Regulation', *Arab Law Quarterly*, **21** (1), 3–34; *Arab Law Quarterly*, **21** (2), 109–34; *Arab Law Quarterly*, **21** (3), 251–68.

Buckmaster, L. (1996), *Islamic Banking, an Overview*, London: Institute of Islamic Banking and Insurance.

Crone P. (1987), *Meccan Trade and the Rise of Islam*, Princeton: Princeton University Press.

Daoualibi, M. (1953), 'La théorie de l'usure en droit musulman', in *Travaux de la semaine internationale de droit musulman*, Paris: Recueil Sirey, pp. 139–42.

Durrez, Ahmed B. (1986), 'Riba', *Islamic and Comparative Law Quarterly*, **VI** (1), 51–71.

Dylan, Ray N. (1995), *Arab Islamic Banking and the Renewal of Islamic Law*, London/Dordrecht/Boston: Graham & Trotman.

Favali, L. (2004), *Qirād Islamico, commenda medievale e strategie culturali dell'occidente*, Turin: Giappichelli.

Foster, N. (2007), 'Islamic Finance Law as an Emergent Legal System', *Arab Law Quarterly*, **21** (2), 170–88.

Hardie, A.R. and Rabooy, M. (1991), 'Risk, Piety, and the Islamic Investor', *British Journal of Middle Eastern Studies*, **18** (1), 52–66.

Iqbal, Ahmad Khan (1999), 'Developing the Country Framework for Islamic Finance', in *Third Harvard University Forum on Islamic Finance: Local Challenges, Global Opportunities*, Cambridge, MA: Harvard University Press, pp. 159–62.

Jawahitha, S., Ab Hamid, N.R. and Ishaq, M.M.M. (2003), 'Internet Banking: A Comparative Analysis of Legal and Regulatory Framework in Malaysia', *Arab Law Quarterly*, **18** (3–4), 291–308.

Kazi, Ashraf U. and Halabi, Abdel (2006), 'The Influence of Quran and Islamic Financial Transactions and Banking', *Arab Law Quarterly*, **20** (3), 321–31.

Khorshid, A. (2004), *Islamic Insurance. A Modern Approach to Islamic Banking*, London: Routledge-Curzon.

Lohlker, R. (1996), *Schari'a und Moderne: Diskussionen über Schwangerschaftsabbruch, Versicherung und Zinsen*, Stuttgart: Harrassowitz.

Moshin, S. (1995), 'Islamic Interest-Free Banking', in *Encyclopedia of Islamic Banking and Insurance*, London: Institute of Islamic Banking and Insurance.

Nomani, F. (1997), 'The Problem of Interest and Banking in Islamic Public Policy', *International Review of Comparative Public Policy*, **IX**, 277–310.

Piccinelli, Gian M. (1996), *Banche islamiche in contesto non islamico*, Rome: IPO.

Piccinelli, Gian M. (1985), 'Mudaràba', in *Digesto*, IV edizione, XI Civile.

Piccinelli, Gian M. (1988), 'Il sistema bancario islamico', *Oriente Moderno*, **LXVIII** (1), 1–164.

Qureshi, Anwar Iqbal (1948), *Islam and the Theory of Interest*, Lahore: Ashraf Publication.

Rodinson, M. (1968), *Islam and Capitalism*, London: Penguin.

Rosly, Saiful Azhar (2000), *Critical Issues on Islamic Banking and Financial Markets: Islamic Economics, Banking and Finance, Investments, Takaful and Financial Planning*, London: AuthorHouse.

Saeed, Abdullah (1996), *Islamic Banking and Interest*, Leiden/New York/Cologne: Brill.

Saleh, Nabil A. (1992), *Unlawful Gain and Legitimate Profit in Islamic Law*, London: Graham & Trotman.

Siddiqi, M.N. (1985), *Insurance in an Islamic Economy*, Leicester: The Islamic Foundation.

Taqi, Muhammad U. (1995), 'Developing an Interest-Free Economy', in *Encyclopaedia of Islamic Banking*, London: Institute of Islamic Banking and Insurance, pp. 104–8.

Vogel, Frank E. and Hayes, S. (1998), *Islamic Law and Finance. Religion, Risk and Return*, The Hague/London/Boston: Kluwer Law International.

Wichard, Johannes C. (1995), *Zwischen Markt und Moschee*, Paderbon: Ferdinand Schoeningh.

Wippel, S. (1994), *Gott, Geld und Staat*, Münster/Hamburg: Lit.

3. Islamic finance: personal and enterprise banking

Frank E. Vogel

INTRODUCTION

In this chapter I offer an introduction to the financial transactions employed in Islamic banking and finance. Also, particularly in the conclusion, I offer some observations about the Islamic banking and finance industry as a whole as viewed from the perspective of contemporary Islamic law.

I offer an introduction to Islamically-denominated transactions that explains them in terms of the Islamic legal basis for them. I believe that if one learns about the relatively few though somewhat obscure Islamic legal principles that play the dominant role in framing Islamic finance operations, then one gains a map that helps one navigate much more easily through the maze of discussions of all these transactions.

Islamic banking and finance applies a number of rules of what I shall call the 'classical' law or jurisprudence of Islam, known as *fiqh*. This is the law of the four Sunni 'schools of law' (Hanafi, Shafi'i, Maliki and Hanbali) as this law was conveyed in the authoritative manuals of these schools stemming from about the thirteenth century CE.[1] This classical law, though still largely framed by these authoritative manuals, has continued to be refined on its own terms ever since, continuing even down to today. Its principles do allow for its innovation, revision and adjustment.

Note that I shall shorten the term 'Islamic banking and finance' to the term 'Islamic finance', but still meaning to include all forms of bank in the term 'finance'.

The chapter proceeds as follows.

I start with a review of some of the revealed texts from which the rules of Islamic finance are said to derive. These are taken from the crucial Islamic legal sources – the *Qur'an* and the recorded example of the Prophet called his *Sunna*. The *Sunna* is known from collections of variably authenticated reports about the Prophet; such a report, taken individually, is called a hadith.[2] Both the *Qur'an* and the authentic *Sunna* are believed to convey literal divine truth.

After reviewing texts from revelation I shall then discuss how modern advocates of Islamic finance have chosen to interpret those texts. I note that, although a group of innovative thinkers in the novel field of 'Islamic economics' made the major early contribution, it is now traditionally trained scholars of Islamic law that have the dominant impact. Turning then to these latter scholars' discipline – classical Islamic jurisprudence or *fiqh* – I explain the interpretations *fiqh* gives to the chief revealed texts, emphasizing certain basic principles that emerge from those interpretations. These principles – though often subtle and difficult to grasp – are actually among the most important determinants of Islamic financial practice from the viewpoint of the law.[3]

Next I shall review some of the rules of particular contracts under Islamic law, choosing the contracts that are of greatest practical importance in modern Islamic finance. From among all these rules I shall focus on rules that pose practical problems for Islamic finance today, many of them dictated by the general principles we will have studied. (Note that I thus emphasize divergences from conventional practice over convergences, which certainly also exist in number.)

Finally I shall explain how modern Islamic finance has used these basic Islamic contracts to construct modern Islamic banking and financial transactions. I summarize the most important of such transactions.

The conclusion is in two parts. First, by way of a sort of indirect summing-up of the chapter's findings, it reviews some common misconceptions one hears about the Islamic law of banking and finance, even from some of those who work in the industry. Second, it ventures an overview of Islamic finance and of its future prospects from the standpoint of Islamic law.

REVIEW OF REVEALED TEXTS SHAPING THE LAW

Our first task, then, is to review the basic revealed texts on which all of Islamic finance claims to stand.

The revelation lays down a number of cardinal precepts that fundamentally shape the law on Islamic finance. Many are not surprising, and align Islamic contract law with other regimes of contract law – such as precepts that parties fulfill their agreements or not act deceptively. But two precepts constrain Islamic finance in unique ways, and understanding them is vital to grasping the rules applying to Islamic finance.

The great Andalusian jurist and philosopher Averroës or Ibn Rushd (d. 1198 CE) observed that there are four causes for the invalidity of contracts: illicitness of the subject-matter of the contract (for example, sale of alcohol or pork); something called *riba*, translated into English as 'usury'; something called *gharar*, translated into English as 'risk'; and 'terms that conduce to one of the last two or some combination of them' (Ibn Rushd 1981, 2: 123–4). In other words if we note now the unlawfulness for Muslims of engaging in transactions involving things unlawful in themselves, such as alcohol, pork, gambling and, out of excess of caution, weapons and tobacco, then we can focus on the other two precepts which need much more explanation.

Riba literally means 'increase', but in the *Qur'an* and *Sunna* it concerns various kinds of gain: gain in loans but also in other transactions where it is deemed unearned. With respect to loans, classical legal scholars were in agreement that *riba* includes any agreed benefit to the lender; loans must be gratuitous.

Gharar literally means 'risk'. It may be surprising to find that a concept besides interest or usury is critical in Islamic finance. But, actually, the prohibition on *gharar* may be even more far-reaching in its impact on the relevant laws than is the prohibition of *riba*.

I now review *qur'anic* verses and hadiths from the *Sunna*, first for *riba* and then for *gharar*.

RIBA

The *Qur'an* contains several weighty verses about *riba*. A verse revealed early in the sequence of revelation of the *Qur'an* reads 'Do not gorge yourselves on *riba*, doubling and re-doubling it' (3: 130).[4] The terms 'doubling and redoubling' are understood to refer to a type of *riba* widely practiced at the time of the Prophet, referred to as 'the *riba* of the pre-Islamic era' or 'pay or increase'. A debtor faced with the due date of his obligation would approach his creditor and ask for an extension of time; the creditor would grant it only in return for a doubling of the principal. Unfortunate debtors were forced into bankruptcy and then slavery.

A later and legally more far-reaching series of verses reads:

> Those who gorge themselves on *riba* behave but as he might behave whom Satan has confounded with his touch: for they say, 'Buying and selling [*bay*'] is but a kind of usury' – the while God has made buying and selling lawful and usury unlawful. Hence, whoever becomes aware of his Lord's admonition, and thereupon desists, may keep his past gains, and it will be for God to judge him; but as for those who return to it – they are destined for the fire, therein to abide! God deprives *riba* gains of all blessing, whereas He blesses charitable deeds with manifold increase. . . . [G]ive up all outstanding gains from *riba*, if you are

believers; for if you do it not then know that you are at war with God and His Prophet. But if you repent, then you shall be entitled to your principal: you will do no wrong, and neither will you be wronged. (2: 275-81)

These verses are interpreted as a clear prohibition of *riba*. 'Believers' give up taking usury; those who do not give it up make 'war on God and His Prophet'. This vehement prohibition is what drives anxiety over *riba* in the minds of pious Muslims.

This passage says little, however, by way of defining *riba*. One can elicit some clues. First, it declares that while *riba* may look like ordinary commerce, as just selling the use of some property, it actually is something else. Only those touched by Satan are confused by this. Second, it strongly implies that *riba* includes any gain in excess of the principal. Third, it creates an opposition between *riba* and 'charitable deeds' suggesting that *riba* may be the opposite of charity, that is, exploitation of the poor.

To turn to the Prophetic *Sunna*, surprisingly we find that legally the most significant hadiths concern sales, not loans. We shall discuss these hadiths later. The best-known (though weakly attested) provision about loans specifically is 'Every loan (*qard*) that attracts a benefit is riba'.[5]

GHARAR

Now to review verses and hadiths on *gharar* or risk, we note first that the *Qur'an* does not contain the term '*gharar*'. But the *Qur'an* prohibits gambling: 'Intoxicants, and games of chance (*maysir*) . . . are but a loathsome evil of Satan's doing: shun it, then, so that you might attain to a happy state! By means of intoxicants and games of chance Satan seeks only to sow enmity and hatred among you, and to turn you away from the remembrance of God and from prayer. Will you not, then, desist?' (5: 90–91)

It is the *Sunna* that condemns *gharar*. One hadith straightforwardly condemns the sale of *gharar*: 'The Messenger of God forbade the "sale of the pebble" [*hasah*, apparently, sale of an object chosen or determined by the throwing of a pebble], and the sale of *gharar*' (Muslim).

There are many other hadiths condemning various specific transactions that are risky or uncertain in various ways (we shall review them shortly).

As in these few examples, the relevant *qur'anic* injunctions often resonate with a moral tone but are vague in terms of the legal rules that might follow from them. *Sunna* texts very often provide more legalistic precision and detail but are more morally obscure. Since even together the *Qur'an* and *Sunna* leave a great deal unsaid, scholars need to interpret and expand on them.

TWO BASIC CONTEMPORARY APPROACHES TO THESE TEXTS OF THE *QUR'AN* AND *SUNNA*

How should modern Muslims understand and apply these texts? One way would be to make a fresh interpretation of them in the light of modern conditions. Another would be to invoke traditional interpretation, most importantly the vast body of rules of the Islamic *fiqh*. One notes an initial parting of the ways among contemporary Muslims, largely along these lines.

Many modern Muslims, seeking to reform the Islamic legal tradition to align better with modern life, choose the first path. Often we find that, to free themselves to make the necessary transformations to the law, such thinkers approach the revealed texts more as indications of ultimate moral purposes that should guide and shape law and legal behavior rather than as laws in and of themselves. This position implicitly aligns them with the idea that human reason has the role and power to discern the ultimate divine moral purposes behind revealed texts. The reformers often focus more on the *Qur'an* and less on the *Sunna* than was traditionally the case.

Such reformist thinkers offer various explanations for the *qur'anic* prohibition of *riba*. For example, a common interpretation is that the ban on interest is to prevent exploitation of the financially destitute borrower, particularly when he is seeking money for basic needs. Note that, if this were the purpose for the *riba* ban, it would rarely apply in commercial settings and bank accounts would be lawful, since in such cases if there is a weaker party it is not the borrower (the bank) but the lender (the depositor). Similarly, reformist scholars argue that the provisions about *maysir* (gambling) in the *Qur'an* should hold over the detailed rules about *gharar* in the *Sunna* – that is, that the real concern is not sale of risk but only excessive risk-taking amounting virtually to gambling, or again exploitation of the foolish or weak.

Many people addressing the *Qur'an* in this fashion find themselves opposing the Islamic finance movement, believing it to be either a backward-looking, literal and legalistic form of devotion to Islam that retards Muslim economic progress or a cynical exploitation of religion preying on pious but ignorant masses.

But other reformist-minded thinkers come out strongly in support of Islamic finance. These include the so-called Islamic economists (Siddiqi 1981). These thinkers believe that, by delving into the *Qur'an*, as well as the *Sunna* and the classical legal and ethical tradition, they can identify moral, social and economic goals or objectives enjoined by God on mankind. Their goal is to develop a new normative economics respectful of these objectives. It is their belief that this economics is the only true and sound economics, and that if followed it would lead not only to prosperity in this world but, through its respect for the spiritual side of human life, to moral and religious benefit in this world and in the next.

Against these varying approaches based on reformist thinking is arrayed the approach of more traditionalist scholars, chiefly contemporary adherents of the tradition of Islamic jurisprudence or *fiqh*. These thinkers in effect rely more on the *Sunna* than the *Qur'an*, since it is more conducive to detailed legal elaborations; approach both the *Qur'an* and *Sunna* with a manner of reasoning that is more legal than moral; and largely forego the search for ultimate divine purposes for the rules, considering these beyond the human capacity to understand. They believe that spiritual, moral and worldly success – and the true Islamic economic order – will follow automatically from devout human obedience to these rules.

While the Islamic economists have made an immense contribution to Islamic finance – in providing its initial inspiration and devising its basic organizational structures – it is the approach of the second group, the legal scholars, that has come to dominate the industry on a day-to-day basis. In practical effect, Islamic finance now can be summed up as an attempt to do modern finance in compliance with Islamic law as understood by these scholars. Islamic finance is, in a way, an experiment to determine whether the classical Islamic law can be made applicable, on its own terms, today.

In what follows we largely adopt the Islamic legal scholars' understanding of the field of Islamic finance.

HOW ISLAMIC LAW – IN THE CLASSICAL TRADITION – HAS CHOSEN TO INTERPRET THE REVEALED TEXTS AS TO *RIBA* AND *GHARAR*

It turns out that Islamic legal rules as to *riba* and *gharar* are not simple or easily stated. They are complex and have ramifications throughout the Islamic law of obligations, and even beyond (Vogel 2006).[6] Here I am going to try an approach that is rather novel. This is to explain *riba* and *gharar* on the basis of certain basic legal principles – principles which Islamic law scholars themselves use to navigate Islamic contract law. This approach, deferring to principles rather than to so many specific rules, may tax patience in the beginning, because these principles seem to follow some new and alien logic and to employ many strange legal conceptions and distinctions. But I believe that it will prove its usefulness in the end.

Riba

One might think that *riba* is nothing but the prohibition of interest on credit. It is not; in Islamic law it is much more far-reaching.

We quoted above the hadith against taking a benefit on loans. But this is not the most important or best-attested hadith on *riba*. The most important *riba* hadiths concern sales, not loans. This may be because the contract of sale itself plays a fundamental role in Islamic contract law. The sale contract is used as a model on which other contracts are regulated by analogy, particularly synallagmatic contracts – contracts in which there is an exchange of pecuniary considerations, including loans.

Here I adopt the approach – a somewhat challenging one – of looking only at a few hadiths, ones that state the sort of basic legal principles we are seeking. Indeed some of these hadiths are just the attribution to the Prophet of basic legal maxims that the scholars uniformly agree upon. These maxims or principles are of great significance throughout contract law.

> Gold for gold, silver for silver, wheat for wheat, barley for barley, dates for dates, salt for salt, like for like, equal for equal, hand to hand. If these types differ, then sell them as you wish, if it is hand to hand (Muslim).

This is actually the most important hadith on *riba*. This hadith prohibits exchanges among certain fungibles – gold, silver, wheat, barley, dates and salt – if there is any delay involved. Sales among these fungibles must be 'hand-to-hand', that is, both performances must be carried out immediately.

Let us set to one side exchanges which are barters of the same species of good: 'wheat for wheat', or 'gold for gold', for example. Let us look instead at the exchanges covered by the last sentence of the hadith – exchanges of different 'types', such as gold for silver.

Islamic legal scholars use analogy to extrapolate from revealed cases. This hadith offers a famous example of the use of analogy. Nearly all the schools of law and scholars studying this hadith decided not to take it literally, as applying only to six specific types of goods (wheat, barley, and so on). They thought it must have wider meaning. Some scholars believed that the six types stand actually for two classes of goods: money (at that time gold and silver were currency par excellence) and foods. Thus, the exchange of any food for any other food, with an agreed-upon delay for performance of one or both considerations, would be prohibited. Others agree with this interpretation, but limiting the class of foods to preservable foods. Still other scholars say that there are three classes of goods: money; objects sold by weight; objects sold by volume.

All the scholars say that the hadith applies at all only if one is exchanging goods within a single one of these classes. For example, one may not exchange wheat for barley with delay because both fall within a single class according to all the schools (either foods, preservable foods, or goods sold by volume). But all the schools say that, because wheat and currency fall into different classes, the hadith does not apply and one may exchange wheat for money even with an agreed delay.

Some consequences of this hadith are that currency exchanges must be presently executed exchanges, with no delay; and that the sale of goods for money with delay – credit sale – is lawful. Note that *riba* has no application to such transactions, even if the delay price is higher than the spot price, and even if negotiations take into account compensation to the seller for loss of use of the price. If the prohibition of *riba* were about denying the time-value of money, then this transaction would be prohibited. Similarly, if *riba* were about the exploitation of the weak, this again would be a highly suspect transaction, but it is not.

'The Prophet forbade sale of the *kāli'* for the *kāli'* [delay for delay]' (Hammad 1986, 12–13, 24).[7] A consequence of this hadith is that contracts may not provide that both performances are not due until the future. One of the parties must be at least obligated to perform at once, whether or not he does so in fact. For example, a conventional futures contract is unlawful. Indeed, so is the ordinary modern contract of sale, by which the purchaser promises to pay in the future and the seller promises to transfer title in the future.

'The Prophet forbade sale of *dayn* for *dayn* [debt for debt]' (ibid.). To understand this hadith and the principle stemming from it one has to plumb the complex notion of *dayn* (Vogel and Hayes 1998, pp. 114–25). Literally, *dayn* means debt; and this is one of its legal meanings. Another legal meaning, however, refers to a type of property. Islamic law distinguishes between two types of property: *'ayn* and *dayn*. *'Ayn* property is property that is unique and concrete, like this watch, that horse. *Dayn* property is generic or abstract property, property known only by a commercial description. *Dayn* property usually (but not always) consists of fungibles. For example, '100 kilos of number one winter wheat'. The distinction between *'ayn* and *dayn* turns out to be vital in dealing both with *riba* and with *gharar*. For *riba* it is vital because, for example, all the goods mentioned in the hadith of the six types, including currency, are fungibles sold by weight or measure. The rules about *gharar* rely on the distinction, as we shall see below.

To return to the hadith against selling a *dayn* for a *dayn,* and combining the two legal meanings of *dayn* mentioned above, the result is far-reaching: one cannot have sales in which both considerations are either debts or property defined abstractly. The old pre-Islamic *riba* of 'pay or increase' falls within this rule, since by this the creditor 'sells' a debt he is owed presently in return for another debt due at a later date. Similarly, a creditor may not sell (that is, discount) an obligation he is owed to another person, either for less or more than the principal. This result obviously throws a shadow over the negotiability of financial securities.

The Prophet said, 'Profit accompanies liability for loss (*al-kharaj bi-l-daman*)'.[8] This hadith means that one may reap the profits (*al-kharaj*) from possession of property only if one also bears the risks of its loss (*al-daman*). It has many applications in Islamic law. One of these is to explain why in some investments – like partnership – it is lawful to take profits, while in others – like loans – it is not. In the case of a loan, the creditor no longer bears the risk of loss (*daman*) of the principal; the borrower bears that risk. (One ignores here credit risk entirely.) Hence profit or *kharaj* – here interest – is unlawful. In a partnership, on the other hand, one's capital investment is subject to risk of loss if the venture goes poorly. Hence taking profit is also lawful. Similarly, in lease, since the lessor remains liable to lose his investment if his property suffers a casualty, he is also entitled to derive a profit – here the rental paid by the lessee.

This is a very far-reaching maxim, offering one of the most penetrating insights into the inner logic of *fiqh* laws as to *riba* and *gharar* (Vogel and Hayes, 1998, pp. 83–3, 112–14).

Maysir (Gambling) and *Gharar*

For the scholars the prohibition in the *Qur'an* of gambling goes without saying. To them this prohibition supports but does not determine the significance of the hadiths on *gharar*. The following are some key hadiths about *gharar*:

- 'The Messenger of God forbade the "sale of the pebble" (*hasah*, apparently, sale of an object chosen or determined by the throwing of a pebble), and the sale of gharar' (Muslim, Cited above, p. 43).
- 'Do not buy fish in the sea, for it is gharar'.[9]
- 'The Prophet forbade sale of what is in the wombs, sale of the contents of their udders, sale of a slave when he is runaway . . . .'[10]
- 'Whoever buys foodstuffs, let him not sell them until he has possession of them' (Bukhari).
- He who purchases food shall not sell it until he weighs it (Muslim).

What do scholars do with these hadiths (Vogel and Hayes 1998, pp. 87–93)? One could explain them as only referring to particularly risky situations virtually equaling gambling. But scholars take them in a different way, as prohibitions of the sale of property affected with particular types of risk. They focus their concern on two types of risk: non-existence (such as when the property inhabits the future) and lack of knowledge. A third commonly mentioned type of risk, lack of control over property (as in a sale of the runaway slave or the sale of what one does not yet own) can be handled by analogy to either or both of the first two.

What are the key consequences of these hadiths? There are two most obvious ones. First, the parties must fully define basic contract terms if the contract is to be binding. For example, the parties cannot ordinarily sell goods without weighing them first, even for a particular price per kilo; or sell 'one of my sheep'. Second, the parties cannot make a contract subject to certain types of contingency or condition. For example, the parties cannot sell 'on condition my ship arrives before Friday' or insure against events, such as 'if casualty A occurs, party B shall pay to C $D'.

Note the oddity that, though it literally means 'risk', in effect *gharar* ends up meaning something else in the hands of the lawyers. It means either non-existence or lack of knowledge. Thus, a prohibition stemming from *gharar* in a particular case may have nothing essential to do with whether the contract is actually risky. There is no assessment here of the quantum of risk. Thus, if a buyer makes a contract to purchase a 'fish in the sea' (a contract axiomatically void as involving non-existence), but adding a condition that the contract shall bind only if the seller actually catches a fish of particular specifications (and thus seemingly curing the risk of non-existence), the contract remains void (according to most scholars). The added condition does not save but rather doubly dooms the contract since it introduces a condition based on a future contingency.

Contracts involving lesser degrees of non-existence or lack of knowledge may still be approved. Thus, scholars provide that one need not inspect inside the walls of a house being sold. Or one may make a transaction as part of a larger deal even if the transaction done separately would be prohibited. Thus, while it is not allowed to sell the fetus of a camel in the womb, it is allowed to sell a pregnant camel – and for more money than a similar but non-pregnant camel.

SOME EXAMPLES OF HOW THESE PRINCIPLES GENERATE ISLAMIC CONTRACT RULES

Even with these few principles one can begin to see how Islamic contract rules that otherwise might seem incomprehensible link together into a comprehensible whole (Linant de Bellefonds 1965; Coulson 1984; Rayner

1991; Saleh 1992; Vogel 2006; Al-Zuhayli 2003). The following are some examples of rules of contract that can be understood as deriving from the hadiths above and the principles arising from them.

Sale of *Salam*

Salam is a contract for advance purchase of fungibles. An example would be 'I buy from you for $200 100 kilos of wheat for delivery at harvest time'. Such a contract appears suspect for four reasons.

First, it appears to offend the hadith of 'six types', being an exchange among two of the six types of goods (here wheat and currency). But, as in the case of credit sale, *salam* is permitted since the two countervalues being exchanged are from different classes of *riba* goods.

Second, what about the hadith prohibiting sales with double delay, seen as prohibiting contracts in which neither party is obligated to perform at once? In this case the prohibition is avoided by requiring, as an essential term of *salam* contracts, that the buyer is obligated to pay the entire purchase price at the commencement of the contract.

Third, this transaction seems prohibited as the exchange of two properties that are both *'dayn'* properties in the sense of properties defined abstractly: money on one side, wheat on the other. It would be so prohibited, but the law avoids this outcome by imposing a second essential term in *salam*. The law requires that the buyer not only becomes obligated to pay the price at once, but that he in fact pays it, during the very session in which the contract is concluded. By this the advance purchase price becomes no longer *dayn*, but something specific – so much actual currency – and hence *'ayn* and outside the reach of the hadith.

Finally, the law requires that the goods being sold, in contrast to the price, must be abstract, must be *dayn*. If one tries to render them more concrete, the sale is void. For example, if one uses *salam* to sell '100 kilos of wheat' but adding that it must come from 'the harvest on my field', the transaction is void because it is a future sale of an *'ayn* that does not exist. This offends the rules against *gharar*. One observes here how *dayn* goods are relatively immune from *gharar* concerns (as long as they occupy only one side of the transaction), since they can be well-defined, and because, being abstract or conceptual, one can largely sidestep the issue of their existence.

Lease

Lease in Islamic law is mostly straightforward, and similar to the law of lease elsewhere. But in a few details it is subject to special constraints that can be seen as dictated by the principles we have laid out.

1. It is a rule that the lessor must bear the risk of loss of the leased property. Any attempt to shift the risk of loss to the lessee (as is commonly done in modern operating leases) is void. This is because of the maxim 'profit accompanies liability for loss'. If the lessor does not bear the risk, he cannot enjoy the profit. (Islamic finance mitigates this constraint by using side agreements with the lessee or insurance.)
2. The rules of *gharar* require that the contract exactly defines the basic terms of the lease. Hence, for example, one cannot fix the rental at a floating rate, pegged to LIBOR for example. (This is gotten around in Islamic finance by making a non-binding 'gentleman's' agreement to renew the lease from time to time throughout its life at the new rate.)
3. Another restriction is that the lessor cannot make the lessee liable for maintenance of leased property. This is seen to impose an undetermined extra rent cost. (Islamic finance gets around this by the lessor appointing the lessee his agent to do maintenance.)
4. One cannot include in the contract either an option or an agreement to sell the leased goods at the end of the lease to the lessor. This is because this would be a contract with neither performance due at once, offending the rule against the sale of 'delay for delay'. (Islamic finance gets around this by making the sale option or agreement either a gift or formality not binding.)

Partnership

In the matter of partnership, Islamic law once again seems very reasonable and familiar. Basically, by partnership several parties contract to contribute either capital or labor to a single venture and share profits by percentages. Islamic law does, however, impose certain specific constraints on all partnerships, these stemming from the principles we have studied.

The first constraint is the absolute requirement that all losses fall solely on those who contribute capital (on a pro-rata basis), and not on those who contribute only expertise or labor. The worker loses only his time. This result stems from the principle that 'profit accompanies liability for loss'. It is the risk of losing his investment that justifies the capital investor's right to profit, while the worker may justify profits by an alternate principle, his work. A related result is that no partner may demand security against a loss in the business.

Second, profits must be shared among the partners by pre-agreed percentages. No partner may specify that he should receive a specific lump sum or, again, receive any guarantee against loss. Either would be an infraction of the rules of *gharar*, since no one knows if the venture will make a profit. It would also make the partner's capital contribution like a loan.

Third, a partner's interest in the partnership cannot be known until the venture is complete and is liquidated. Until then, its value being subject to future vicissitudes, it is *gharar* and cannot be sold. This problem has been overcome in modern times by treating the value of an interest in an ongoing partnership as adequately determined by the accounts of the company and thus permissibly bought and sold.

BASED ON THESE RULES, WHAT ARE THE TRANSACTIONS USED IN ISLAMIC FINANCE?

The contracts used for Islamic finance (Vogel and Hayes 1998; Saeed 1996; Warde 2000; El-Gamal 2006)[11] fall into two major groups: sale contracts (and contracts derived from sale like credit sale and lease) and partnership contracts (in various forms).

Islamic economists strongly favor the partnership contract as the ideal form for Islamic credit and investment, since it defines a model for investment they consider unique to Islam: return equals a pre-agreed percentage of actual net revenues; capital losses fall solely on capital and not on labor. This model is heralded as a third way between capitalism and socialism, and as far fairer and more productive than interest-taking.

But lawyers – and the historical and contemporary practice of Islamic finance – rely on sale and its derivatives as the more natural alternative to interest and the more practical medium for investment and credit. Sale contracts have many advantages over partnerships, including allowing compensation for credit, security against loss, use of collateral and fixed obligations enforceable in court.

The following are some contracts in use in Islamic finance.

Sale-based Transactions

Mark-up sale (*murabaha bi-amr li-al-shira'*, literally mark-up sale with commission to purchase)
This trade finance transaction accounts for from 80 to 95 per cent (estimates vary) of Islamic bank revenue. A customer desiring to finance purchase of goods asks the bank to purchase the goods and then resell them to him. The bank's purchase from a supplier will be for cash, and the customer's purchase from the bank, the second purchase, will be on time, usually in installments. The bank calculates the price of the second sale as an agreed mark-up over its own costs.

From an economic point of view, *murabaha* may seem identical to the financing of a purchase of goods. But from a legal point of view it does differ, specifically insofar as the bank must take title, however momentary, of the goods.

There are several problems with *murabaha* stemming from the principles we have reviewed. The customer's promise to purchase the goods from the bank (the second sale) cannot be made binding since this would be a contract in which neither side is obligated immediately to perform. This problem is solved by a narrow *fatwa* (that is, authoritative Islamic legal opinion) allowing banks engaging in such transactions to demand compensation for any losses incurred from a customer's breach of promise. Based on this *fatwa* banks take collateral against this type of liability.

A second problem with *murabaha* is that, once the transaction is complete and an obligation to pay in installments is created, the bank cannot then sell that obligation because of the maxim against sale of *dayn* or debt. A partial solution has been found, however: a *fatwa* declares that if lawfully traded interests are pooled with interests that may not be lawfully traded, then as long as the latter are less than half of the pool, interests in the whole pool may be traded. Thus, a bank may mix its *murabaha* accounts-payable with an equal or greater amount of properly tradable assets, such as interests in lands subject to lease. This *fatwa* is being used to securitize large quantities of Islamic bank assets into freely traded securities called *sukuk*.

Lease (*ijara*)

Lease or *ijara* is also considered a sale transaction – the sale of the right to use property. *Ijara* has become a vital transaction for Islamic banks since it is very flexible, easily adapted to financing, and creates its own collateral. I discussed above the restrictions on leases from the viewpoint of Islamic law, and how Islamic banks adapt to them. Islamic leases are increasingly being standardized and treated much like conventional leases.

Ijara wa-iqtina' is a transaction whereby the lessee not only pays rent but progressively buys a share in the leased property, reducing the rent as he does so. This is a very common transaction, and is now being used for home mortgages in the United States.

Commissioned manufacture (*istisna'*)

Another important transaction, named *istisna'* meaning 'commissioned manufacture', is used to finance manufacture or production. Typically, by this contract a customer gives specifications for a manufactured good to a manufacturer who produces the good for a price and delivery date fixed in the contract. The rules about sale of delay for delay would seem to require the purchaser to pay the price in full at the time of the purchase, as in *salam*. But *istisna'* is an exception in this respect. Traditionally it was accepted by only one school, and by not all scholars within that school.

Istisna' is useful for banks wishing to provide finance for construction or for new equipment purchases. For example, a bank finances an airplane by selling the plane according to specifications to its customer for payment over a number of years. Then, as Islamic law allows, the bank makes a second, mirroring *istisna'* contract with a manufacturer, this time paying in cash.

Advance purchase (*salam*)

Salam is an increasingly important transaction, typically for financing agriculture.

Services

Islamic banks may readily sell their services, virtually without restriction. For example, they may earn fees for letters of credit, payment and collection services, or investment advice. Similarly, agency relationships may be compensated in various ways, even by a share of profits.

Partnerships

Mudaraba

Mudaraba is considered the most Islamically pristine form for Islamic finance, the one that Islamic economists hold out as epitomizing the Islamic ideal. Known in medieval Europe as *commenda,* it is a transaction by which one party, called the capital owner, invests only capital and remains a silent, non-managing partner. The other partner, the entrepreneur, invests time and effort, but no capital. As explained above, Islamic rules enjoin that, if there are losses, they fall entirely on the capital owner. If there are profits, the parties share them according to a percentage determined in advance in their contract.

This contract is the one on which the Islamic commercial bank itself is modeled. The bank's depositors are considered capital investors, owners of capital, and the bank is the entrepreneur. A problem arises in that deposits in this conception may sustain losses, a result obviously opposed to the ordinary expectation elsewhere as to bank deposits. Moreover, since Islamic law prevents guaranteeing capital investors against loss, deposit insurance faces a stumbling block. If a depositor wishes to be secure against losses, then Islamic law construes his investment as a true deposit or bailment (*wadi'a*) which under Islamic law earns no return.

Mudaraba is important also on the other side of the bank's balance sheet, as a basis on which Islamic banks extend credit to customers, a substitute for loans. For example, the bank contributes to the customer's business a quantity of inventory and earns a share of the profits from the sale of that inventory.

Mudaraba can be arranged as diminishing (*mutanaqisa*), meaning a contract by which the customer progressively purchases the bank's ownership share by making payments of principal in addition to profits owed.

Mudaraba faces certain problems in practical use. First, it makes banks investors in their customers' businesses, drawing them into the need to supervise in various ways. Second, as early experiments with *mudaraba* investments showed, Islamic banks risk losses when *mudaraba* is used extensively. Since the bank must bear all losses, customers are tempted to increase costs or to distort accounts. Third, as noted above, banks may not take security against investment losses. But they may, and do, take security against a customer's engaging in negligence or impropriety. Fourth, given the availability to most borrowers of an interest-based alternative, a problem of adverse selection arises: borrowers will tend to finance ventures with worse risk–reward profiles Islamically and get interest-loans for the others, since in the latter case they get to keep 100 per cent of gains above the fixed interest rate for themselves.

A third important use of *mudaraba* is as the model by which the modern legal institutions of share corporation and common stock have been understood by Islamic law and declared lawful. Islamic finance builds on this result by using *mudaraba* to justify numerous types of funds and securitizations. These form a large and growing part of Islamic finance business. Islamic mutual funds exist that invest in conventional equity securities after applying an Islamic 'filter' to screen out companies that have too high a debt to equity ratio (since otherwise the fund would be deemed to be paying or receiving interest) or that invest in pork, alcohol, gambling, and so on. In this respect such funds resemble various socially conscious funds.

Musharaka

Another form of partnership, *musharaka*, differs from *mudaraba* in that capital investors are also active in management. This term is used when a bank not only contributes money to a business but also takes a hand in its management or when the customer contributes not only management but also capital.

TRANSACTIONS RENDERED DIFFICULT BY ISLAMIC LAW

Clearly, contemporary interpretations of Islamic law allow a great many useful bank and finance transactions. But much remains problematic or impossible. Examples include deposit insurance, since this offends basic principles of partnership; currency futures contracts, which are unlawful as sale of *dayn* for *dayn* or on grounds of *gharar*; hedging risks through options and other derivatives, since these contracts are ordinarily unlawful either because of *gharar* or sale of debt; and most bonds, which usually are unlawful as interest-based or are financial obligations (*dayn*) which cannot be traded, (note, however, that Islamic bonds or *sukuk* are possible using securitized lawful and tradable returns such as from ownership or leased property or *mudaraba* ventures).

CONCLUSIONS

First, by way of summing up some of our findings, let me present a list of some of the statements often heard about Islamic banking that we have learned are either not true or are half-truths.

One often hears that Islam does not recognize any time value for money. This is true if one considers solely debt obligations such as loans. They may not grow over time. But Islamic law does recognize the time value of money in sale transactions such as credit sale, *salam*, and lease.

Gharar is often equated to risk in the modern economic sense. It is not; it consists of certain particular types of uncertainty or contingency with respect to the subject matter or other essential terms of a contract.

It is sometimes asserted that investments are compensable only in return for either assuming risk or performing service. But one is not compensated in Islamic law specifically for assuming risks. The issue of bearing risks arises instead in deciding, as to a particular property, who may derive rents or other gain from possession of that property.

Many accept as a principle that Islamic banking investments must be profit-and-loss based to be fully sound. However, most Islamic finance transactions, both in medieval times and at present, are based in sale, not partnership. From a legal perspective there is nothing per se wrong or even flawed about this practice.

A frequent aspiration, and justification, for Islamic banking is that it will serve the social good or welfare of the Muslim community. Though this aspiration is no doubt widely shared by Islamic economists and many others involved in Islamic finance, yet, viewed legally, Islamic banking is merely a profit-making private-sector enterprise which is distinguished solely by its claim to comply with Islamic laws of contract, property and commerce.

Many outsiders, Muslim and non-Muslim, disdain Islamic finance as a mere shell-game, which, however much it decks itself out superficially in Islamic form, remains in substance no different from conventional interest-based finance. If one adopts a distant enough perspective and analyses functions only economically, this claim is true for many transactions. But from a closer perspective, and particularly from the standpoint of lawyers, one cannot assume this. These contracts operate under different rules than do conventional instruments, and generate somewhat different rights and obligations. To accomplish the same purposes as some particular conventional transaction while still complying with Islamic legal rules is frequently difficult (if not impossible), and achieving it often takes complex legal arrangements and numerous *fatawa* from the scholars who oversee Islamic financial institutions. Moreover, those who oversee or regulate Islamic finance, not only the Islamic scholars whose *fatawa* determine the Islamic legality of transactions but also outside regulatory officials and accounting professionals, routinely acknowledge practical legal and functional distinctions between Islamic and conventional finance. But, on the other hand, for several highly engineered or synthetic contractual arrangements, for which ever more sophisticated legal refinements bring the resultant transaction ever closer to exact conformity with its conventional counterpart, even lawyers come to doubt whether the actuality of Islamic law is being preserved or only its outward form. This has led to revival of the medieval debate about the permissibility of legal artifices (*hiyal*) that seek to achieve an unlawful result by a series of individually lawful maneuvers.

As a final word, allow me to venture an overview of the prospects of the Islamic finance industry from the relatively narrow viewpoint of this chapter concerned with Islamic law. The long-time dilemma of Islamic finance has been how much it should approximate itself to – and eagerly compete with – conventional finance, particularly in commercial banking. But the resolution of the dilemma is actually preordained. If Islamic finance practice were ever to become indistinguishable from conventional interest-based finance, even succeeding in reducing to negligibility the extra transaction costs to maintain Islamic form, then, while its integration within the world financial system would be assured, its chief competitive advantage over conventional finance would also be lost. Complying with Islamic law, particularly in avoiding interest, remains the main motivation of its core customer base, and gives the industry a powerful marketing advantage so far overcoming the disadvantage of added costs. Success in conforming to conventional finance, especially as this success becomes better known amongst its customers, would in the end destroy this advantage. It seems unlikely that Muslims of this day and age will accept that the *riba* prohibition, so vehement in the *Qur'an*, is only a matter of intricate legal formalism without substantive effects. If such an impasse were reached, Islamic finance could persist only as a family of institutions with a useful but dwindling entrée and expertise in particular regions and among a few narrow customer groups.

The alternative to this result is to insist on conformity with an evolved but still traditional *fiqh*, even when it is inconvenient either in barring transactions altogether or in imposing on them added transaction costs. This approach still allows for close conformity with conventional finance in those spheres where Islamic law raises few or no obstacles, such as fund investments in equities, venture capital, services, and trade finance. Signs are that Islamic finance as a whole will end up closer on average to this second result, rather than the first. One such sign is that, as growth continues at a rapid pace, as calls multiply for greater standardization, transparency, institutionalization, regulation and self-regulation, and as better specialized infrastructures emerge (for example, securities laws and markets), one observes a tendency among both practitioners and consumers to insist that Islamic *fiqh* be followed more rigorously, not more leniently.

Given all of this, there appears to be no reason why Islamic finance should not succeed on its own terms. It must be understood, however, that these are not the terms of either the various reformers of Islam (who often argue that Islam properly understood allows interest-based banking and finance); the idealists, typically economists, of Islamic banking (who hoped that profit–loss-sharing principles would catalyze far-reaching social and economic transformations in modern life); or the political Islamists (who push for Muslim states to embrace Islamic law – understood still largely as the traditional *fiqh* – expecting from this alone manifold reform and revival in Muslim societies). Rather, the terms in question are those of religious lawyers interested in the conformity of particular transactions with particular traditional legal rules and principles. Islamic finance as so practiced is unlikely to lend much momentum to Islamic reformation (much less revolution) as to other pressing Islamic issues of the day – whether political ideology, international relations, constitutionalism and the rule of law, economic development, women's issues, or human rights.

It is more likely that an enduring success of Islamic finance on these terms will have an encouraging but also moderating effect on Islamically-denominated thought and practice in private and civil-society spheres. It will display Islamic law – and its traditionally trained scholars – gradually evolving from their traditional origins, strengthening claims of authenticity and loyalty to tradition while igniting no economic, political or religious upheavals, and working successfully in mundane, routine matters without ushering in any form of utopia or converting all to their side.

NOTES

1. Shi'i law plays little role in Islamic finance outside of Iran (Yasseri 2002; Khan and Mirakhor 1987).
2. In this chapter, hadiths will be cited to one or more of the best-known, most authoritative collections of Sunni hadith, citing to these collections only by their author. The works (by author) cited here are (with death dates C.E.) Bukhari (d. 870), Muslim (d. 874), Abu Dawud (d. 888), Tirmidhi (d. 892), Nasa'i (d. 915), Darimi (d. 868), Ibn Maja (d. 886) and Ibn Hanbal (d. 855). If found in either or both of Muslim or Bukhari (the most authoritative works), citations to similar hadiths in other works are not added.
3. For examples of such principles (*qawa'id*) in the law, see the famous first 100 articles of the Ottoman codification of the law of obligations *Majallat al-ahkam al-'adliyya,* available in English translation by C.A. Hooper (1930). These articles were taken mainly from Ibrahim bin Muhammad Ibn Nujaym (d. 1563 CE) (1985).
4. Translations from the *Qur'an* are adapted by the author from Muhammad Asad (1980).
5. This particular hadith does not appear in any of the major hadith collections. It is narrated by the most respected scholars as a statement only of companions of the Prophet, not the Prophet himself. As a prophetic hadith, scholars reject it as false. See al-Shawkani (n.d. 5: 262). Its content is, however, universally upheld by *fiqh* schools.
6. In my article (Vogel 2006), I show how the revealed strictures of *riba* and *gharar* pervasively influence Islamic contract law and go far to forge its unique character.
7. This hadith has only weak attestation.
8. Abu Dawud, Tirmidhi, Nasa'i, Ibn Maja.
9. Ibn Hanbal, noting that its most correct version is handed down on the authority of Ibn Mas'ud, a companion of the Prophet, not the Prophet himself.
10. Ibn Maja, with weak authentication.
11. Many sources describe the basic contract rules defining the transactions used in Islamic finance, while at the same time, according to the thesis of the author, either advancing or critiquing the justifications offered by Islamic finance for its activities. See, for example, Saleh (1992), Vogel and Hayes (1998), Saeed (1996), Warde (2000, which also covers the history of the industry) and El-Gamal (2006). A very useful detailed guide to Islamic legal rules used in the industry (in somewhat aspirational form, that is, as best practices adopted by few institutions fully as yet) are the Islamic legal standards adopted by the Accounting and Auditing Organization for Islamic Financial Institutions (AAOIFI).

REFERENCES

Accounting and Auditing Organization for Islamic Financial Institutions (2007), *Shari'a Standards*, Bahrain: AAOIFI.

al-Shawkani, Muhammad b'Ali (n.d.), *Nayl al-awtar*, Cairo: Mustafa Babi al-Halabi.

Al-Zuhayli, Wahbah (2003), *Financial Transactions in Islamic Jurisprudence*, Trans. A. Mahmoud El-Gamal and S. Muhammad Eissa, 2 vols, Beirut: Dar al-Fikr al-Mouaser.

Asad, M. (1980), *The Message of the Qur'an*, Gibraltar: Dar al-Andalus.

Coulson, Noel J. (1984), *Commercial Law in the Gulf States: The Islamic Legal Tradition*, London: Graham & Trotman.

El-Gamal, Mahmoud A. (2006), *Islamic Finance: Law, Economics, and Practice*, Cambridge: Cambridge University Press.

Hammad, Nazih Kamal (1986), *Bay' a-kali'bi-al-kali'*, Jedda: King Abd al-Aziz University.

Hooper, C. (1930), trans. *The Law of Civil Procedure of Iraq and Palestine*, Basrah: Times Printing & Publ. Co.

Ibn Nujaym, Ibrahim bin Muhammad (1985), *al-Ashbah wa-al-naza'ir*, Beirut: Dar al-Kutub al-'Ilmiyya.

Ibn Rushd, Muhammad b. Ahmad (1981), *Bidayat al-mujtahid wa-nihayat al-muqtasid*, Cairo: Mustafa al-Babi al-Halabi.

Khan, M. and Mirakhor, A. (1987), Islamic Banking, IMF Occasional Paper No. 49, Washington, DC: International Monetary Fund.

Linant de Bellefonds, Y. (1965), *Traité de droit musulman comparé*, 3 vols, Paris: Mouton.

Rayner, S. (1991), *The Theory of Contracts in Islamic Law,* London: Graham & Trotman.

Saeed, A. (1996), *Islamic Banking and Interest*, Leiden: EJ Brill.

Saleh, N. (1992), *Unlawful Gain and Legitimate Profit in Islamic Law*, 2nd edn, The Hague: Kluwer Law International.

Siddiqi, Muhammad Nejatullah (1981), *Muslim Economic Thinking*, Jedda: The Islamic Foundation.

Vogel, Frank E. (2006), 'The Contract Law of Islam and of the Arab Middle East', *International Encyclopedia of Comparative Law*, **VII** (7), 1–155.

Vogel, Frank E. and Hayes, Samuel L. III (1998), *Islamic Law and Finance: Religion, Risk, and Return*, The Hague and Boston: Kluwer Law International.

Warde, I. (2000), *Islamic Finance in the Global Economy*, Edinburgh: Edinburgh University Press.

Yasseri, A. (2002), 'Islamic banking contracts as enforced in Iran', in M. Iqbal and D.T. Llewellyn (eds), *Islamic Banking and Finance: New Perspectives on Profit-Sharing and Risk*, Cheltenham, UK and Northampton, MA, USA: Edward Elgar Publishing.

4. Islamic banking in Europe: the regulatory challenge

M. Fahim Khan

It can hardly be disputed that the growth of Islamic banking and finance in Europe is a welcome development in view of the fact it is effectively contributing to increased penetration of financial services and hence contributing to what is being referred to as 'social inclusion'. The members of the large Islamic community in Europe, who refrained from benefiting from financial services on religious grounds, are now able to benefit from the financial market without violating religious norms.

The emerging institutions offering Islamic banking services, however, are creating a challenge to the supervisory and regulatory bodies. The challenge posed by the emergence of these institutions is quite different from the challenge that regulatory bodies face with respect to supervising and monitoring the conventional financial institutions. The distinct regulatory challenge arises because of the methods these institutions adopt to mobilize funds and to deploy them to earn income on them.

The ways in which Islamic banks can and do mobilize funds are all non-conventional and in some ways new to the regulators. Several issues and questions arise in the minds of regulators confronted with the task of supervising and regulating Islamic banks. Some methods for mobilizing funds, for example, would require asset management. Involvement of commercial banks in asset management is entirely a new phenomenon in the context of the conventional concept of commercial banking. Regulatory authorities will be rightly worried about how to define firewalls to keep asset management and commercial banking separate, legally, administratively and operationally, in order to ensure proper monitoring and supervision of the bank's activities.

On the side of mobilizing funds, what *Shari'ah*-compatible modes of operating Islamic banking should be provided within the European banking framework by an institution to be called a 'bank'; and what products offering *Shari'ah*-compatible services be left for institutions that may not be called bank, are issues that regulating authorities and lawyers of Islamic banks will always find a challenging task to deal with.

Similarly, in the context of utilizing funds, Islamic banks will use contracts that will include stipulations and provisions that will not interface with the conventional banking system in Europe. The questions arise: how far are these contracts in line with the European Directive to protect the clients of the Islamic finance industry? Are the Islamic financial products offered by these banks as professionally sound and competent as of those institutions that use conventional contracts in defining their financial products?

The use of non-conventional contracts to offer products for financial services can create a whole range of issues concerning corporate governance standards, sources of new risks and how to manage them, and how to make Islamic banks conform to the market discipline created for the conventional banks. For example, risk profiles of some financial products may be quite distinct and may not have been addressed by the Basel II agreement that addressed only the conventional banking activities. The new dimensions of risk emerge on both the assets side as well as the liabilities side of the Islamic banks' balance sheet. On the assets side Islamic banks will use contracts known as *ijara, murabaha, istisna'* and *salam* which have more complex implications towards risk management than those of the products on the assets side of the conventional bank's balance sheet. On the liabilities side, Islamic banks will be offering profit-sharing investment accounts to the depositors. These depositors are assumed to share the profits/losses of the bank but neither fall into the category of the capital of the bank nor can be regarded as liabilities of the bank, in the accounting sense of the term. This raises complications for the formula for capital adequacy and for other indicators and measures. How to make the accounts of Islamic banks conform to the banking laws of Europe without violating *Shari'ah* provisions will be a challenge for the lawyers of Islamic banking intending to do banking in Europe as well as a challenge to regulators who will be evaluating the proposals for establishing Islamic banks in Europe.

Broadly speaking, the regulatory challenge has three main dimensions as highlighted by the Managing Director of the UK Financial Services Authority (FSA) while speaking at a conference in the Middle East:

1. protection of customers of Islamic Banks;
2. transparency (including issues relating to Corporate Governance);
3. professional competition (in differential and distinct aspects of Islamic banking in addition to competence in the conventional aspects of banking).

In the UK, where the FSA deals with the whole range of financial services, this may not be as difficult a task as it may prove in other European countries where there are different regulatory bodies for different financial services. For example, Islamic banks often will be combining what are known as 'banking activities' with what are known as 'investment activities'. In many parts of the world, and Europe is no exception, the two activities are regulated by different bodies.

Islamic banks offer two types of accounts to mobilize funds from depositors. One is the equivalent of the conventional concept of the current account where Islamic banks' liabilities are exactly the same as those of conventional banks with respect to the deposits that they have. Such accounts with the Islamic banks pose no additional challenge for the regulators. The other account is called a profit-sharing investment account (PSIA) where the depositors are supposed to share the profits of the bank instead of receiving a fixed return on their deposits. This account has no equivalent in conventional banking.[1] Such deposits can neither be considered part of the bank's capital nor are they the liabilities of the bank. Holders of these accounts, and not the Islamic bank, bear the risk of loss on the use of these deposits by the banks. This has repercussions for corporate governance, besides implications for risk management.

Regulators will need to look at PSIAs from the investors' protection point of view and not merely the depositors' protection point of view as in the case of commercial banking. PSIAs are considered to have implications for the capital adequacy ratios and the risk management approach adopted for conventional banks and the regulators will wonder how to modify the capital adequacy requirement to take care of the nature of PSIAs and risks involved therein.

In order to have a better picture of the nature of distinctive features of Islamic banks and their regulatory implications, let us look at the balance sheet structure of a typical Islamic bank in comparison with the balance sheet of a conventional bank. A conventional bank's balance sheet is shown in Table 4.1. The column of uses of funds has been arranged in order of decreasing liquidity. It may be noted that while the items are in the decreasing order of liquidity, they are also in the increasing order of riskiness. The greater the volume of the items in the lower half, the more vulnerable is the asset side of a conventional bank. A similar situation is observable when the two sides (assets side and liabilities side) are compared. There is a high possibility of mismatch between the two sides of the balance sheet. Any shock in the lower part of the asset side will throw the whole balance sheet 'off balance'. This has a potential of triggering a run on the bank. And if that happens there may be a contagion effect. The whole banking system may face a risk of collapse. This is what would keep the regulatory authorities on their toes in watching the banking activities

Table 4.1   Balance sheet of conventional banks

Assets (Uses of Funds)*	Liabilities (Sources of Funds)
Reserves	Current accounts
Cash and equivalent (e.g. items in process + deposits at other banks)	Non-transactions savings deposits like time deposits
Securities	Time deposits
Government and agency	Borrowings
State and local government	
Other securities	
Loans	Bank capital
Commercial and industrial	
Real estate	
Consumer	
Interbank	
Other	
Other assets (for example, physical capital)	
Total	Total

Note: *In order of decreasing liquidity.

and regulating them to minimize the probabilities of banks' balance sheets going 'off balance'.

Compared to this, let us have a look at the balance sheet structure of a typical Islamic bank. In a very simplified form, the balance sheet will have the structure shown in Table 4.2.

USES OF FUNDS

The column of uses of funds shows the items in order of decreasing liquidity and increasing riskiness. The following lists the differences from conventional banks: we now compare the individual items from the use of funds column.

1. Receivables (generated by real transactions) in place of loans that are merely financial transactions not linked with any real transactions. Receivables form the bulk of the assets.
2. *Ijara* and *Ijara Muntahia Bittamleek* (IMB) will require holding interest in real assets to make long-term investments as opposed to long-term loans in conventional banking that does not require retaining ownership in assets.

Table 4.2   Simplified structure of the balance sheet of a typical Islamic bank

Assets (Uses of Funds)*	Liabilities and Capital (Sources of Funds)
Cash and cash equivalents	Current account deposits
Receivables	Investment accounts
Investment	Borrowings
Other assets	Bank capital

Note: * In order of decreasing liquidity.

3.   *Salam* and *istisna'* give rise to non-financial assets and investment.

   - *Salam* – positions in commodities (and where permissible, hedged by *parallel salam*)
   - *Parallel istisna'* – work-in-progress inventories
   - There is no counterpart activity in conventional banks
   - *Musharaka* and *mudaraba*
   - There are risk-bearing investments and conventional banks do not have any counterpart activity

Cash and Cash Equivalent

This item is exactly the same as in a conventional balance sheet bearing the same features with respect to liquidity and riskiness.

Receivables

'Receivables' is a counterpart of the loans and securities as shown in the conventional balance with similar features with respect to liquidity and significance. These mostly arise from *murabaha* transactions. The bank authorizes the client to buy goods on behalf of the bank which are immediately resold to the client with a mark-up. The client will pay the bank in installments or with a lump sum at a later date. Collateral is obtained to ensure repayment of obligations in time. There are other modes of financing based on the concept of *ijara, istisna'* and *salam*. The contracts based on these concepts can be structured in a way that their liquidity and riskiness features remain the same as those of receivables under *murabaha* transactions and hence similar to those of 'loans' in the balance sheet of conventional banks. The regulators and lawyers of Islamic banks can easily work out modalities to ensure this. The problem arises due to the fact that Islamic banks, in applying the above-mentioned modes of financing are required, by *Shari'ah* rules, to assume the role of a trader or a lesser. This may not be permissible within the banking laws in Europe. The central banks of a Muslim country where Islamic banks and conventional banks are operating parallel to the conventional bank can add a clause to the effect that would permit the bank to assume the role of a trader only if it is needed for the use of a training-based mode of financing. How far central banks in Europe will be willing to make this provision in banking will be a complex question for them.

Another problem would arise from the non-tradability or non-negotiability of 'receivables', on the asset side of the Islamic banks. These 'receivables', according to law, cannot be sold in the market on discount. The 'receivables' therefore are not as liquid as 'loans' are in the balance sheet of a conventional bank. To what extent this element introduces risk in the banking business and how Islamic banks plan to mitigate this risk will be another question that regulators will particularly be interested in resolving while granting a license to conduct Islamic banking.

It may also be instructive to note that the application of Islamic modes of financing requires the Islamic banks to assume at some stage the ownership of the underlying assets. Though in some cases it may be made effective only for an extremely short period (such as in the case of *murabaha*-based financing), the ownership of assets, for whatever period it is assumed, involves bearing the risks associated with the ownership. These risks, of course, can be insured but that will involve additional cost. (The insurance of third party risks could be quite expensive.) This is not only an issue of efficiency in providing an alternative product, but there is also the question of who will pay this cost. If depositors pay the cost, it will have implications on the rate of return of their deposits. There will, therefore, be an issue of transparency about all costs and their implications on return for the depositors of the bank and costs to the clients seeking finances from the bank. Receivables have always been and still are the overwhelmingly dominant item, representing more than 75 per cent of the assets. As explained earlier the risk profile of receivables is not significantly different from that of 'loans'. The only risk element in receivables is their limited liquidity feature. The main issue with respect to this item relates to allowing the 'banks' to be involved in the sale, purchase and renting of assets as a part of the financing operation. The liquidity aspect, though important, is being dealt with by Islamic banks at the global level. This is further discussed later in the chapter.

Investments

The next item in the uses of funds column in the balance sheet is 'investments'. These are risk-bearing investments and hence this item is peculiar to Islamic banks and does not exist in the balance sheet of conventional banks. This may include direct investment in the equity of the clients and may also include provision of financing on the basis of modes called *mudaraba* and *musharaka* under which the bank will share in the profits and losses of its clients by virtue of meeting their financing needs. The significance of this item in the balance sheet is an empirical question. The experience of Islamic banks so far suggests that there is not much willingness on the part of banks as well as on the part of clients to deal on this basis. But irrespective of whether there is low or high demand for such modes, the regulators will need to look into how to allow the banks to perform such activities within the banking laws of the country.

The item is high in riskiness and hence another concern for the regulatory authority. The practice of Islamic banks, however, has succeeded in developing contractual stipulations as well as a system of internal and external controls to minimize even to a negligible extent the risks (for the Islamic bank) in *musharaka*-based financing. *Mudaraba* and equity participation, however, remain high-risk profile items in the balance sheet but very little amounts against these items appear, if any, in the balance sheets of existing Islamic banks (see the Glossary at the end of this book).

Other Assets

This is an item similar to those in the conventional banks' balance sheets and include bank's own assets, real estate, equipment etc. It poses no extra challenge to the regulators.

SOURCES OF FUNDS

The sources of funds in terms of liabilities acquired by Islamic banks include two main categories: current account deposits (on which no return is given to the depositors and the deposits are guaranteed) and investment accounts for which the bank shares its profit with depositors (and depositors will also share losses of the bank in case the eventuality arises and neither the principal amount of deposits nor the return thereupon are guaranteed). Some Islamic banks have a large proportion of current accounts which are liabilities.

This is a challenge for the Islamic banks before it is a challenge for the regulators. In an environment where depositors have become used to having a guarantee of their principal amount, Islamic banks will face a great challenge in attracting deposits that would carry a risk of being lost.

Islamic banks, however, can offer two types of profit-sharing investment accounts (PSIA).

1. restricted profit-sharing investment accounts;
2. unrestricted profit-sharing investment accounts.

PSIAs:

- take the place of interest-bearing deposits;
- do not represent liabilities, are accepted on a *mudaraba* basis;
- constitute the bulk of funding;
- in principle, bear the credit and market risk on the assets they finance, but not the operational or funding risks of the bank.

The deposits received under the restricted accounts are used in pre-specified projects using pre-specified modes. For such accounts, Islamic banks have succeeded in developing products that will ensure a return to the depositors varying only in a very narrow range and an almost non-existent possibility of loss. Thus despite being profit–loss-sharing accounts, the depositors can have their deposits in Islamic banks with the same risk profile that clients of a conventional bank will get on their savings accounts. Whether Islamic banks will be able to provide some sort of return profile as conventional banks provide to their depositors is an empirical question. Such accounts thus pose no significant regulatory challenge with respect to the protection of depositors' money. But the mode of operation of these accounts would require Islamic banks to enter into risk bearing that involves investment activity on the part of the bank for which a provision is to be found in the banking laws of the country.

Unrestricted profit-sharing investment accounts, however, is an item that offers the major and most complicated regulatory challenge. This is an account where the depositors authorize the bank to invest their deposits in any investment that banks find suitable and the depositors agree ex-ante to share the profits/losses arising from these investments.

First, this account guarantees neither any rate of return on deposits nor the principal amount of deposits. This violates the basic definition of a 'bank' in a conventional sense. For such accounts guaranteeing a principal amount will violate the *Shari'ah* principle. Some compromise solutions are, however, possible on this issue. The regulatory authorities and lawyers of the Islamic banks can find such solutions. The way this problem has been solved in the establishment of an Islamic bank in the UK is an example.

Another major issue that arises out of the nature of this account relates to corporate governance. The bank will be using the deposits of account holders in investments selected by the bank and account holders will not have any say in this choice. The possibility of moral hazard may arise in the use of depositors' money which may be used more in the interest of the bank than in the interest of depositors. Though depositors share the profits made by the bank as the shareholders do, unlike shareholders, depositors are not represented on the board and no Islamic bank so far been able to develop a mechanism of internal controls strong enough to take care of the interest of investment account holders *vis-à-vis* the interests of shareholders and bank management. In the disciplined financial and investment environment of Europe, this issue will be a serious challenge to the regulators.

The corporate governance issue in this respect may not be resolved simply by prudential regulations. There are aspects that relate to ethical issues also in this respect. For example, investment account holders put their money in Islamic banks to do banking according to their religious belief. The protection of interest of PSIAs, without adversely affecting the performance of Islamic banks, perhaps will best be served by strict adherence to a carefully designed code of ethics that is normally given to investment companies rather than by prudential rules governing banking activities. Also it would be the duty of the Islamic banks that they be transparent in declaring all such details that will satisfy account holders that their religious concerns are being respected in deploying their funds. This is, however, not simple in view of the diversity of opinion in religious perceptions of what is Islamic and what is un-Islamic. This would require a religious board to specify clear rules and ethical standards to make the appropriate declarations.

Another item in the sources of funds is reserves. The only distinction in this item is that some Islamic banks like to keep part of the bank's profit (before sharing it with the depositors) as a 'profit-equalization reserve'. These reserves are intended to be used to smooth out wide fluctuations in the return on the profit-sharing investment accounts. They are used to compensate the depositors for abnormal decline in profits in any year. Some prudential and ethical standards are needed to ensure that no moral hazards takes place on this account and that some depositors are not compensated from what is genuinely due for other depositors.

On the liabilities side, investment accounts dominate in an overwhelming proportion. This item poses a concern only with respect to unrestricted investment accounts. The main issues in this item are:

(a) How to conceive 'banks' that will not guarantee the deposits of the depositors.
(b) How to ensure a standard of corporate governance that will restrict the banks to match and synchronize their risk appetite with those of investment account holders.

However, it needs to be noted that the structure of the Islamic banks' balance sheet reflects a built-in stability factor which is absent from conventional banks. Any shock on the asset side can not be expected to lead to a run on the bank as much as it would in case of conventional banks. Since investment account holders share the profits and losses with the bank, they will resist their temptation to run on the bank as it would mean sharing the loss. Waiting a bit to allow the bank to recover from the shock may yield a dividend and may save investors from bearing the loss. In the case of conventional banking, depositors have no reason to wait. Running on the bank will be more advisable as those coming first will have a greater probability of not losing their money. This brings us to discussing other crucial elements of regulatory challenge, such as capital adequacy, liquidity management, corporate governance and so on.

For financial institutions, particularly the banks, capital adequacy is a major concern for regulatory authorities in order to minimize the probability of failure of a bank. This is for two reasons.

First, banks in a conventional sense always operate on a razor edge. A shock on the asset side can lead to a run on the bank and may cause the bank to collapse, though it may have the capacity to sustain the loss and recover if there is no run on the bank to withdraw the deposits. The collapse becomes inevitable if the bank does not have adequate capital to meet the unforeseen demands for withdrawals. It is the responsibility of regulatory authorities to protect depositors from loss. Ensuring capital adequacy is one instrument to ensure depositors protection.

Second, the collapse of one bank may lead to a contagion effect. Banks have liabilities on each other. The collapsing bank may impose abnormal withdrawal demands on other banks, and the collapse of one bank may send chilly waves to depositors of other banks who, fearing that other banks may also collapse, hence cause a run on other banks too. Thus the whole bank system is at risk if the banks do not maintain adequate capital to meet unexpected withdrawal demands. Regulatory authorities, in the interest of protecting the depositors and protecting the banking system, always remain preoccupied with the concern about the capital adequacy in the banking institutions. The Basel Committee on Banking Supervision which is a body of the Bank of International Settlements has worked out a framework for assessing capital adequacy, known as the Basel I and

Basel II documents. The framework, though complex and also controversial in several respects, provides regulators with guidelines to assess the capital adequacy of banking institutions. Since the latest version of the framework (Basel II – 2004) covers banking institutions which continue banking operations with securities (investment) operations (such as universal banks in Germany) and provides different capital adequacy criteria for the two categories of operation, this framework becomes relevant for the Islamic banks also. The capital adequacy for such non-banking operations as trading operations, mutual funds as well as non-financial investments through s*alam, istisna'* and *ijara* operations, can be assessed using the Basel II guidelines for the securities operations of banking institutions. But whether there is a case to subject Islamic banks to capital adequacy as rigorously as the conventional banks are subjected to, and whether Islamic banks should face the same limits of capital adequacy as imposed on conventional banks is a question that is yet to have a clear answer.

Capital adequacy requirements are meant to address two serious problems:

(a)   protection of depositors from the loss of their money;
(b)   protection of the banking system from collapse that may be caused by a contagion effect.

For Islamic banks, depositors do not stand protected by capital adequacy. They deposit their money with the understanding that they may lose their deposits. It is not the capital adequacy that can save the depositors from bearing losses. The depositors' protection in Islamic banking requires prudent rules and corporate governance standards that will not allow Islamic bank managers to satisfy their risk appetite with the depositors' money. It is the moral hazard issue that would need to be handled by prudential rules and overseeing the investment strategies of Islamic banks rather than imposing stringent capital adequacy requirements.

There is also no case for stringent capital adequacy requirements on the grounds of the contagion effect as failure of an Islamic bank is not likely to pose a threat to the entire banking system. It has also been explained earlier that the probability of a collapse of an Islamic bank due to a run on the bank is much lower than that of the conventional banks. The case for a rigorous capital adequacy requirement to mitigate the possibility of the contagion effect of collapse of a bank does not exist.

Another argument for capital adequacy is to impose market discipline on banks when there is a deposit guarantee scheme in effect which may cause banks to take more risks than depositors would like to bear. In the presence of a deposit guarantee scheme, the market may not penalize banks for keeping inadequate capital to bear the risk by investing depositors' money in risky projects. The case does not stand for imposing a capital adequacy requirement as far as PSIA deposits are concerned. Islamic banks do not subscribe to a deposit guarantee scheme, as it will have *Shari'ah* implications. Though Islamic law permits a third party (like a central bank) to guarantee the deposits, the *Shari'ah* issue will arise with respect to who will pay the cost of insurance. There is a possibility that in some Muslim countries a central bank may provide Islamic banks with a guarantee for deposits free of charge. Such a possibility in the European context probably can be ruled out at least at this stage. Hence, there is no additional care for capital adequacy because of any deposit insurance scheme.

It can be argued that despite the ability of PSIAs to absorb the shocks on the asset side, Islamic banks still cannot be assumed to be immune from 'runs' and a large volume of panic withdrawals. Such a possibility would exist if an Islamic bank happens to face a serious liquidity crisis. Islamic banks' investments in *murabaha, ijara, salam* and *istisna'* type activities generating 'receivables' on the asset side of the balance sheet are considered to be illiquid and cannot be readily disposed of to meet the withdrawal demands. Liquidity crisis is thus a genuine possibility in the context of Islamic banks. Capital adequacy, however, is not the right solution because additional capital will also be deployed in the same modes of investment unless Islamic banks are advised to keep a greater proportion of their assets in liquid form which will be an inefficient solution. The efficient solution for facing a possible liquidity crisis would be to have proper liquidity management on the asset side. Presently Islamic banks have limited choice for efficient liquidity management. But several institutions and instruments are coming up to help Islamic banks to manage their liquidity. These developments will be helpful for Islamic banks in Europe also. Malaysia and Bahrain are the most active countries where institutions and instruments for liquidity management are being developed for Islamic banks.

There is a tendency among the consultants to the regulatory authorities to suggest a capital adequacy requirement as a solution to all these peculiarities. This does nothing but put an undue burden on both the regulators as well as Islamic banks which in turn may lead to creating an unfavourable environment for Islamic banking.

There are, however, other peculiarities of Islamic banking that do require special attention from their supervision point of view. Some of the conventional methods of risk mitigation such as hedging and use of derivatives are not available on *Shari'ah* grounds. Some other *Shari'ah*-compatible alternative methods of risk management are to be explored.

There is a lack of *Shari'ah*-compliant instruments for the inter-bank market. As in commercial banks, there is a counterpart of an interest rate risk arising out of the mismatch between liabilities and assets. The rate of return on receivables in the balance sheet arises from *murabaha* (mark-up) and *ijara* rentals that are fixed in advance and cannot change with the changes in the market, while PSIA holders' expectations on the rate of return will depend on current market conditions. If expectations of PSIA exceed the return contracted by the Islamic banks on receivables, there will be a 'profit-rate squeeze' on the Islamic bank comparable to the interest-rate squeeze for conventional banks. This risk, called displaced commercial risk, has implications on the performance and efficiency of Islamic banks that supervisors would like to monitor as a part of their concern for the health of the financial sector in the country.

Several of the risks in Islamic banking can be managed by Islamic banks adopting suitable risk management strategies and tools. Financial engineers and experts are continuously helping Islamic banks on this. Supervisory authorities only have to oversee these efforts so that Islamic banks do not lapse on this account. Besides, there are prudential rules and ethical standards that can be laid down to regulate the activities and to ensure the protection of depositors.

Capital adequacy will remain important but needs to be worked out in totality, with other measures of risk management and good corporate governance, and not merely as a mechanical calculation on the framework of conventional banks. This is important if Islamic banking is to be promoted as a complementary but integral part of a country's financial structure in the spirit of broadening what is called 'social inclusion', and not as a marginal activity on the periphery of the financial structure. Islamic banking, on its own merit as well as in terms of its importance in Europe to meeting the needs of European Muslim communities, deserves to be integrated in the mainstream of the financial system rather than being left as a marginal activity. Taking an alienated approach towards the supervision of Islamic banking and making capital adequacy as the only or main tool for its regulation will deny the Islamic financial industry a level playing field and impose unnecessary additional costs on Islamic banks and hence will constrain the industry's potential to integrate in the mainstream global financial market.

To help the regulators and supervising bodies in providing a level playing a field for Islamic banks without compromising on the efficiency and ethical standards already in vogue in the national and global financial markets, a body named as the Islamic Financial Services Board (IFSB) has been established which is governed by the central bank governors of countries where Islamic banking exists. The membership of the Board also includes the IMF, World Bank and Bank for International Settlements. IFSB is rigorously reviewing international standards and developing standards from Islamic banks in the following areas:

- capital adequacy
- risk management
- corporate governance
- transparency and market discipline.

The Board is in the process of developing prudential and supervising standards in these areas for the purpose of promoting best practice for the industry at the national as well as global level. These standards are meant to complement the guidelines issued by bodies such as the Basel Committee on Banking Supervision and the International Organization of Securities Commission.

Besides the establishment of the Islamic Financial Services Board, there are other important infrastructural developments taking place to provide institutional support to the Islamic banking industry. The establishment of the International Islamic Financial Market is another such infrastructural development. One of the most important elements of risk management in Islamic banks is related to liquidity management. The problem of liquidity management arises because of the fact that most available conventional instruments for liquidity management are interest-based and therefore cannot be used by Islamic banks. The absence of an Islamic money market and an Islamic inter-bank market is, therefore, a serious hurdle in the way of proper liquidity management. The development of the International Islamic Financial Market in Bahrain which will provide a secondary market with Islamic instruments will provide a good opportunity to Islamic banks for liquidity management.

The Accounting and Auditing Organization for Islamic Financial Institutions (AAOIFI), based in Bahrain, plays an important role in integrating and harmonizing the accounting and auditing practices. The Islamic Rating Agency (IRA) is another emerging infrastructural institution.

NOTE

1. The Islamic Bank of Britain contract for depositors did mention the mandatory guaranteed interest rate (2 per cent) to be paid to the depositors on their saving accounts. If the actual rate of return on deposits calculated by the bank comes out to be more than 2 per cent, the depositors claim the actual return. If the actual rate of return turns out to be less than 2 per cent, the Muslim depositors abiding by *Shari'ah* will claim only the actual

return and will forego their legal right to claim the minimum guaranteed return of 2 per cent. Even if the bank posts the minimum guaranteed return of 2 per cent to the account of the saving deposit holders, they will keep only the part that is equal to the actual rate of return on savings deposits declared by the bank and will give the remaining part to a charity.

BIBLIOGRAPHY

Ayub, M. (2007), *Understanding Islamic Finance*, Wiley Finance Series.

Čihák, M. and Heiko, H. (2008), 'Islamic Banks and Financial Stability: An Empirical Analysis', *IMF Working Paper*, No. 16

El-Gamal, Mahmoud A. (2000), *A Basic Guide to Contemporary Islamic Banking and Finance*, Rice University, June.

El-Gamal, Mahmoud A. (2001), *An Economic Explication of the Prohibition of Riba in Classical Islamic Jurisprudence*, May 2, http://www.ruf.rice.edu/

Foot, M. (2003), *The Future of Islamic Banking in Europe*, Second International Islamic Finance Conference Dubai, September, http://www.fsa.gov.uk/Pages/Library/Communication/Speeches/2003/sp150.shtml

Institute of Islamic Banking and Insurance (IIBI) (2000), *A Compendium of Legal Opinions on the Operations of Islamic Banks, London*, edited and translated by Yusuf Talal DeLorenzo, Volume II.

Khan, Fahim M. (1991), *Comparative Economics of Some Islamic Financing Techniques*, Islamic Research and Training Institute, Islamic Development Bank, Research Paper No. 12.

Khan, Fahim M. (1995), *Islamic Futures and Their Markets*, Islamic Research and Training Institute, Islamic Development Bank, Research Paper No. 32.

Khan, Fahim M. (1999), 'Financial Modernization in the 21st Century and the Challenge for Islamic Banking', *International Journal of Islamic Financial Services*, **1** (3).

Khan, Fahim M. (2001), *Time Value of Money and Discounting in Islamic Perspective, Islamic Studies*, Islamic Research and Training Institute, Saudi Arabia: Islamic Development Bank.

Khan, Fahim M. (2005), 'Islamic Alternative Tools for Islamic Borrowing and Monetary Management', in Hassan and Lewis (eds), *Handbook of Islamic Banking and Finance*, Cheltenham, UK and Northampton, MA, USA: Edward Elgar.

Khan, Fahim M. (2006), 'Setting Shari'ah Standards for Shari'ah Application in the Islamic Finance Industry', in Hassan and Lewis (eds), *Critical Writings in Islamic Finance*, Cheltenham, UK and Northampton, MA, USA: Edward Elgar, and also in *Thunderbird International Business Review* (2007), **49** (3).

5. Islamic finance and ethical investments: some points of reconsideration

Valentino Cattelan

An apparent correspondence between Islamic finance and ethical investments is commonly argued. More precisely, Islamic finance is usually deemed to be an example of the loose realm of ethical investments, according to a *genus/species* logical relation (see Figure 5.1). But criticism of this assumption may provide a more comprehensive understanding of Islamic finance. Indeed, it seems to me that the depiction of Islamic finance as intrinsically ethical stems from two concurrent factors that have hindered any sensible investigation on the matter: first, a misleading conception of 'Islamic law' as an ethical code of behaviour; second, the idealization of Islamic finance as part of a superior social system, fostered by an enthusiastic economic scholarship.[1]

Leaving aside these assumptions, this chapter aims at proposing a more critical distinction between the categories of 'ethical investments' and 'Islamic finance' as bearer of an autonomous ethics. Consequently, I will argue for the opportunity to distinguish in academic research the notion of 'Islamic finance', as a branch of the international financial market, from the sub-category of 'ethical investments' supported by Islamic financial institutions.

ISLAMIC FINANCE AND 'ISLAMIC LAW'

Islamic finance, as is well-known, is based on the application of classical 'Islamic law' in the management of money: this implies the prohibition of interest (*riba*), of excessive risk (*gharar*), of gambling (*maysir*), the exclusion of investments in arms, alcohol, casinos, tobacco, pornography and pork, and a major attention on social welfare. As Vogel emphasizes, 'one of the more striking facts about the rise of Islamic banking and finance is that it represents an assertion of religious law in the area of commercial

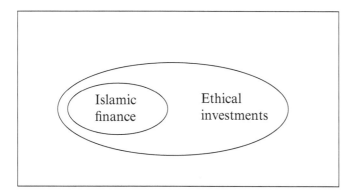

Figure 5.1   Islamic finance/ethical investments relation as commonly argued

life, where secularism rules almost unquestioned throughout the rest of the world' (Vogel and Hayes 1998, p. 19). Through the application of *Shari'ah*, 'the sacred Law of Islam' reflecting 'the divinely ordained pattern of human life', Islamic finance pursues 'a fairer distribution of wealth, greater support for the poor and needy, and less corruption and dishonesty' (Vogel and Hayes 1998, p. 26).[2]

This self-feeding description of Islamic finance and law as intrinsically ethical is widespread in Western and Islamic scholarship; it is well-accepted by Muslim believers, as it emphasizes the moral superiority of Islam; it is useful for Islamic financial institutions, which can enjoy a 'moral reputation' advantage over their 'secular' competitors. Moreover, the description can be comfortably justified by the assertion that 'faith and conscience have always been influential amongst factors encouraging to invest ethically' (Alam 2004, p. 7).

But does the application of Islamic law (which is the only peculiarity of Islamic finance) really guarantee *per se* the achievement of ethical performance? I strongly doubt it. In my opinion, this description of Islamic finance as ethical *per se* is lacking in proper hermeneutical concern. The same (conscious or unconscious) employment of 'Islamic law', *Shari'ah* and *fiqh*, as synonymous by much academic literature has certainly contributed to thickening the layer of uncertainty that continues to dominate the matter.[3]

Making up for this interpretative weakness requires focusing, first of all, on the meaning of Islam as 'submission to God's Will', a submission which is conceived by Islamic theology as unconditional and complementary to God's absolute omnipotence.[4] The Merciful has revealed the Way, *Shari'ah* (literally, 'the road leading to water'), giving the Book and sending the Prophet as reminders of the Message. But the clarity of the Truth does not mean that it is manifest, and *fiqh* (literally 'comprehension', 'understanding'[5]) is the discipline which aims specifically at 'making manifest' God's Will as 'clearly' revealed in the *Qur'an* and exemplified by the Prophet. *Fiqh* implies an effort, an endeavour (*ijtihad*) of interpretation that does not aim at acquiring any 'firm' knowledge or at constructing a systematization of God's Will, but at achieving its better understanding for the goodness of the whole Muslim community. From this standpoint, the better definition of *fiqh* is that of a 'hermeneutic discipline which explores and interprets revelation [. . .] (within the) tradition' (Calder 1996, p. 980)[6] (of one of the recognized schools (*madhahib*)[7]: in the Sunnite universe, Hanafi, Maliki, Shafi'i, Hanbali).

The above analysis leads to some critical reflections.

First, the use of *Shari'ah* and *fiqh* as synonymous is misleading, given the nature of *Shari'ah* as divine, fixed and perfect, and that of *fiqh* as human and improvable.

Second, translating *Shari'ah* into 'divine law' implies the transformation of a Merciful Path that man should decide to follow[8] without any imposition (*Qur'an*, 2: 256: 'Let there be no compulsion in religion') into a system of imposed legal rules. Then, a dramatic leap from 'God's mercy' to 'God's burden' may be apodictically brought about.

Third, translating *fiqh* into 'knowledge of divine law' or, worse, 'Islamic law' determines a mystification of its main purpose. The phrase 'Islamic law' finds its origin in the Western world-view, and it could find an equivalent only in *al-qanun al-islami,* its Arabic calques. *Fiqh*, instead, as the hermeneutical juristic theology, has historically found its chief objective in the exploration of God's Will, giving practical ends less attention. I am not arguing that *fiqh* rules have never been shaped for practical application,[9] but this was not their direct purpose, as the Western phrase 'Islamic law' could suggest. For this reason, in traditional *fiqh*, systematization is scarce; elaboration of abstract rules is avoided, as human reason cannot dare to compete with divine will; the method is heuristic and casuistic; the language is often rhetorical; and norms drawn out from interpretation combine elements that the Western perception would define as religious, ethical or legal.

This does not mean, anyway, that the concept of 'law' cannot describe *fiqh* at all, whose methodology, *usul al-fiqh*, in fact, provides it with a codified juristic reasoning. As Schacht perceived,

> though it was incorporated into the system of religious duties, the legal subject-matter was not completely assimilated, legal relationships were not completely reduced to and expressed in terms of religious and ethical duties, the sphere

of law retained a technical character of its own, and juridical reasoning could develop along its own lines. (Schacht 1964, p. 201)

Accordingly, *fiqh* was able to maintain its independence as a 'legal discipline', focusing much more on the requirement of validity according to normative reasoning rather than on ethical research for justice (Johansen 1999):

> for the Muslim, law is that which God wishes to be such. [. . .] Law, morality and social behaviour are all encompassed by religion and cannot be known without its light nor outside its framework. But this does not prevent the law from having an existence independent of the rules of morality. Actions blameworthy according to religion (*makruh*) remain nevertheless legally valid and in the same way the failure to do something recommended by religion (*mandub*) produces effects in law. Sinfulness and validity are able to co-exist. (Afchar 1973, p. 96)

As Chafik Chehata remarks, 'Islamic jurisconsults have always made a clear distinction between the domain of law and that of morality and religion' (Chehata 1970, p. 138).

To conclude this introductory section:

1. the idea of an intrinsic 'ethical' nature of *fiqh* should be rectified: as a specific 'normative discourse' based on reasoning, *fiqh* focuses on the category of 'normative validity' (according to the 'grammar' of *usul al-fiqh*), and not on morality;
2. the 'legal' nature of this 'normative discourse' does not exist *per se*, even if the identification of the *fiqh* with 'Islamic law' has become a sort of tautology at present. As I tried to show, the hermeneutical premise of *fiqh* does not match perfectly with the Western category of 'law', whose practical orientation (law does exist to be applied, as an authoritative system of rules) is merely incidental in the cultural premise of *fiqh*, and, moreover, risks transforming it into a sort of *al-qanun al-islami*, with a shift from the realm of the interpretation of the divine will into that of secular legal systems. Certainly, we can speak of *fiqh* as 'Islamic law', but in this case we have to be conscious that we are shaping it as a '"positive" system of law [. . .] applied over the centuries, in varying degrees of flexibility, like *any other living legal system*', and, coherently, that 'it is right to say, not that there are a number of schools of Islamic law, but rather that there are a *number of legal systems*, each of which rightly claims to be a *system of Islamic law*' (directed to application and without any divine self-proclaimed orientation/authority).[10] In other cases the translation risks traducing its nature.

WHICH 'ETHICS' ARE BEHIND ISLAMIC FINANCE?

Thus, the identification of *Shari'ah*, *fiqh* and 'Islamic law' (that has led many authors to interpret Islam as the legalistic religion *par excellence*[11]) and the interpretation of Islamic finance as ethical *per se* as manifestation of religious ideals need to be reoriented.

In particular, two points need thorough examination.

1. First of all, the contemporary attempt to reassert the eternal validity of *Shari'ah* thanks to the application of *fiqh* risks confusing, as already suggested, the religious foundation of Islamic ethics with an authoritative imposition of legal rules. To be more precise, if the *ijtihad* of traditional *fiqh* was certainly 'God-oriented', the present reality of Islamic finance seems to be dominated by the application of what I have defined *al-qanun al-islami*, with a net prevalence of a 'practice-oriented' attitude on ethical concerns.[12] Indeed, it seems to me that the present situation does not show the reassertion of *Shari'ah* values, but a persistent spreading of *hiyal* ('legal devices', 'stratagems', 'evasions')[13] in Islamic commercial activities. This statement finds evidence in the overwhelming prevalence of profit mark-up (*murabaha*, *salam*, *'ina*, . . .) and leasing (*ijara*) instruments over *profit–loss-sharing* (PLS) financial products (*mudaraba* and *musharaka*) in the investments strategy of Islamic financial institutions. Even if censured by Islamic scholarship for the dissimulation of interest, fixed return techniques of financing continue to represent the main Islamic finance operative mode (Siddiqui 2002, pp. 11–24). Then, it should be honestly recognized that despite their *al-qanun al-islami* validity, these modes are *Shari'ah*-undesirable, and they do not seem to provide any ethical improvement in the management of money, as their PLS alternatives could do.
2. Nevertheless, in spite of these evident drawbacks, authoritative scholarship continues to praise without reserve Islamic finance, depicting its shortcomings as transitory and bearable since the 'application' of *Shari'ah* will ensure a future of prosperity to all mankind.[14] Why? Is this not an ideological position rather than a scientific statement?

An explanation may come from a reflection on the ethics that animates Islamic finance.

If historically Islam has experienced different theories on the ontological status of ethical values (Hourani 1985), the 'normative ethics' that Islamic jurists adopt focuses on the complete submission to God's Will as intended by Ash'arite moral theology. According to the Ash'arite theology, which corresponds to Sunnite orthodoxy, values have no objective existence that can be perceived by human reason (Mu'tazilite position[15]): they are whatever God commands and can be known only by scriptural and prophetical tradition, in other words, by 'following *Shari'ah* according to the juristic interpretation of *fiqh*'.

The assertion strongly diverges from the Western conception of ethics as based on universal (objective) moral values stemming from rationality and free will. The idea is, more or less, that men act rationally according to certain values and that the 'right' action reflects a perception of 'objective' justice which belongs to 'human nature'. Historically this paradigm has led to the belief in a set of 'objectively true' norms governing human behaviour, namely 'natural law',[16] focusing on the prevalence of truth (*veritas*) on human contingent power (*auctoritas*), which has shaped the opposite category of 'positive law'.

Well, what instead is the role of rational behaviour in Islamic juristic ethics? As anticipated, in Ash'arite moral theology man has no possibility to distinguish 'good' from 'evil', since they do not exist *per se*, as part of an objective natural order. They are, instead, mercifully identified by God's Will: *veritas* and *auctoritas* (or mercy?) do converge. Consequently, following *Shari'ah* is acting well; infringing *Shari'ah* is acting badly. No recourse to the Western 'invention' of natural law is needed for Islamic ethics, which is completely focalized on God's Will. The outcome of this juristic ethics is the development of the 'impératif de l'obligation pure, dans lequel les valeurs du sentiment et meme du jugement [. . .] (sont) totalement annihilées' (Vadet 1982, p. 236). The only role given to human reason is to discern the clarity of the Message and then to devote to it; no 'rational' evaluation about good and evil is possible, since they are already determined by *Shari'ah*.

ISLAMIC FINANCE AND (ISLAMIC) ETHICAL INVESTMENTS

The juristic conception of ethics that belongs to Islamic moral theology and dominates Islamic *fiqh* provides us with a strong hermeneutical tool for explaining the aprioristic description of Islamic finance as intrinsically ethical: if the 'good' is defined by *Shari'ah*, then its application will ensure ethical results in the end, regardless of present shortcomings.

I have already raised criticism on this assumption. Moreover, it is likely to provoke at least three undesirable effects.

First, this 'messianic' connotation of Islamic finance[17] in opposition to 'secular' welfare practices may undermine an objective examination of its

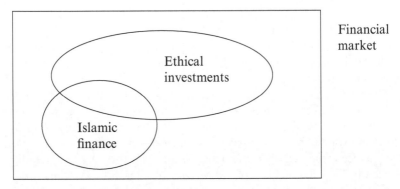

Figure 5.2   Islamic finance/ethical investments relation: neutral approach

real economic achievements, in terms of wealth increase, raising of productivity, and reduction of inequalities.[18] Second, the formal application
of *hiyal* may easily subordinate the substantial objectives that incontest-
ably belong to Islamic ethics (support for the poor, avoidance of exploitation. . .) to a formal application of *fiqh* (*al-qanun al-islami*) rules. Third,
regarding social cohesion and improvement, Islamic finance assertors risk
preventing Muslims from achieving a serene integration into contemporary multi-valued societies and economies, due to a negative consideration
of conventional interest-based financial products.[19]

To conclude, let me propose two reasonable remedies to the second and
third inconveniences (the avoidance of the first one being under the personal responsibility of each scholar).

On the one hand, the 'ethical' performance of Islamic finance should be
evaluated according to a 'substantial' approach: that is, it should not be
derived from the application of *fiqh* rules *per se*, but from the substantial
destination of the funds. This implies the need for labelling as 'ethical'
not any investment managed by Islamic financial institutions, but only
those that realize forms of PLS partnerships (in microfinance projects,
for instance) or that sponsor social responsible ventures: those that are,
in other terms, really 'ethically oriented'. In other terms, the qualification
of 'ethical investments' would derive from a 'neutral' approach[20] and not
from the label of the application of 'Islamic law'. This, of course, will
weaken the 'reputation factor' that Islamic financial institutions have
opportunistically enjoyed till now. Accordingly, the initial scheme should
be reconstructed as shown in Figure 5.2.

On the other hand, a renewed perception of Islamic finance would be
promoted. Non-Islamic interest-based investments would not be classified
as 'bad' by Islamic scholars. At the same time, Islamic investments would

not be interpreted or intended as a means for reasserting a purer Islamic way of life, but as one of the several branches of the contemporary financial system, whose techniques, if really ethically orientated, do contribute to a more just economical system (as their interest-based 'cousins' can do: the experiences of Grameen Bank, micro-credit and elimination of collaterals prove the assertion).

Of course, this requires that Islamic finance renounces its brand identity and its self-proclaimed status of 'exceptionalism', with the recognition that the application of *fiqh* (*al-qanun al-islami*/Islamic law) is not a legal duty but a free choice of Muslim/non-Muslim investors (which becomes a manifestation of worship towards God for Muslims, if sustained by a sincere intention, *niyya*).

NOTES

1. This attitude is clear, for instance, in Chapra (1992). Here the author radically contrasts the imperfections of 'secularist' welfare states with the ideal operation of an economic system derived from Islam.
2. Islamic law is said to be 'an all-embracing body of religious duties, the totality of Allah's commands that regulate the life of every Muslim in all its aspects', 'the epitome of Islamic thought, the most typical manifestation of the Islamic way of life, the core and kernel of Islam itself' (Schacht 1964, p. 1). In similar terms, Coulson defines Islamic law as an 'ideal code of behaviour', while 'jurisprudence (*fiqh*) [. . .] is [. . .] a composite science of law and morality, whose exponents (*fuqaha'*; sing. *faqih*) are the guardians of the Islamic conscience' (Coulson 1964, p. 83).
3. As Norman Calder notes, 'Western scholarship (even when written by Muslims) has rarely presented Islamic law in such a way as to demonstrate its values rather than the values of the observer. It is legal practice in the Western sense [. . .] that dominates the standard introductions to the subject [. . .]. Certain features of Muslim juristic discourse, those perhaps which are most revealing of its nature and its intentions, are in such works disregarded in favour of a search of practical rules (certainly present, but strangely hard, sometimes, to find)' (Calder 1996, p. 979).
4. The assumption is the result of the historical triumph of Ash'arite over Mu'tazilite in the sphere of the *kalam*, the Islamic speculative theology. If the Mu'tazilite (influenced by the Hellenistic philosophy as proven by Gutas (1998) initially argued the correspondence of God's Will to an objective reason, which human intellect could conceive, sharing with God the same perception of natural justice, the Ash'arite eventually promoted an orthodoxy based on an absolute freedom of God, as manifestation of His undeniable omnipotence.
5. As Patrick Glenn remarks, *fiqh* is 'sometimes referred to in western writing as the "science" of Islamic law or jurisprudence, though its literal meaning is simply that of "understanding"' (Glenn 2004). Also the usual translation of *'fiqh'* into 'knowledge' may be misleading: for the reason that I stress in the text, in fact, there is no 'certain' knowledge in *fiqh*.
6. This hermeneutical discipline may be better perceived, in its effort of expressing submission to God through juristic literature, next to Sufism, where rationality is abandoned in favour of contemplation, asceticism, introspection and meditation on God (ibid., p. 997). For further reference, see Leaman and Nasr (1996, pp. 367–525) and Kiliç (1996, pp. 947–58).
7. For an interpretation of the *fiqh* as a hermeneutical/linguistic discipline, aimed at understanding the revealed 'legal Speech', see the introduction by Éric Chaumont to Al-Šīrāzī (1999). The introduction deserves a quotation for the constant attention of the author

to the meaning of Islamic terms in their *own* cultural context (see, for instance, p. 4, note 5: 'La métaphore du "chemin à suivre" est omniprésente en Islam. Le terme *šarīʿa* lui-même, que nous traduisons communément par "loi", signifie plus immédiatement la "voie"; le *madhab*, le "chemin" si l'on veut, désignant l'une des manières possibles de "cheminer" sur cette "voie"').

8. The metaphor of the solitary traveller in the desert and of the road leading to water, and therefore salvation, is strongly stuck in Arabic culture and Islamic thought. The title of one of the most relevant books of Shafi'i tradition (Ahmad Ibn Naqib al-Misri 1997, d. 769/1368) confirms this image of salvation.

9. The attention to the necessities of the commercial traffics is strongly demonstrated by the well-known literature of *hiyal*, 'legal devices', to which many contractual schemes of Islamic finance actually belong.

10. In fact this was the specific and conscious interpretative approach by Chafik Chehata, to whom the quotations in the text refer (ibid., italics original).

11. Denny, for instance, believes that Islam should be characterized as a religion of ortho-praxy instead of orthodoxy (Denny 1985, pp. 1069–84).

12. The length of the present chapter does not allow investigating whether the reconfigura-tion of the God-oriented *fiqh* into the practice-oriented *al-qanun al-islami* will be irre-versible for the future or not.

13. *Hiyal* (pl. of *hila*) 'can be described, in short, as the use of legal means for extra-legal ends [. . .]. The "legal devices" enabled persons who would otherwise [. . .] have had to act against the provisions of the sacred Law, to arrive at the desired result while actually conforming to the letter of the law. For instance, the Koran prohibits interest [. . .] while at the same time there was an imperative demand for the giving and taking of interest in commercial life. In order to satisfy this need, and at the same time to observe the letter of the religious prohibition, a number of devices were developed' (Schacht 1964, pp. 78–9).

14. 'In any event, if its interpretation of God's law is correct, Islamic finance should experi-ence great worldly success, yielding moral, financial, and social rewards, thus proving to the world the superiority of Islamic norms [*sic*!]. Its successes should not only be individual, but social, leading to a more just society' (Vogel and Hayes 1998, p. 26).

15. See note 4, above.

16. In the Tomistic conception of natural law, for instance, 'goodness is understood as the fulfilment of a thing's proper function, that is, the fulfilment of a thing's nature. While the nature of the human person is understood most fully in light of the revelation [. . .], the basic aspects of human nature are accessible through ordinary human experience and reason' (Beabout and Schmiesing 2004, p. 86; Schwartz, Tamari and Schwab 2004, pp. 76–82).

17. 'Islamic banks, being enlightened by Islamic norms, should enjoy Muslims' support and patronage [. . .] The success of Islamic financial institutions would be the harbinger of a host of other advances toward a more integrated Islamic way of life' (Vogel and Hayes 1998, p. 28).

18. Spread criticism on the 'messianic' character of Islamic finance can be found in Kuran (1986, pp. 135–64; 1989, pp. 171–91) and Behdad (1989, pp. 185–211).

19. '. . . in pursuing cultural protectionism Islamic economics [. . .] (fights assimilation by) the guild that it fosters by characterizing certain universal economic practices as un-Islamic' (Kuran 1996, p. 438).

20. To be clear, 'neutral' does not mean 'secular', in my mind.

BIBLIOGRAPHY

Afchar, H. (1973), 'The Muslim conception of law', in *International Encyclopedia of Comparative Law*, Vol. II, *The Legal Systems of the World, Their Comparison and Unification*, Chap. 1, *The Different Conceptions of the Law*.

Aggarwal, Rajesh K. and Yousef, T. (2000), 'Islamic banks and investment financing', *Journal of Money, Credit and Banking*, **32** (1).

Ahmad ibn Naqib al-Misri and Nuh Ha Mim Keller (eds) (1997), *The Reliance of the Traveller: a Classic Manual of Islamic Sacred Law*, by Nuh Ha Keller and Nuh Ha Mim Keller (translators), Amana Publications.

Alam, N. (2004), *Islamic Finance – Issues and Opportunities*, EIRIS.

Al-Šīrāzī, A. (1999), *Kitāb al-Luma'fī usūl al-fiqh, Le livre des rais illuminant les fondements de la compréhension de la Loi, Traité de théorie légale musulmane*, Berkeley: Robbins Collection Publications.

Beabout, Gregory R. and Schmiesing, Kevin E. (2004), 'Catholic perspectives: social responsible investing: an application of Catholic social thought', in *Convergence: New Directions in Islamic finance?*, The Arab Financial Forum.

Behdad, S. (1989), 'Property rights in contemporary Islamic economic thought: a critical perspective', *Review of Social Economics*, **47** (2), 185–211.

Calder, N. (1996), 'Law', in O. Leaman and O. Nasr Seyyed (eds), *History of Islamic Philosophy*, London and New York: Routledge, pp. 979–98.

Chapra, Muhammad, U. (1992), *Islam and the Economic Challenge*, Islamic Economic Series, Leicester and Nairobi: Islamic Foundation.

Chehata, C. (1966), 'L'equité en tant que source du droit hanafite', *Studia Islamica*, 25.

Chehata, C. (1970), 'Islamic law', in *International Encyclopedia of Comparative Law*, Vol. II, *The Legal Systems of the World, Their Comparison and Unification*, Chap. 2, *Structure and the Divisions of the Law*.

Coulson, N. (1964), *A History of Islamic Law*, Edinburgh: Edinburgh University Press.

Cowton, C. (1994), 'The development of ethical investment products', in A. Prindl and B. Prodhan (eds), *Ethical Conflicts in Finance*, Oxford: Blackwell Finance.

Denny, F. (1985), *An Introduction to Islam*, London and New York.

Denny, F. (1994), 'Islamic theology in the new world: some issues and prospects', *Journal of the American Academy of Religion*, **62** (4), 1069–84.

DiVanna, J. and Strategies, M. (2004), 'Will Islamic banking appeal to non-Muslims?', in *Convergence: New Directions in Islamic Finance?*, The Arab Financial Forum, pp. 72–4.

Dusuki, Asyraf W. and Abdullah, Nurdianawati I. (2007), 'Why do Malaysian customers patronise Islamic banks?', *International Journal of Bank Marketing*, **25** (3), 142–60.

El-Gamal, Mahmoud A. (2007), '"Interest" and the paradox of contemporary Islamic law and finance', http://www.ruf.rice.edu/~elgamal/files/interest.pdf, 25 July.

Ellison, R. (1997), 'Corporate governance and ethical investment: legal aspects of the role of financial institutions in the UK', in A. Pezard and J.M. Thiveaud, *Corporate Governance. Les perspectives internationales*, Paris: AEF, pp. 217–303.

Glenn, Patrick H. (2004), *Legal Traditions of the World, Sustainable Diversity in Law*, Oxford: Oxford University Press.

Gutas, D. (1998), *Greek Thought, Arabic Culture: the Graeco-Arabic Translation Movement in Baghdad and Early 'Abbāsid Society (2ⁿᵈ–4ᵗʰ/8ᵗʰ–10ᵗʰ c.)*, Routledge.

Hallaq, Wael B. (1984), 'Considerations on the function and character of Sunni legal theory', *Journal of the American Oriental Society*, **104** (4), 679–89.

Hallaq, Wael B. (1984), 'Was the gate of ijtihad closed?', *International Journal of Middle East Studies*, **16** (1), 3–41.

Hallaq, Wael B. (1986), 'On the origins of the controversy about the existence of mujtahids and the gate of ijtihad', *Studia Islamica*, **63**, 129–41.

Hallaq, Wael, B. (1997), *A History of Islamic Legal Theories*, Cambridge: Cambridge University Press.

Hourani, G. (1985), *Reason and Tradition in Islamic Ethics*, Cambridge: Cambridge University Press.

Johansen, B. (1999), *Contingency in a Sacred Law: Legal and Ethical Norms in the Muslim Fiqh*, Studies in Islamic Law and Society, Leiden.

Kamali, Mohammad H. (1996), 'Methodological issues in Islamic jurisprudence', *Arab Law Quarterly*, **11** (1), 3–33.

Kiliç, M.E. (1996), 'Mysticism', in O. Leaman and S.H. Nasr (eds), *History of Islamic Philosophy*, London and New York: Routledge, pp. 947–58.

Kuran, T. (1986), 'The economic system in contemporary Islamic thought: interpretation and assessment', *International Journal of Middle East Studies*, **18** (2), 135–64.

Kuran, T. (1989), 'On the notion of economic justice in contemporary Islamic thought', *International Journal of Middle East Studies*, **21** (2), 171–91.

Kuran, T. (1996), 'The discontents of Islamic economic morality', *The American Economic Review*, **86** (2), 195–206.

Leaman, O. and Nasr, S. (1996), 'Philosophy and the mystical tradition', in O. Leaman and S. Nasr (eds), *History of Islamic Philosophy*, London and New York: Routledge, pp. 367–525.

Lynch, J. (1991), *Ethical Banking: Surviving in an Age of Default*, New York: Macmillan.

Makdisi, G. (1979), 'The significance of the Sunni schools of law in Islamic religious history', *International Journal of Middle East Studies*, **10** (1), 1–8.

Makdisi, G. (1985), 'Freedom in Islamic jurisprudence, ijtihad, taqlid, and academic freedom', in *La notion de liberté au Moyen Age: Islam, Byzance, Occident*, Paris: Les Belles Lettres, pp. 79–88.

Makdisi, J. (1984), 'The juridical theology of Shāfi'ī: origins and significance of usūl al-fiqh', *Studia Islamica*, **59**, 5–47.

Makdisi, J. (1985), 'Legal logic and equity in Islamic law', *The American Journal of Comparative Law*, **33** (1), 63–92.

Rahman, F. (1979), *Islam*, Chicago: University of Chicago Press.

Wilson, R. (1997), 'Islamic finance and ethical investments', *International Journal of Social Economics*, **24** (11).

Saleh, Nabil A. (1992), *Unlawful Gain and Legitimate Profit in Islamic Law, Riba, Gharar and Islamic Banking*, London: Graham & Trotman.

Schacht, J. (1964), *An Introduction to Islamic Law*, Oxford: Clarendon Press.

Schwartz, Mark S., Tamari, M. and Schwab, D. (2004), 'Ethical Investing from a Jewish Perspective', in *Convergence: New Directions in Islamic Finance?*, The Arab Financial Forum, pp. 76–82.

Siddiqui, S.H. (2002), 'Islamic banking: true modes of financing', *Journal of Islamic Banking & Finance*, **19** (1), 11–24.

Smirnov, A. (1996), 'Understanding justice in an Islamic context: some points of contrast with Western theories', *Philosophy East and West*, **46** (3), Seventh East–West Philosophers' Conference.

Vadet, J.C. (1982), 'Controverses théologiques autour de la notion d'obligation morale chez les Arabes', in *La notion d'autorité au Moyen Age, Islam, Byzance, Occident*, Colloques Internationaux de la Napoule, Session des 23–26 octobre 1978, Press Universitaires de France.

Vogel Frank, E. and Hayes, S.L. (1998), *Islamic Law and Finance. Religion, Risk and Return*, The Hague, London, Boston: Kluwer Law International.

PART III

The challenge

6. Islamic banking versus conventional banking

Claudio Porzio

INTRODUCTION

Conventional and Islamic banking activity had different evolutions, although they have common origins and foundations in interest prohibition: historically, these have been essentially connected to the extreme poverty of some borrowers; in non-mercantile societies it was necessary and ethically right to protect 'the weak counterpart'.

In the banking activity which has shaped itself in the western context, characteristics of the traditional banking transactions have been influenced by requirements directly connected to the limits in applying the usury prohibition and banks have progressively been 'separated' from risks inherent to customers' activities. On the contrary, in the Islamic context the interest-based system is replaced by a system based on creditor participation in the profits and risks of the activity (a corporate model?). The impossibility of applying predetermined interest rates has not prevented the Islamic credit institutions from offering financial instruments able to satisfy the economic needs and preferences of customers. The main alternative method is risk sharing used in relationships between bank and depositors on one side and borrowers on the other, while profit and loss sharing represents the alternative to calculating interest rates (Piccinelli 2002). The fact that Islamic laws prohibit paying and receiving interest does not imply that they frown on making money or encourage reverting to an all-cash or barter economy: all parties in a financial transaction have to share risk and the profit or loss of the project.

Adopting such a model, the proceeds of both deposits and investments are not predetermined but calculated *ex-post*, according to incomes really achieved: deposits are considered similar to a stock purchase and, similarly, the withdrawal of money like the selling of the said stocks; lending money, the bank participates in the profits or losses of the financed companies. Depositors, banks and entrepreneurs find themselves being 'associates' in specified business activities, sharing profits and losses.

A loan provides the lender with a fixed return irrespective of the outcome of the borrower's venture: it is much fairer to have a sharing of profits and losses. Fairness in this context has two dimensions: the supplier of capital possesses a right to reward, but this reward should be correspondent to the risks and efforts involved and thus be governed by the return on the individual project for which funds are supplied. Hence, what is forbidden in Islamic is a predetermined return; the profit sharing is legitimate.

To describe the Islamic financial system exclusively as interest-free, would be misleading. The *Shari'ah* rules that give Islamic banking its distinctive religious identity and must be observed also include: the prohibition of economic activities involving speculation (*gharar*); the obligation of paying the *zakat*; the discouragement of the production of goods and services which contradict the value pattern of Islam (*haram*, the sacrality of contracts); and the prohibition to invest in activities forbidden by the *Qur'an* law.

Since common origins have taken different evolutionary paths, but banks have the same economic function of funds' transfer between economic units, is Islamic finance coherent with the financial intermediation theory according to which the bank is typical because risk transformation is realized through the balance sheet interposition between depositors and borrowers (Porzio 2009)? Moreover, is the Islamic banking activity compatible with the current evolution of the supervision regulation?

Concerning typical banking contracts, on the asset side, borrowers' screening and monitoring, also with respect to *riba*, give place to contracts (*mudaraba, musharaka, ijara*) which are similar to conventional ones, at least from the economic point of view. On the contrary, a typical contract for collecting money is characterized by the absence of any guarantee on capital reimbursement and by the presence of the profit-sharing mechanism.

In terms of risks, the profit- and loss-sharing mechanism reduces the impact of the financial risks transformation carried out by any financial intermediary: channelling funds from middle–low-risk depositors to long-term lending in favour of middle–high-risk borrowers transforms the Islamic bank into a market liability intermediary. As there is no longer a need for transformation to make the needs and preferences of lenders and borrowers coherent and compatible, an integrated asset and liability management approach becomes less important than in the conventional bank but it requires a distribution policy based on its stability.

TYPE OF OPERATIONS AND CONTRACTS

Are Islamic funding and lending operations similar to, or at least compatible with, conventional banking activity? Anticipating some more analytic considerations, we can assert that the problem is, from the liability side, limited and mostly related to 'nominal' aspects while, from the asset side, of a more complex resolution.

Current accounts satisfy the traditional need for services related to cash and payments management and the bank supplies the traditional payment instruments, but a credit card cannot be used since it can cause payment delays which accumulate eventual interest. Rather, funds accumulating in these accounts can only be used to balance liquidity needs and for short-term transactions under the bank's responsibility.

Savings accounts also operate under the *al-wadi'a* principle and have no guarantee concerning return or capital reimbursement even though it is possible to withdraw: for this reason, it is possible to think about a certain kind of 'segregation'. Savings accounts differ from current deposits because, depending upon financial results, the Islamic bank may discretionally decide to pay 'dividends' periodically calculated on the basis of the profitability of related investments. As they are not liabilities at the nominal value, there is not a problem of depositors' protection and banks use collected resources for short–medium low-risk investments, even if the risk level still remains higher compared to traditional banks. Depositors have fewer guarantees: but the possibility to withdraw causes the bank a management problem in terms of both liquidity and risk control of lending operations.

The profit sharing investment accounts (PSIAs) have limited or unlimited maturity and, according to the type of investment, can be restricted and unrestricted. The bank can only use customers' funds for financing specific initiatives, playing the role of agent and monitoring the development of the initiatives: so, such contracts are improperly called and considered as time deposits. Periodically, or at year-end, the bank withdraws a part of the profits or losses of the investment to the depositors, according to a previously established agreement. In practice, investment accounts represent a hybrid instrument between equity and debt.

The amount of funds effectively invested is calculated considering liquidity reserves. Meanwhile, the profit share due to depositors is a part, net of *mudarib,* of the total profit that also includes all revenues for services and is net of both all operating expenses and provisions against risk. This means that the bank regulates the relationships between shareholders and depositor-investors in the so-called pooling method; such a method implies relevant problems concerning the potential conflict of interest and the implementation of complex corporate governance models. Alternatively, according to the so-called separation method, depositors only participate in the financial results, profits, losses and costs of the risk arising from the investments, while revenues from services and operating costs are fully charged to shareholders. The quota for *mudarib* is deducted from the profits due to depositor-investors and included in the profit due to shareholders only if the result of the portfolio management is positive; on the contrary, if the lending activity generates loss, the *mudarib* is equal to zero and provisions against market and credit risks are shared between shareholders and depositor-investors.

It is not clear which are the effective barriers isolating risks and perform-ances pertaining to the different stakeholder categories: in fact, assets are generally managed like a pool, in which it is not possible to distinguish between investments related to specific categories of depositors, while total revenues, arising from the investment of all funds, including money depos-its, are shared between shareholders and depositor-investors according to their respective participation in the capital invested.

Islamic banks try to assure to PSIA a rate of return almost in line with market interest rates applied by conventional banks on similar instru-ments; moreover, the probability for depositors to incur a capital loss is largely reduced by the fact that most banks, under the control of the national supervising authorities, have two different voluntary reserves:

1. the investment risk reserve used to absorb potential losses and playing the same function of loan risk provisions in conventional banks;
2. the profit equalization reserve to level off the rate of return during the economic cycle, similar to the equalization reserve used by insurance companies for smoothing economic results.

For PSIA subscribers, the *mudaraba* contract introduces many elements of ambiguity, mainly due to the discretionary powers of the bank arising from the lack of transparency concurred from the combined management of funds (the pooling method). Such discretion is used, in particular: in establishing the criteria for shareholders' and depositor-investors' capital allocation; in modifying the profit share as compensation for the activity carried out as *mudarib*; in choosing the methods for calculating the money reserves deducted from the invested capital (and therefore also from the profit and loss share), and, above all, in deciding to cover losses using self-financed provisions or the investment risk reserve.

In lending activity, Islamic law expresses a clear preference for equity financing compared to debt financing. Contracts, limited in number, are all based on schemes that can be distinguished between those indirectly and those directly participating in the profits and losses of the financed company.

In the first case, contracts (mainly *murabaha* and *ijara*) are substantially similar to a term sale that could characterize the bank as a trade intermediary that takes title and risks also on the underlying sold good; in the second case, contracts (mainly *mudaraba* and *musharaka*) are substantially similar to an association in participation that always requires the borrowers' analysis, as in the case of the loan portfolio of a conventional bank.

In the *mudaraba*, the *sahib al-mal* entrusts funds to the entrepreneur (*mudarib*) to undertake an activity: in this case, the entrepreneur brings non-financial resources (his or her job, creativity and engagement) and is the only manager of the activity while the financial resources remain the property of the bank that has no direct role in organizing and managing the investment project. The bank cannot interfere in the company's business policy, although it can contribute with non-financial resources, but only if it is clearly possible to determine the monetary value of its contribution before its effective employment.

Mudaraba represents a PLS contract where the return to lenders is a specified share in the profit/loss outcome of the project in which they have a stake, but no voice. Only profits are shared among counterparts according to a proportion already defined and agreed, because losses are exclusively the responsibility of the bank and the entrepreneur is considered sufficiently penalized by the lack of gain and by the wasted investment in the job.

Mudaraba also describes the relationship between the bank and the depositors who, through investment accounts, participate directly in the profits eventually gained by the bank. The bank itself plays the role of *mudarib* managing depositors' funds according to the rules of a *mudaraba* agreement. In so doing, the bank creates a double *mudaraba* contract, assuming the functions of *mudarib* in collecting funds and *rabb al-mal* in financing customers. Moreover the bank can stipulate contracts of *musharaka* with borrowers, sharing the profits and the eventual losses. *Mudaraba* contracts, since they are generally high risk in that the associate is responsible for the losses, are used almost exclusively for short-term financing as import–export and the purchase of raw materials.

Similar to a joint-venture, *musharaka* is considered to be the economic instrument with the greater degree of Islamic 'purity and harmony' hence its prominent role in many Islamic countries. The entrepreneurs add some finance of their own to that supplied by the investors, so exposing themselves to the risk of capital loss; the bank can directly take part in the decisions concerning the ordinary project's management and sometimes participates in its execution, perhaps by providing managerial expertise. Profits and losses are shared between the parties according to pre-fixed proportions – these proportions need not coincide with the ratio of financing input but also relate to the principle of the effective contribution to the development of the plan or the enterprise; and conversely, eventual losses are distributed between contractors in proportion to the capital given.

The *musharaka* contract can have a fixed maturity (in this case, funds are progressively reimbursed according to profits realized) or an undetermined maturity (in this case, the invested capital does not give place to periodic dividends in the short term). Among terms that must be decided on before the conclusion of the contract are those related to the possible termination of the contract – for defining whether the participants' unanimity is necessary or the will of one single party is sufficient – and those regarding the possibility to establish compensation or fixed salaries related to the functions and tasks carried out.

Murabaha, similar to a sale with a profit mark-up, still remains prevalent in the Islamic world even if it is criticized since many retain that it is no more than a 'masked' use of the interest rate. For being *murabaha* Islamic compliant, the good, even for a short period, must be in the possession of the lender who takes on the risks connected to its maintenance in good condition until a definitive transfer. In particular cases, it is the customer who has to find the good, acting as an agent of the bank. Then, the customer will ask to sell and only as a result of an explicit acceptance will the passage of property and of the implicit risk consequently happen.

At each stage of the contract, the customer and the bank assume different roles and functions. At the beginning, there is a promise of sale and, correspondingly, a promise of purchase based on an agreement of *murabaha*, therefore the roles are those typical of a guarantor and a promissee. In the case in which the customer is managing the process of finding the good, a relationship between the agent (customer) and principal (bank) is created; afterwards, it is followed by the true sale, in which the two parts become, respectively, seller (the bank) and buyer (the customer). Only in the final step, with the passage of ownership of the good, is there a true financial relationship between a creditor and a debtor, in the transfer of the possession and the payment. Only at this time can the bank require its customer to make an obligation to guarantee the payment. This possibility is denied in the previous steps since there is no a credit relationship between the parties.

In case of delay in payment in full or in defined instalments, no increase in the amount due is allowed, so the price remains equal to that established when the contract was signed. The only recognized and admitted exception is tied to the case in which the parties have decided to donate the possible increase produced in the various steps of the project, but the sum in surplus must never form part of the earnings of the lending counterpart (the bank). According to Islamic law, the contract of *murabaha* does not include penalties, for delays of payment or lack of execution of the defined obligations. To avoid this problem, in some countries the concept of mark-down, the opposite to mark-up, has been introduced. Through this method, for payments in advence a reduction of the amount due is applied.

The *ijara* is accepted by Islamic law because revenues for the bank originate from the rental of a real good: the property and the connected risk remain in the bank while the customer has only the right to use the good. *Ijara* is similar to an operating leasing contract, typically carried out in the western context, by specialized financial companies but not, at least not directly, by banks. The *ijara wa iqtina* is similar to a contract of sale with limited ownership in which the customer is obliged, at the expiration of the prefixed period, to buy the good previously acquired by the financial institution. The customer opens a banking account that cannot be subject to withdrawal but receives periodic deposits that the bank can use and reinvest. Only when the account balance reaches an amount equal to the cost of the purchase of the good plus the cost of the bank's services is it possible to carry out the exchange of property with the consequent transfer of the funds.

The *istisna'* is a contract to acquire goods on behalf of a third party where the price is paid to the manufacturer in advance and the goods produced and delivered at a later date. The agreement is applied to contracts of deferred exchange, with particular regard to assets produced on specific request. With no obligation to pay the agreed price in advance or at delivery, this contract can be conveniently used by small and medium enterprises and by families. Generally the *istisna'* is applied in two steps: (a) a contract within the bank and the buyer who needs a particular good (for example, machinery, a new plant, or a house); (b) a contract between the bank, transforming itself into a buyer, and a third party that will become completely responsible for the correct procedure of the project according to the predefined terms and conditions.

The *bay al-salam* today continues to play a prominent role in financing the agricultural sector even if its use has been progressively extended to the commerce of raw materials and fungible products. *Bay al-salam* is really the opposite of *murabaha*: there the bank gives the commodity first, and receives the money later, here the bank pays the money first and receives the commodity later. It represents, together with *ijara*, the only exception to the *Qur'an* prohibition of exchanging goods and assets that are still nonexistent. For instance, it is necessary to specify the amount to be exchanged because a change due to uncontrollable or explicitly expected events is not permitted unless the transformation of the contract is an aleatory one. The buyer has the right to request the subscription of an obligation conditioned to the successful conclusion of the transaction, and in case of non-fulfilment by the counterpart he can proceed to the cancellation of the contract without lessening its validity.

In terms of risk, in contracts substantially similar to forward sales (mainly *murabaha* and *ijara*) the bank could be defined as a trading intermediary that assumes, therefore, the underlying risks (risk of obsolescence, risk of depreciation, and so on). Conversely, in both PLS and association in participation contracts the analysis of the risk profile of the borrower is always involved, as in the loan portfolio of a conventional bank: profits are shared according to a predefined formula, losses are totally loaded to the customer and the bank runs, theoretically, the risk of not being paid for the lending activity. On the opposite side, it is possible that the bank assumes the role of a borrower that manages funds on behalf of the customer.

Mudaraba and *musharaka* are difficult to classify according to the principle of conventional banking activity since they seem to introduce, at least apparently, some characters similar to those typical of private equity or corporate banking operations. From the legal point of view, they cannot be considered as credit or financing operations but as trading activities in which the bank actively participates in the profit and loss sharing. Thus, under these two contracts, the project is managed by the client and not by the bank even though the bank shares the risk. The bank, as a partner, has the right of full access to the books and records, and can exercise monitoring and follow-up supervision. Nevertheless, the directors and management of the company retain independence in conducting the affairs of the company.

Their typical conditions have the characteristics of non-voting equity capital. From the viewpoint of the entrepreneur, there are no fixed annual payments needed to service the debt as under interest financing, while the financing does not increase the firm's risk in the way that other borrowings do through increased leverage. Conversely, from the bank's viewpoint, the returns come from profits – much like dividends – and the bank cannot take action to foreclose on the debt should profits not eventuate.

The most common type of investment is differentiated even if the sharing contracts seem to only represent a limited part of the bank's assets (Vogel, Chapter 3 this volume): a preference is observed for agreements of *murabaha, bay al-salam* and *ijara*, while the *musharaka* plays a secondary role. If, therefore, *murabaha* has much greater importance than *mudaraba* and *musharaka*, under the economic profile they seem to reduce the concern of compatibility. The main problem seems therefore of prevalence of the shape, the sale itself, on the substance, giving a financial facility. However it affects the risks of the bank because it could be considered, using 'Basel compliant' language, not only a credit risk but also an operating risk.

Table 6.1   The functioning of Islamic and conventional banks

Islamic banks	Conventional banks
Prohibition to apply interest rates both on borrowing and lending operations	Use of interest rates both on borrowing and lending operations
Profit and loss sharing	No profit and loss sharing
Bank as partner of depositors and borrowers	Bank as principal and agent of its customers
No profit if the financed counterpart has a loss	Interest has to be paid even if the financed counterpart has a loss
It is not possible to invest in companies operating in industries not compliant with the *Qur'an* law	It is possible to invest with no limits
Speculative activities are prohibited	Speculative activities are allowed
Banks are controlled by Central Bank, other supervisory authorities and an internal board responsible for compliance to *Shari'ah* and *Qur'an* law according to AAOIFI standards	Banks are controlled by Central Bank and other supervisory authorities; typically there is no internal ethics committee
It is necessary to create a special reserve in which put the Islamic tax (*zakat*) to be used for charity	Charity is discretional

There is, in fact, a problem of correct pricing, and therefore of convenience of the operation, from the point of view of the beneficiary rather than from the point of view of the bank.

MANAGEMENT OF THE TYPICAL RISK/RETURN PROFILE

After having summarized the main characteristics of borrowing and lending operations in the typical Islamic context, it is possible to outline the main differences in the functioning of Islamic and conventional banks (Table 6.1). The intermediation model based on participating contracts can follow two schemes:

1. one defined as two-tier *mudaraba* in which both funding and lending are carried out according to the profit-sharing scheme between the investor-depositor, the bank and the financed entrepreneur;

2. the other defined as two-windows that differs from the previous
    because liabilities are shared in two parts (windows): one for mon-
    etary deposits and one for investment deposits, the choice between
    these two being left to the customers' will.

In the first case the bank is the agent of the depositors and principal of
the entrepreneurs similar to an investment company. The economic results
are shared between the borrower, the bank itself and the depositor. For
banking operations, the *mudaraba* concept has been extended to include
three parties: the depositors as financiers, the bank as an intermediary, and
the entrepreneur who requires funds. The bank acts as an entrepreneur
when it receives funds from depositors, and as financier when it provides
the funds to entrepreneurs. In other words, the bank operates a two-tier
mudaraba system in which it acts both as the *mudarib* on the saving side
and as the *rabb al-mal* (owner of capital) on the investment portfolio side.
As such, an Islamic bank acts as a *mudarib* which manages the funds of the
depositors to generate profits subject to the rules of *mudaraba*. The bank
may in turn use the depositors' funds on a *mudaraba* basis in addition to
other lawful (but less preferable) modes of financing, including mark-up
or deferred sales, lease purchase and beneficence loans. The funding and
investment avenues are now listed.

In the second case, 100 per cent of monetary deposits are placed into
liquid reserves and risky assets are financed with the total amount of
investment-deposits. From this point of view, the Islamic bank could be
considered an institutional investor but this does not consider the operational risks assumed on the asset side and the non-perfect comparison
between a depositor and an underwriter. Economic theory and regulation traditionally justify the peculiarity of the banks mainly based on the
importance of nominal liabilities, that is the obligation to reimburse issued
liabilities to their nominal value in contrast to the fair market value liabilities of institutional investors.

The combined asset/liability analysis of typical risk/return profiles
arising from funds' collection and lending through Islamic contracts
poses some remarkable methodological problems since the model based
on profit and loss sharing is difficult to reconcile with the economic function traditionally carried out by banks. Thanks to loan portfolio frac-
tioning and to diversification, the intermediaries are able to reduce the
non-systematic risk of their liabilities compared to those of their assets.
A bank, but not an investment company, is also able to transform and to
reduce its portfolio risks since non diversified risks are transferred from
depositors to shareholders.

In the Islamic context, in many cases, there is no risk assumed by the intermediary in collecting funds. That means no risk transformation, at least in terms of maturity, but the bank is free to use and lend these resources, choosing the best investment opportunities without limits. Can it be asserted that, in this case, any mixture of commercial banking and typical asset management activities is non-existent? If Islamic banks are not true institutional investors but operate like conventional banks without any risk transformation, how do they carry out their intermediation functions? For this reason, it is necessary to refer to a more complex and diversified context (Iqbal and Molyneux 2005).

Progressively, the intermediation model has differed from the two original paradigms both characterized by a clear distinction of the asset portfolio into different categories, each one strictly related, in terms of risk levels, to the funding contracts: current accounts, term deposits, restricted or unrestricted investment accounts and equity (Chapra and Khan 2000; El-Hawary, Grais and Iqbal 2004; Montanaro 2006). The prevailing operating model is more complex considering both funds' collection and assets. Beside contracts of *mudaraba* and *musharaka*, bank assets predominantly include indirectly participating contracts while liabilities, even if essentially based on funds collected according to the *mudaraba* scheme, include a meaningful quota of sight and short-term deposits that the customer can withdraw at short notice.

This model involves different financial risks, mostly similar to those faced by conventional financial institutions, and, for this reason, appropriate prudential regulation is necessary. The simultaneous presence among liabilities of money deposits and investment accounts implies peculiar systemic risks that could extend from the latter towards the former, characterized by the bank's obligation to reimburse at nominal value: for this reason, it is necessary to define a segregated capital as a firewall between the two categories of liabilities.

Considering liquidity management according to *Qur'an* rules, because of the prohibition of *riba*, the main difficulties are access to the interbanking deposits market and the underwriting of short-term and low-risk securities characterized by high liquidity. Designing Islamic instruments for monetary operations has proven conceptually difficult. The liquid nature of banks' liabilities, related to the predominance of deposits of short-term maturities, predisposes the system to hold substantial liquid assets and excess reserves. Difficulties in defining the rates of return on these instruments have also constrained the development of money and interbank markets. Developing these markets is indispensable for the conduct of monetary policy and financial market deepening. The inadequate development or absence of these markets in many countries constrains central bank intervention through indirect instruments and has occasionally encouraged the use of direct controls on credit. The absence of well-organized, liquid interbank markets – that can accept banks' overnight deposits and offer them lending to cover short-term financial needs – has exacerbated banks' tendencies to concentrate on short-term assets.

Progress in effective liquidity management calls for adopting a comprehensive, integrated approach to developing money and securities markets. It would also require establishing an efficient lender of last resort facility; developing well-suited interbank instruments and operations; actively utilizing securitization techniques to manage the maturity and risk of assets and liabilities; and making available risk management and hedging instruments, which presupposes the resolution of various legal, institutional and accounting issues. To a certain extent, the use of equity funds can solve the problem, as it is a lawful alternative to conventional bonds not permitted by the *Shari'ah* (Miglietta 2006). In addition, Islamic banks use Islamic bonds (*sukuk*), liquid financial instruments rather, very similar to traditional bonds but *Shari'ah*-compliant because they represent not a debit, but a property right on a specific asset and their return is linked not to the interest rate, but to the underlying asset.

Liquidity management is strictly connected to monetary policy management in the context of Islamic countries; without further investigation, it can be observed that in those countries, beside the basic functions, the Central Bank pursues some objectives and uses some operating instruments closely related to the peculiarity of Islamic banking activity:

- to establish reserves and liquidity ratios differentiated according to the different types of deposits;
- to re-finance commercial banks according to sharing agreements;
- to determine the profit-sharing quota and its admitted range;
- to determine the maximum profit quota that banks can obtain from non-participating contracts (*ijara, murabaha, bay al-salam*);
- to fix the maximum amount of management costs the bank can debit to customers;
- to indicate the minimal percentage of potential profit a project must produce to be financed;
- to define the minimum and maximum amount of loan granted, subdivided by type of contract.

There are several peculiarities of credit risk in Islamic banking activity:

- the case of default restructuring based on credit compensation is the best known kind of *riba* (specifically *riba to the Jahiliyah*) but it requires a complex credit risk management;

- some moral objections against the constitution of reserves for credit losses;
- restrictions on the use of financial instruments (for example government bonds) reduce the quality of the collateral.

Considering each lending contract, it can be observed that in *mudaraba* and *musharaka* the default event is indefinite and collaterals (or guarantees) are not allowed; both *bay al-salam* and *istisna'* imply a risk that can be defined as counterpart/performance risk and, moreover, it is difficult to subdivide market risks from credit risks and there is a high catastrophic risk. For *murabaha* the default risk is probably lower compared to other lending contracts even if it is necessary to consider the counterpart risk due to the existing implicit option to buy.

In other words, for the Islamic bank, the lending activity determines:

- the emergence of relevant market risks connected to the holding of real assets until the maturity of the 'lending' contract or until the property is transferred to the customer (the borrower);
- a strict connection between market and liquidity risks;
- transformation of credit into market risk and vice versa in the different steps of the contract;
- a different bundling of both credit and market risks between the bank and its financed customer;
- a different regulation of default.

In conventional banks, market risk is mostly concentrated in the trading book; on the contrary, in Islamic financial institutions, such a risk is concentrated in the banking book, particularly in *mudaraba*, *ijara*, *bay al-salam*, *musharaka* and *murabaha* contracts: for this reason, market and credit risks are more intensely interdependent and connected. Considering again each single contract jointly with the impact of their technical characteristics on market, operating and liquidity risks it emerges that:

- the credit risk is the highest for *musharaka* followed by *mudaraba*;
- the contracts absorbing higher market risks are *istisna'*, *salam* and *musharaka*;
- the liquidity risks derive mainly from *ijara*, *salam* and *musharaka*;
- the operational risks have a significant impact on *musharaka*, *istisna'* and *salam*.

With reference to the typical asset portfolio characteristics, it is necessary for any bank to strictly respect *Shari'ah* restrictions, not considering the merit control carried out by the *Shari'ah* board. These restrictions typically impose negative selection criteria (first level filter: prohibition to invest in the entertainment and the tobacco industries, and so on) and asset ratios (second level filter: the liabilities cannot exceed one third of the total asset, and so on). These limits reduce the investment field with consequences both at the micro level – mainly in terms of lower portfolio diversification – and the macro level – the active role of the banks in economic development.

The reduction of possible investment opportunities for ethical reasons (even if of Islamic origin) is undoubtedly similar to the principles that inspire socially responsible investment. Two main differences must be considered: (a) the obligation of the prohibition set up by the *Shari'ah* board is higher than that imposed by the agencies that are recognized to a greater or lesser degree, giving an ethic at 'certification'; (b) in the Islamic context investment limits are not uniform because *Qur'an* prohibitions are not unanimously interpreted; in the western economy many organizations are trying to identify a single agency able to 'certify' the ethical character of the business or the financial instrument.

The liquidity risk is not very high because of the provisions that impose the maintenance of a higher proportion of liquid assets (current accounts at the central bank) so balancing the potential higher return/higher risk of lending operations; such an obligation, fixed by the supervising authorities, is due to the (obvious) absence of traditional instruments (for example, the interbanking market and the credit of last resort) used for adjusting liquidity shocks from which it would be reasonable to fear a potential increase of the systemic instability risk.

The need for the banks themselves to reduce the so-called displaced commercial risk, that is the risk of losing collected funds in case their rate of return is lower than that recognized by competing banks, has been recognized as relevant also by the AAOIFI, and refers to a situation in which the bank is subject to competitive pressure that obligates it to pay investment account holders a rate of return in order to induce them to maintain their funds at the bank, rather than withdrawing them and investing them elsewhere.

The Islamic Financial Services Board has allowed the displaced commercial risk to be covered by equity capital, justifying, also for reasons of systemic stability, the praxis to renounce (partly or completely) the profit share due as *mudarib*, when it is necessary to increase the rate of return for the investment accounts' holders. To maximize the stability of funding and to avoid a run on deposits two constraints are common to the management of both Islamic and conventional banks. This explains the policy, supported by prudential regulation, to reduce the volatility of the rate of return offered to the depositors, also through reserves.

THE IMPLEMENTATION OF THE PRUDENTIAL REGULATION

The previous remarks are strictly connected to the widest topic of risk management techniques that can be used in the Islamic context and, consequently, of how prudential supervision can be exercised by the competent authorities. The possibility of applying prudential regulation has to be verified considering the disclosure degree and the governance model typical of Islamic banks. The risk of moral hazard is only one of the most critical aspects strictly connected to the intermediary modus operandi. In fact, the profit and loss sharing limits the level of disclosure and the historical series of returns paid with the bank's full discretion are only partly meaningful.

The market rules require the regulation of possible conflicts of interest, a breadth of disclosure and the adoption of specific operating procedures (that is internal controls, risk management, compliance procedure). In my opinion, in the context of Islamic banking activity, the mixture of typical and peculiar financial risks, the instruments used for their mitigation, the average level of transparency, the typical corporate governance models, seem, at the moment, to be deeply different from those in relation to the models of regulation and risk management now prevailing in the western context (particularly the new Basel Agreement on capital adequacy) that have been considered.

Without segregated capital facing investment accounts, the governance of the Islamic banks poses a relevant question concerning the impact of sharing contracts on bank capital and its adequacy; in fact, it is not clear if these contracts are financing operations carried out by the bank though without any portfolio risk transformation. One of the main characteristics of *mudaraba* is the segregation of the asset holding, with the financial and non-financial risks involved, not only from the bank's asset and liability management, but also by any control on the quality and the results of its management.

Considering PSIAs' holders:

- as shareholders, they have no right to interfere on how funds are managed because this is under the *mudarib*'s (the bank) exclusive control which, as compensation, earns a profit;
- differently from shareholders, they do not have any power of control over management's behaviour;
- they have the right to withdraw the deposited sums: though limited by the often short maturity and by the absence of the bank for advanced refunding, it represents a kind of control over the

behaviour of the management, through which the depositors can express their dissent, if the rate of return is lower than that offered by competitors or than that expected.

Concerning the problem of adopting the same prudential regulation as western countries, the Islamic Financial Services Board on 15 March 2005 published two draft papers: *Guiding Principles for Risk Management* and *Capital Adequacy*.

The first document points out 15 principles for implementing risk management procedures in the Islamic banks. The approach adopted considers the risks of the prevailing banking activity and the risks of the different types of contracts offered by Islamic banks. In particular the principles have been grouped with reference to six different risk categories: credit, equity investment, market, liquidity, operating and rate of return; the last risk is peculiar because it is related to the potential impact of market factors on the rate of return expected by the investment accounts holders.

The second document, instead, represents a successful attempt at the homologization of Islamic finance to the requirements established by Basel II: in fact, where the new rules are perfectly compatible with *Shari'ah* principles, the Basel Accord is applicable, while for all the other specific aspects the IFSB proposes specific rules. As an example, for each contract the following was determined: the typical risks, the weighting coefficient for calculating the total asset ratio and the possible presence of risk mitigation mechanisms.

Corporate governance in banking has been analysed almost exclusively in the context of conventional banking markets. For example, there has been discussion of the role of 'market discipline' exerted by bank shareholders and depositors in constraining the risk-taking behaviour of bank management. By contrast, little is written on governance structures in Islamic banking, despite the rapid growth of Islamic banks. Islamic banking is radically different from conventional banking, and from the viewpoint of corporate governance it embodies a number of interesting features since equity participation, risk and profit and loss-sharing arrangements form the basis of Islamic financing.

Governance structures are quite peculiar because the institution must obey a different set of rules and meet the expectations of the Muslim community by providing acceptable financing contracts. First, and foremost, an Islamic organization must develop a distinctive corporate culture, the main purpose of which is to create a collective morality and spirituality which, when combined with the production of goods and services, sustains the growth and advancement of the Islamic way of life.

Islamic banks have a major responsibility to shoulder . . . all the staff of such banks and customers dealing with them must be reformed Islamically and act within the framework of an Islamic formula, so that any person approaching an Islamic bank should be given the impression that he is entering a sacred place to perform a religious ritual, that is the use and employment of capital for what is acceptable and satisfactory to God. (Janachi 1995)

In addition, any Islamic bank is subject to an additional layer of governance since the suitability of its investment and financing must be in strict conformity with Islamic law and the expectations of the Muslim community. For this purpose, Islamic banks employ an individual *Shari'ah* Advisor and/or Board. Central to the conceptual framework of corporate governance for an Islamic bank is the *Shari'ah* Supervisory Board (SSB) and the internal controls which support it. The SSB is vital for two reasons. First, those who deal with an Islamic bank require assurance that it is transacting within Islamic law. Should the SSB report that the management of the bank has violated the *Shari'ah,* it would quickly lose the confidence of the majority of its investors and clients. Second, some Islamic scholars argue that strict adherence to Islamic religious principles will act as a counter to the incentive problems outlined above. The argument is that the Islamic moral code will prevent Muslims from behaving in ways which are ethically unsound, so minimizing the transaction costs arising from incentive issues. In effect, Islamic religious ideology acts as its own incentive mechanism to reduce the inefficiency that arises from asymmetric information and moral hazard.

CONCLUSIONS

In financing the economy, the profit and loss share contracts give Islamic banks a more direct role because, assuming a capital share, they have to effectively carry out the business activities of the company. The bank's role is no longer to 'give and collect money' but to be a true entrepreneur who, engaged in the effective management and at the same time part of the business risk, is interested in how the business plan is carried out. Moreover, the different financial obligations of the two parties involved, bank and borrower, heavily influence the behaviour of the subject that can make use of the funds lent by the bank.

The typical case of credit granted by conventional banks penalizes initiatives characterized by high risk and high potential in terms of innovation. In the Islamic model, on the contrary, capital and other resources obtained through the bank still have a cost but this is no longer independent from the economic and entrepreneurial results achieved. The essential element to be judged and evaluated is no longer the borrower's creditworthiness but the expected profitability of the project/the business/the company. Lenders and borrowers have a common interest in undertaking a profitable project together and the choice among different financial instruments is no longer exclusively the task of the entrepreneur, but becomes a common aim shared with the bank.

A critical point is represented by the correctness of the management and execution of activities and contracts. Simply because of their intrinsic characteristics they appear to be more vulnerable and more difficult to control with regard to the conditions and presumptions for regular execution. Independently from the ability of Islamic banks to be competitive with institutions operating in a western context, they also introduce some advantages and opportunities that can represent a release from static economy that currently characterizes many Islamic countries.

The profit- and loss-sharing model could support and promote entrepreneurship more effectively by stimulating economic development even though a new approach is necessary to support as well as to speed up medium- and long-term investment. Differently from the theoretical approach, Islamic banks seem to concentrate their lending activity on real estate management, trade financing and import/export financing that do not require a strong role of *musharaka* and *mudaraba* but guarantee a satisfactory profit.

Financing a greater number of medium- and long-term projects introduces a higher credit risk and a level of complexity that require more specialized human resources. It appears, therefore, necessary to create a basis for the development of a secondary market for the Islamic finance instruments, without which the future of the Islamic model and banking would be destined for certain failure or a marginal loss in economic life.

In conclusion, it can be asked: should Islamic banks gradually become equivalent to western commercial banks? Or should they become specialized financial institutions favouring the areas of business where Islamic law is most congenial: mutual fund investments, venture capital, investment funds, services and trade finance? From the theoretical point of view, considering the economic functions typically carried out by banks, is an intermediation process different from the conventional one, typically based on the interest rate, possible and feasible? An Islamic credit institution is able to carry out the same operations and functions as a commercial bank, using and applying different methods and management techniques.

An optimistic, but at the same time unrealistic, opinion about the difficult relationship between traditional Islamic and conventional banks states that for banks their Islamic nature would be enough to be chosen by the Islamic population all over the world. The religion, without doubt, plays an important role, although it is undeniable that the same role is played by the achieved and achievable economic results. Selecting the best investment or financing opportunities, the profit and the rate of return are, for the customers, the most effective parameters. It should also be noted that Islamic economic models can be developed, reaching acceptable levels of effectiveness and efficiency only in countries in which an explicit prohibition of the interest rate and of every type of transaction based on does not apply. The markets for Islamic instruments and government securities remain shallow and an organized international Islamic financial market is still nascent. The sector must improve the range and sophistication of asset and liability classes and develop new instruments that would enable Islamic banks to diversify their balance sheets.

Resolving these important issues, as well as adopting best practices for supervision and accounting, are critical for future market and industry development. For the foreseeable future, supervisory authorities will continue to face the dual challenges of understanding the industry and striking a balance between providing effective supervision and facilitating the industry's legitimate aspirations for further growth and development. These challenges can be overcome if the central banks and institutions concerned enhance their multilateral cooperation, and create the appropriate environment and conditions. These conditions would create a level playing field and provide the infrastructure needed for the industry's market-driven development. A sound, well-functioning Islamic financial system can pave the way for the regional financial integration of the countries involved. It can also contribute to their economic and social development, by financing the economic infrastructure and creating job opportunities.

Some remarks on the evolution of Islamic finance and financial engineering complied with Western financial engineering which, trying to widen investment opportunities, mostly orients itself with instruments closely related to speculation (from which there is an increase in the vulnerability of the economy to financial shocks). Conversely, Islamic finance while trying to create new *Shari'ah*-compliant instruments, has introduced new instruments transforming the ones already existing (equity investment funds) or creating completely new ones (*ijara* funds and Islamic bonds) that are based on underlying principles that already exist and are closely linked to the real economy.

In conclusion, I offer some remarks on the overall adequacy of the portfolio of opportunities Islamic finance is able to offer – on one side to savers, and on the other to corporations and SMEs involved in the trading of their countries' typical goods and raw materials – and, consequently, on the adequacy of such a model to support the economic development of those countries.

If we agree to the opinion that the financial system must have an active function supporting overall economic development (according to Schumpeter), the great challenge for Islamic finance is mainly to find the best ways to mobilize existing financial resources and to employ them for the development of the Islamic population and countries, safeguarding its peculiar ethical characteristics. It is, in fact, obvious that the financial engineering necessary in order to adapt Islamic finance to conventional finance – avoiding, at the same time, not being compliant with religious principles and rules – has a substantial implicit or explicit cost charged to the collectivity.

How long will it be economically and socially sustainable? How long will the existing and traditional Islamic banking activity be compatible with the needs of those Islamic countries that still have large problems of development? How can we mobilize financial resources among the population that, because of the presence of quantitative limits, is not able to gain access to investment accounts? And, then, is it correct to consider as similar Islamic finance on one side, and ethical finance, social banking, banking services access and microcredit on the other? In our opinion, typical Islamic banking activity seems to be extremely complicated and has little transparency on both the assets and liabilities side and is far from all the above-mentioned scenarios, however different it is from conventional banking activity.

BIBLIOGRAPHY

Archer, S. and Karim, Rifaat A. (eds) (2002), *Islamic Finance, Innovation and Growth*, London: Euromoney Books and AAOIFI.

Blair, M. and Aliga D. (2006), 'A new framework for collective investment funds in the Middle East', *Journal of International Banking Law and Regulation*, (8).

Chapra, M. and Khan, T. (2000), *Regulation and Supervision of Islamic Banks*, Islamic Research and Training Institute, Occasional Paper n. 3, Jeddah: Islamic Development Bank.

DeLorenzo, Talal Y. (2002), 'The religious foundations of Islamic finance', in S. Archer and Rifaat A. Karim (eds).

El-Hawary, D., Grais, W. and Iqbal, Z. (2004), *Regulating Islamic Financial Institutions: the Nature of the Regulated*, World Bank Policy Research, WP n. 3227.

El Qorchi (2005), 'Islamic finance gears up', *Finance & Development*, **42**(4).

Fadeel, Mahmoud N. (2002), 'Legal aspects of Islamic finance', in S. Archer and Refaat A. Karim (eds).

Forte, G. and Miglietta, F. (2007), *Islamic mutual funds as faith-based funds in a socially responsible context*, Lecce: Proceedings of ADEIMF Conference, Lecce, 15–16 June.

Giustiniani, E. (2006), *Elementi di Finanza Islamica*, Turin: M. Valerio Editore.

Iqbal, M. and Llewellyn, D. (eds) (2002), *Islamic Banking and Finance: New Perspective on Profit Sharing and Risk*, Cheltenham, UK and Northampton, MA, USA: Edward Elgar Publishing.

Iqbal, M. and Molyneux, P. (2005), *Thirty Years of Islamic Banking. History, Performance and Prospects*, New York: Palgrave MacMillan.

Janachi, A.L. (1995), *Islamic Banking, Concept, Practice and Future*, 2nd edition, Manama: Islamic.

Khan, M. (1986), *Islamic Interest-free Banking: A Theoretical Analysis*, IMF Staff Papers, Vol. 33, No. 1.

Maroun, Y. (2002), 'Liquidity management and trade financing', in S. Archer and Rifaat A. Karim (eds).

Miglietta, F. (2006), *I prodotti bancari per la clientela immigrata: analisi di contesto e prospettive*, WP 05/06, Milan: Newfin Università Bocconi.

Montanaro, E. (2006), 'Quale reglamentazione per le banche Islamiche', in G. Gimigliano and G. Rotondo (eds), *La Banca Islamica e la Disciplina Bancaria Europea*, Milan: Giuffrè.

Piccinelli, Gian M. (2002), *Etica e prassi delle Banche Islamiche*, Rome: ABI.

Porzio, C. (ed.) (2009), *La finanza islamica: opportunità o minaccia?*, Rome: Bancaria Editrice.

Ussmani, M. (2002), *An Introduction to Islamic Finance*, The Hague: Kluwer Law International.

7. Islamic banking: a challenge for the Basel Capital Accord

Elisabetta Montanaro

INTRODUCTION

Every type of financial innovation forces regulators to question their limits and the effectiveness of the existing rules for financial institutions, instruments and cultures different from those for which the rules were initially devised (Merton 1995).

In this perspective, the increasing spread of Islamic banks in the Western banking system represents an interesting test on the ability of the Basel capital discipline to reconcile a discretionary and flexible approach, necessary for coping with this type of intermediation, with the objective of safeguarding a level playing field through standardised and uniform regulations.

For prudential capital rules, Islamic banking is in many ways a paradox. On the one hand, it is understandable that its operations, so different from the conventional models with which the regulatory authorities are used to dealing, are deemed potentially riskier,[1] and therefore subject to stricter capital rules. On the other hand, the essence of profit-sharing contracts seems to make this type of intermediation better able to bear unexpected losses than conventional banks, questioning the same logic of capital requirements.

In the *Core Principles for Effective Banking Supervision*, the minimum capital requirements are clearly stated as central among the global standard principles of banking regulations. According to Principle 6, 'Banking supervisors must set prudent and appropriate minimum capital adequacy requirements for all banks. Such requirements should reflect the risks that banks undertake, *and must define the components of capital, bearing in mind their ability to absorb losses*' (Basel Committee 1997, emphasis added). While the regulatory authorities have much discretion in the application of the rules, it is prescribed that 'at least for internationally active banks, these requirements [capital adequacy] must not be less than those established in the Basel Capital Accord and its amendments' (Basel Committee

1999). Therefore, the solutions to the problem of the applicability of the Basel Capital Accord to Islamic banks are of strategic importance, particularly considering the inevitable and in many ways welcome increasing integration of Islamic with conventional finance.

These solutions must bring together two contrasting needs. On the one hand, there is the need to standardise the prudential and supervisory rules, in order to limit regulatory arbitrage, to ensure minimum common best practices as foundations for the global financial system, and to make the cross-border collaboration of the supervisory authorities possible. On the other hand, applying uniform rules to different financial institutions and functions, to countries at different stages of economic development and with different cultures, can create inefficiencies and/or unfair competitive disadvantages, with negative consequences for collective welfare (Merton 1995).

The ability to mediate between these two needs has laid the foundations for the wide consensus that has given the Basel regulation global recognition, much further than the original Accord, which was binding only for the international banks of the G-10. It is worth remembering that this ability to mediate is the result of an extended consultation (especially for Basel 2) that included supervisory authorities, financial operators and academics, mainly from the G-10 and EU. The same has happened for the preparation of the three Quantitative Impact Studies, simulation exercises done between 2001 and 2004, in which more than 350 large and medium-sized banks have taken part, again mainly operating in the G-10 and EU. None of the countries where Islamic banking is dominant or even significant was included in the list of countries of the banks taking part in the Impact Studies. This tells us that to date Islamic finance has been at the margin of the consultation process on the rules of Basel 2. This is due not only to the modest weight in financial market that Islamic banks have relative to conventional ones, but also to insufficient 'political representation' within the Basel Committee, worsened by the fact that, in reality, there is not *one* model of Islamic bank but many, often very different from the original 'pure' version. Rules and supervisory practices differ among the various Islamic countries; the accounting standards used for financial contracts and their associated risks are reported and measured for regulatory purposes very differently; there are five schools of thought, each with its own interpretation of financial transactions and banking products compatible with the *Shari'ah* rules (El-Hawary, Grais and Iqbal 2004).

Islamic intermediation, based on profit-sharing, seems, however, difficult to tie in (on not only practical but also theoretical grounds) with the fundamentals and the objectives of the prudential regulation based on minimum capital requirements. For stability purposes, the greater is the risk transformation by the intermediary, the more relevant is capital.[2]

If the regulation forces on the shareholders a financial burden that grows with the intermediation risk, it not only limits the moral hazard relating to the coexistence of the explicit and implicit deposit insurance and of the lending of last resort, it also limits the conflict of interest among depositors and shareholders typical of banking characterised by opaque assets and high leverage (Alexander and Duhmale 2001).

We may then ask what could possibly be the prudential role of capital for an Islamic bank, and, more in general, if it is justified to limit its financing function since the bank, funding its assets with profit-sharing contracts, does not perform a portfolio risk transformation function, with the result that the investment account holders and shareholders jointly bear the credit and market risks.

The chapter is organised as follows. In the second section we present the main features of the two traditional models of the profit-sharing contracts. In the third section we discuss the problems posed to the banks' governance by the more recent evolution of Islamic banking. In the fourth section we analyse the role of shareholders as vicarious supervisors for investment account holders in the traditional model of Islamic banking, with their consequences for regulation. In the fifth section we discuss why, due to systemic fragility, the traditional profit-sharing principles are in practice partially violated, and why the commercial displacement risk weakens the role of the investment accounts as Tier 1 capital, taking the Basel regulatory perspective. In the sixth section we analyse the proposal on capital regulation advanced by the Islamic Financial Services Board. The final section offers some conclusions.

PROFIT-SHARING IN INTEREST-FREE BANKING

The usual definition of Islamic banking as interest-free must be interpreted considering that Islam not only admits but also praises profit, as reward for entrepreneurial activity to the benefit of the whole society.

Islamic banking based on profit sharing has in fact its foundations on the need to reconcile the entrepreneurial goals,[3] which legitimate financial intermediation, with the ban on *riba* (interest) in the *Qur'an*. It is difficult to understand the significance of this ban without reminding ourselves of the ethics behind Islamic economics. It is worth briefly mentioning, however, its fundamental principles (Khan 1986; Zaher and Hassan 2001; El-Hawary, Grais and Iqbal 2004).

1. Risk sharing: the terms of the financial operations must reflect a symmetrical distribution of risks/rewards among the counterparts.

2. Reality of contracts: all financial transactions must be directly or indirectly linked with the real economy.
3. Prohibition of exploitation of the debtor by those who have financial means.
4. Sanctity of contracts: every economic relationship must follow standard contracts, whose correct application must be assessed on the basis not of the actual achievements but of the good faith and equitability of the parties' behaviour.

The profit-sharing contract, or *mudaraba*, represents the foundation of Islamic banking. Following this contract, the funds' owner gives to the entrepreneur the capital necessary to finance his/her enterprise or a specific investment project. The entrepreneur receives a reward (*mudarib*) for his/her work and managerial skills; rewards which become zero in the case of losses. The profits are shared between the funds' owner and the entrepreneur following a formula set in advance; if there are losses, these are borne only by the funds' owner, while the entrepreneur, if in good faith, is not obliged to return the capital received. We have then two main styles of Islamic banking: two-tier *mudaraba* and two-windows *mudaraba*.

In the two-tier *mudaraba*, both fund raising and investment follow profit sharing among the investment account holders, the bank and the entrepreneurs. The bank operates as an agent of the depositors and principal of the entrepreneurs, somewhat similar to conventional investment banking; the returns of funds are shared among the entrepreneurs, the bank and the depositors.

In the two-windows *mudaraba* instead, banks' liabilities, including money deposits without interest, are split into two 'windows': one for the money deposits and one for the investment accounts, leaving the choice between these two windows to the bank's customers. In this type of banking, the bank keeps 100 per cent of the money deposits as liquid reserves (as a 'narrow bank') and invests all the investment deposits (Sundararajan and Errico 2002; El-Hawary, Grais and Iqbal 2004).

THE EVOLUTION OF ISLAMIC BANKING AND ITS GOVERNANCE

The foremost experts in Islamic finance (Archer, Karim and Al-Deehani 1998; Chapra and Khan 2000; El-Hawary, Grais and Iqbal 2004) agree in highlighting that profit-sharing contracts have evolved from these two original models. Both of these models are characterised by a clear separation of the investment portfolio according to the risk levels and contract type of the different investors: money depositors; investment account holders[4] (restricted[5] and unrestricted investment accounts); shareholders.

In current practice, there is no longer a clear separation of the risks and performance pertaining to the different stakeholders. The assets of a typical Islamic bank are managed as a whole portfolio, within which there is no distinction between the investments made by the different types of funds providers.[6] The proceeds from the investment of all the available funds, including money deposits, are then shared among shareholders and the investment account holders according to their relative share of capital.[7] The share given to the investment account holders is net of the percentage of *mudarib* due to the bank – and therefore to its shareholders – as a reward for the investment management, a reward that goes to zero in case the return of the investment is zero or negative. Therefore, the shareholders and the investment account holders bear the credit and market risk pro-quota. Only the shareholders bear the operating risk, that is, the potential losses resulting from negligent or illegal behaviour by the management of the bank.[8]

Thanks to the joint intermediation of money deposits and investment accounts, Islamic banking is therefore something in between a commercial bank and an investment bank and closer to a universal bank. However, differently from a classic universal bank, there are no legal, financial and managerial firewalls between the commercial and investment banking activities. Hence the investment portfolio managed by the bank as trustee of the owners of the profit-sharing accounts is not kept separate from the shareholders' funds.

Intuitively, this is one of the most critical aspects from a regulatory point of view, given that the different stakeholders need different safeguards, according to the level of risk transformation that the bank performs by law or in practice: a uniform regulatory approach may be insufficient or otherwise too restrictive.

Moreover, from the point of view of the holders of the profit-sharing accounts, the actual application of the *mudaraba* contract has many ambiguities, linked to the great freedom given to the bank management, mainly due to the lack of transparency following the joint management of the funds. This freedom is particularly evident: in managerial investment choices when pooling the funds coming from shareholders and from profit-sharing depositors; in managers' ability to change the share of profit taken as reward for the *mudarib*; in the allocation methods of the liquidity costs between investment account holders and shareholders; and particularly in the choice between absorbing losses with internal reserves or passing them on to the investment holders accounts and/or the shareholders.

Especially when there is no separation of assets, governance in Islamic banking suggests, therefore, contrasting interpretations as to whether the profit-sharing contracts are to be considered as capital, that is, as funds intermediated without portfolio risk transformation, excluding operational risk.

One of the main characteristics of the *mudaraba* contract is the separation of the ownership not only from the management but also from the control of the quality and proceeds resulting from such management; this separation poses financial risks. Like the shareholders, the investment depositors have no right to interfere with the fund management: this is the exclusive domain of the *mudarib*, that is the bank, which, as a reward for its entrepreneurial activity, gets a share of the profits, as long as they are positive. Unlike the shareholders, however, the investment account holders are not entitled to directly monitor the management: they have no voting rights for either the approval of financial statements or the nomination or dismissal of members of the board of directors, members of the *Shari'ah* Supervisory Board[9] or external auditors.

The investment account holders, however, can 'vote with their feet' by taking away their funds, given that, unlike shareholders, their contract has a maturity, often a short one. This exit right, even if limited to the expiry of the contract and/or the possible agreement with the bank to an early exit, represents a form of external control (or market discipline) on management behaviour; this is how depositors can show their dissatisfaction if the returns received are lower than the ones expected or obtainable from competitors.

Do these difference in governance mechanisms associated with profit sharing reduce or increase the risk of opportunistic behaviour? Do they reduce or increase the conflict of interests between investment account holders and equity holders?

A SIMPLIFIED MODEL OF INTERNAL AND EXTERNAL CONTROLS IN ISLAMIC BANKING

From a theoretical point of view, if one accepts that shareholders and investment account holders have the same risk/return objectives (Al-Deehani, Karim and Murinde 1998), the type of governance in Islamic banking seems to allow an efficient interaction between the market discipline and internal controls, even without regulating the capital structure of banks.

The shareholders, thanks to their share of *mudarib*, get an increase in the profitability of the invested capital without additional risks as the funds obtained by the bank with the *mudaraba* deposits grow. This should induce them to use their control powers on management even in the interest of the investment account holders in order to attain adequate performance levels, to avoid the risk of loss of funds and to maximise the ability of the bank to collect deposits. Therefore, there should be a sort of virtuous 'bilateral dependency' between shareholders and investment account holders, thanks to which the shareholders depend on the investors-depositors as a source of profits via the bank's share in *mudarib*, while the investors-depositors depend on the shareholders for the control on management.

According to this view, the insolvency risk of the bank does not increase with the degree of funding via profit-sharing deposits. The actual basis for the capital discipline tends to lose its original prudential content and the regulation's focus moves to the requisites for entry, the efficiency of the internal risk-control mechanisms, and the disclosure and transparency levels adequate for market discipline to function (El-Hawary, Grais and Iqbal 2004).

As a governance tool, the role of the minimum capital constraint becomes that of ensuring for the investment account holders an adequate level of commitment on the part of the shareholders in their vicarious supervisory role and in operational risk bearing; for the supervisory authorities its role is only that of ensuring to the conventional banks a level playing field with Islamic banks.

From this interpretation it derives that, for the Basel rules, the investment accounts represent a buffer (cushion) which can be counted on in order to absorb (to cover) unexpected losses in the same way as pure equity. How these functions should be accounted for when calculating the minimum capital coefficient would depend ultimately on the accounting principles chosen to settle the profit-sharing relationship between shareholders and depositors. If the net profit is shared (when the pooling method is applied), the investment deposits should be considered as true components of Tier I, which is to the numerator of the coefficient. Otherwise, if only the financial result of the investments is shared (when the separation method is applied), they cannot be added to Tier I, but should be subtracted from the risk-weighted assets, to the denominator of the ratio (Karim 1996).[10]

FORMS OF SYSTEMIC RISK IN ISLAMIC BANKING: THE ROLE OF PURE EQUITY

According to the previous view, financing with investment deposits should not only make Islamic banks better able than conventional ones to absorb external shocks, but also represent an effective governance tool in order to jointly protect the interests of all the stakeholders without intervention from prudential regulation.

In practice, however, many institutional and market factors contrast the rigorous application of the profit-sharing principles. These seem difficult to replicate in their integrity, when the objectives of fair wealth distribution and social cohesion, which are at the roots of the profit-sharing principles, take second place to the maximisation of profits and market shares (Zaher and Hassan 2001).

The actual nature of the relationship between the bank and the investment account holders is nowadays very different from the original model: and this is the case not only in the more advanced banking systems, where the Islamic banks coexist with the conventional banks (Errico and Farahbaksh 1998; Chapra and Khan 2000; Martens 2001; El-Hawary, Grais and Iqbal 2004), but also in officially pure Islamic systems such as Iran, where often a vast informal market towards foreign financial institutions, however, operates (Lewis and Algaoud 2001; Zaher and Hassan 2001; Yasseri 2002; Elhiraika 2004).

While the opening of 'Islamic desks' by large Western banks[11] shows that the demand for banking products following the *Shari'ah* from Muslim savers is continually growing all over the world, no empirical research suggests that the cultural and religious motives are so strong as to make irrelevant the conventional demand for stable and high returns (Haron and Ahmad 2000).

The profit-sharing contracts seem to be the investments preferred by the savers in systems characterised by particularly high inflation and/or by financial exclusion, where the main or only way to access banking services is via mutual financial institutions (Dar and Presley 2000; Cook, Deakin and Hughes 2001; Elhiraika 2004). However, when Islamic banks operate in a relatively sophisticated market or even in competition with the conventional banks, their market power is based not on the management ability to select the projects worthier of financing for the society they serve, but on the ability to offer to its investors a product that not only follows the *Shari'ah* rules, but also has a competitive return (Haron and Ahmad, 2000).

Therefore, as an alternative to market rating, the return offered to the investment account holders becomes a sort of protection against the reputation risk of the bank: its worsening can generate, if not true bank runs, accelerated processes of disintermediation, with negative effects on the performance and stability of the credit system. The need to protect the economic value of the investment deposits, even if not stated in the contracts, reappears in reality, often as a basis for a tacit agreement among the monetary authorities, the banks and the public (Zaher and Hassan 2001).[12]

Indeed, there is some agreement among Islamic scholars on the hypothesis of extending also to this category of savers some form of deposit insurance (even if in contrast with the *Shari'ah* principles) in light of the systemic instability risks deriving from the lack of conventional adjustment mechanisms to liquidity shocks, such as the inter-bank market and the credit of last resort (Chapra and Khan, 2000).

As also shown by recent empirical analysis based on the interview method (Khan and Ahmed, 2001), Islamic banks are strongly aware – maybe even more than conventional banks[13] – of the major need to mini-mise their liquidity risk, which for them means displaced commercial risk, for example the risk of losing deposits when their profitability is lower than that paid by the competing banks.

The relevance of this risk has been expressly recognised by the Accounting and Auditing Organization for Islamic Financial Institutions (AAOIFI),[14] which associates the situation where an Islamic bank 'is liable to find itself under commercial pressure to pay a rate of return to its profit sharing investment account holders which is sufficient to induce those investors to maintain their funds with the bank rather than withdrawing them and invest them elsewhere'[15]. In its recent proposal of capital regulation for Islamic banks, the Islamic Financial Services Board (IFSB)[16] confirmed the possibility that the displaced commercial risks were borne by the shareholders, even considering justified for reasons of system stability the practice of 'renouncing in part or all the profit share for *mudarib* when it is deemed necessary as a result of commercial pressure to increase the return rate to the profit sharing investment account holders' (IFSB 2005).

Maximising funding stability and avoiding bank runs are therefore managerial constraints that Islamic banks and conventional banks have in common. Considering this, one understands the established prac-tice of market strategies (promoted by the same prudential regulation) aimed at reducing the variability of the return rate offered to investment account holders, even through the establishment of internal reserves of self-insurance.[17] The empirical evidence confirms that the return rates on investment deposits tend to be stable and relatively uniform among the various banks, notwithstanding variable portfolio profitability in time and among the different banks.

WHAT CAPITAL REGULATION DO ISLAMIC BANKS NEED? THE ISLAMIC FINANCIAL SERVICES BOARD'S PROPOSAL

Performance smoothing, with the aim to strengthen the bank's reputation and the market value of the bank's licence, and to avoid the contagion of liquidity risks for money deposits, shows that the profit-sharing principle is at least partially violated in practice.[18] Therefore, the implicit safeguard of deposits' economic value forces even Islamic banks to do some portfolio risk transformation in favour of investor-depositors. This implies the re-emergence of the usual conflicts of interest between shareholders and creditors, typical of universal banks; this also makes profit-sharing funding less able to complement fully shareholders' capital as loss absorber.

Obviously, this conclusion changes the role of the prudential capital regulation of Islamic banks and, in particular, the treatment of investment accounts for the calculation of the minimum Basel capital adequacy requirements. Given that in these conditions the investment account holders have preferences asymmetric relative to the shareholders, their participation in the profits and losses does not exclude the need for prudential regulation to safeguard the solvency of banks and the system's stability.

The minimum capital requirement is one of the tools[19] available to the regulator – even if not necessarily the most efficient – in the hypothesis, which is valid empirically even for Islamic banks, that conflicts of interest between shareholders and other investors exist, and that neither governance mechanisms nor the market discipline are sufficient to create enough incentives to 'healthy and prudent management' necessary to protect society from systemic risk (Chapra and Khan 2000; Sundararajan and Errico 2002).

In order to take into account the weaker capital function of the investment deposits, due to the fact that the bank must bear the operational risk and more importantly the commercial displacement risk, Islamic scholars and regulatory authorities propose two solutions.

The first is to equate the investment accounts to the hybrid capital instruments included in Tier II (Karim 1996). However, this solution is difficult to reconcile with the technical characteristics of the investment deposits, which are not negotiable in the financial markets and can have short maturity, even cut short with the bank's agreement.

The second solution, which nowadays is favoured, was found by the AAOIFI in 1999 (Chapra and Khan 2000) and proposed again by IFSB in the New Agreement for Capital Regulation in Islamic Banks (IFSB 2005). This acknowledges the fact that Islamic banks, for market needs but mainly for the prudential supervisory requirements, must bear a share of credit and market risks pertaining to the investment deposits 'as a measure of investor protection and in order to mitigate potential systemic risk resulting from massive withdrawals of funds by dissatisfied investment account holders'.[20] To this end, the IFSB suggests computing the Basel solvency requirement as the ratio of pure equity capital on risk-weighted assets. These should include not only the assets financed with shareholders' capital and money deposits, but also a percentage of the portfolio pertaining to the investment deposits, which the national regulatory authorities can fix to no more than 70 per cent at their discretion.[21]

CONCLUDING REMARKS

From a merely quantitative point of view, like every compromise solution, the one suggested by the IFSB does not pretend to be rigorous,[22] but simply 'reasonable'. From a theoretical point of view, this solution is nonetheless extremely relevant for at least three reasons:

1. It recognises that the intermediation through the profit-sharing deposits can lead to a portfolio risk transformation function similar, at least in part, to that of the conventional banks.
2. It recognises that the supervisory authorities of the countries where the Islamic banks originate have ample discretion in the valuation of the capital function of investment accounts and therefore in the application of the Basel capital regulation.
3. It suggests the possibility of an explicit separation, from an accounting point of view, of the portfolio financed with the investment deposits[23] from that financed with shareholders' capital and money deposits, that is, from the investment and the commercial banking activities. If the separation is possible for the purposes of the application of prudential capital requirements according to the proposal of the ISFB,[24] why should it not be also from the legal and operative points of view?

According to many Islamic scholars (Chapra and Khan 2000; El-Hawary, Grais and Iqbal 2004), this is the direction towards which Islamic banks with international aims could move to reconcile their specificity with the Basel prudential regulatory requirements: the investment deposits – or, at least, part of them – could be allocated to a legally separate portfolio managed by an associate company, similar to an investment company with variable capital.

The compartmentalisation of Islamic intermediation could limit the probability of systemic contagion due to the displacement of commercial risks inherent in the profit-sharing contracts, making the performance valuation more transparent and therefore investors' choices more informed. This would probably make the task of the supervisory authorities easier, avoiding inappropriate superposition between systemic stability and investor protection objectives. The entry requisites, the governance processes and proper disclosure rules are much more relevant for investors than a regulation based on quantitative requirements and controls.

In my opinion, however, regulation cannot take Islamic banks back to their original pure operational model, based on the separation between the risks pertaining to different types of financers.

From a managerial point of view, the integrated model of modern Islamic banking results not only from the need to exploit the advantages of diversification and joint production economies, but also from the difficulty with renouncing managerial freedom in allocating resources to maximise overall performance, which probably affects the real profitability of the profit-sharing contracts.

The raising of savings through mutual funds obliged to invest in portfolios of assets following the *Shari'ah*[25] cannot be functionally equated to the functions fulfilled by modern Islamic banking, as is shown by the fact that where Islamic mutual funds and Islamic banks coexist they have different markets.[26]

At present, therefore, the hypothesis that in Western countries standard Basel capital rules can be applied to the Islamic banks seems not only premature but perhaps also unwise. To safeguard consumers, a pragmatic and discretionary approach based on a deep knowledge of the peculiarities and the risks of profit-sharing intermediation can be more useful than the pretence of forcing this model of financial intermediation within the conventional banking format.

NOTES

1. 'Less apparent understanding of the new environment can create a sense of greater risk even if the objective level of risk in the system is unchanged or reduced' (Merton 1995, p. 462).
2. Risk transformation means, properly, that risks borne by bank's creditors are lower than the risks accepted by the bank in its lending activity. All intermediaries perform a risk transformation function thanks to risk pooling and diversification, therefore lowering the non-systemic risk of their portfolio. The bank – but not for instance a mutual fund – performs a further portfolio risk transformation, guaranteeing the certain nominal value of its liabilities with its own capital. Non-diversified portfolio risks are, in other words, transferred from the depositors to the shareholders (Baltensperger 1980, pp. 4 ss.).
3. It is interesting to highlight that even the most rigorous Islamic economic literature recognises the bank as an enterprise aiming to get a legitimate and needed profit (Zaher and Hassan 2001).
4. By investment accounts (or investment deposits) we mean the different types of profit-sharing investment accounts, including the saving investment accounts, which, even if coming under the same type of *mudaraba* contract, are usually more liquid.
5. To be precise, from an economic or accounting point of view the restricted investment accounts are not real liabilities, and have consequently to be treated as off-balance sheet liabilities.

6. We must consider that for the investment accounts, but not for the shareholders' capital, the invested funds are usually calculated net of a discretionary share of reserves, kept by the bank against liquidity risks (Al-Deehani, Karim and Murinde 1998).

7. The share of profits due to the investment deposits is a fraction, net of the share for *mudarib*, of the total profit; that is, if the bank uses the *pooling method*, it includes fees from the services provided by the bank and is net of all managerial expenses and provisions. An alternative is the *separation method*, according to which the investment account holders participate only in the financial revenues of the assets they have financed. In this case, the non-interest income and the operating costs are given wholly to the bank, and therefore the shareholders (Karim 1996).

8. This risk is also defined as 'fiduciary risk', as negligent or illegal behaviour by management in the execution of the duties deriving from the *mudaraba* contract must result in the loss of trust from the investment account holders and therefore in the withdrawal of their deposits (Chapra and Khan 2000). Fiduciary risk is in reality one of the categories included in Basel 2 operational risk, as also specified in the regulation of capital for Islamic banks proposed by the Islamic Financial Services Board (IFSB 2005), par. 74: 'The IIFS (Institutions offering only Islamic Financial Services) is liable for losses arising from its negligence, misconduct or breach of the investment mandate, and the risk of the losses arising from such events is characterized as a fiduciary risk. The capital requirement for this fiduciary risk is dealt under operational risk.'

9. This Board is fundamental in the governance structure of all the Islamic financial intermediaries since it is responsible for evaluating the admissibility of the contracts relative to the *Shari'ah* and to monitor their correct execution (Archer, Karim and Al-Deehani 1998).

10. This, even if only in principle, is the view adhered to by the proposal for regulation of capital for Islamic banks issued by the IFSB (par. 74): 'In principle . . . the commercial risk on assets financed by PSIA (Profit Sharing Investment Accounts) do not represent risk for the IIFS's own (shareholders) capital and thus would not entail a regulatory capital requirement for the IIFS. This implies that assets funded by either unrestricted or restricted PSIA would be excluded from the calculation of the denominator of the capital ratio' (IFSB 2005).

11. These 'Islamic desks' are departments or branches of conventional banks, usually located in Islamic countries, offering financial products and services permitted by the *Qur'an*. Nowadays there are many multinational banks that have 'Islamic desks'; among the main ones are Citibank, Bank of America, Commerzbank, Deutsche Bank, Merryl Lynch, ABN AMRO, BNP Paribas, UBS, HSBC.

12. 'The PLS (profit and loss sharing) principle is never strictly applied. There are various degrees of non-compliance with respect to the PLS principle in current banking practices. In some cases, the bank guarantees the expected rate of return on investment deposits. Moreover, this rate of return is de-linked from banks profit' (Zaher and Hassan 2001, p. 181).

13. This due to the Islamic banking book mainly containing non-financial assets (consumable goods or real estate). The two main categories of investments of Islamic banks stem from the *murabaha* and *musharaka* contracts. The first one (defined as cost-plus or mark-up financing) implies the acquisition of an investment good or consumable by the bank, with the promise by the person receiving the finance to buy it back at maturity, paying to the bank the price plus the mark-up. This type of contract, born to finance the working capital of business, is today applied also to real estate. The *musharaka* contract is instead similar to a form of venture capital or joint venture (Lewis and Algaoud 2001; Zaher and Hassan 2001).

14. This international agency was formed in 1991 by the main Islamic banks and financial institutions; at present it has 115 members from 27 countries and is located in Manama (Bahrain).

15. AAOIFI, Statement on the purpose and calculation of the Capital Adequacy Ratio for Islamic Banks, 1999, quoted in Karim (2001).

16. This is an institution, based in Kuala Lampur (Malaysia), founded in 2002 with the blessing of the Accounting and Auditing Organization for Islamic Financial Institutions and of the International Monetary Fund, similar, in many ways to the Basel Committee. It includes the Islamic Development Bank and the central banks of Bahrain, Indonesia, Iran, Kuwait, Lebanon, Pakistan, Qatar and Sudan.

17. It is interesting to see that, for example, the Central Bank of Malaysia has recently mandated Islamic banks to have a Profit Equalisation Reserve:

> To generate rates of returns that are competitive and stable, the Profit Equalisation Reserve acts as a mechanism to mitigate the fluctuation of rate of return arising from the flow of income, provisioning and total deposits. This reserve is appropriated out of the total gross income and is shared by both the depositors and the banking institution. In a dual banking environment, the ability to maximise risk-adjusted return on investment and sustain stable and competitive returns is an important element for the development of a competitive Islamic banking system. (Central Bank of Malaysia, 2004)

This confirms what many scholars have stressed: the central banks find many ways to discourage wide fluctuations in the rates that the banks are authorised to offer to the depositors in order to avoid destabilising movements in the shares of deposits within the system (Zaher and Hassan 2001).

18. Many theoretical and empirical analyses come to the same conclusions with reference to the asset management; these show how Islamic banks tend to prefer mark-up contracts to profit-sharing agreements because of the need to smooth performance, especially in the presence of adverse selection and moral hazard (Aggarwal and Yousef, 1996; El-Hawary, Grais and Iqbal 2004).

19. It goes beyond the objectives of this study to analyse which is the most effective mix among capital regulation, internal controls and market discipline; nor do we intend to discuss whether the minimum capital requirements are really – for Islamic banks as well as for conventional banks – the most efficient form of quantitative control relative to other alternatives, such as, for example, minimum liquidity requirements. For non-conventional analyses of this problem see Merton (1995) and, specific to the US, Ball and Stoll (1998).

20. IFSB, 2005, par. 74 and Appendix A.

21. When the banks constitute internal reserves in the form of profit equalisation reserve or investment risk reserve (the first, charged pro-quota to both the shareholders and the investment accounts; the second, charged wholly to the second), the risk-weighted assets financed by such reserves can be taken away from the denominator of the solvency coefficient up to a maximum of 30 per cent as established by the supervisory authorities (IFSB, 2005, par. 79 and Appendix A).

22. This is also true for the 8 per cent minimum value of the Basel coefficient.

23. Including particularly those unrestricted.

24. The adjustments to the denominator of the Basel coefficient suggested by the IFSB can result in a big reduction in the capital constraint. A simple simulation exercise shows that taking away in full the portfolio financed with the investment deposits can result in the intermediation growing, for a given primary capital, about three times more than that allowed to the conventional banks (in the hypotheses of constant assets weights and the investment deposits on average 60 per cent of the total liabilities). This calculation does not take into account the operational risks (Karim 1996).

25. See Zaher and Hassan (2001, pp. 177 ss.) for an analysis of the ethical and managerial principles of the Islamic investment funds.

26. A significant example is the UK, where financial institutions offering Islamic mutual funds have been operating since the 1990s and where in August 2004 the Islamic Bank of Britain was founded, the first Islamic bank authorised to operate in a Western country (FSA 2004).

REFERENCES

Aggarwal, R. and Yousef, T. (1996), 'Islamic banks and investment financing', Unpublished Paper, Harvard University.

Al-Deehani, T., Karim, Rifaat A. and Murinde, V. (1999), 'The capital structure of Islamic banks under the contractual obligation of profit sharing', *International Journal of Theoretical and Applied Finance*, **2**(3), 243–83.

Alexander, K. and Duhmale, R. (2001), *Enhancing corporate governance for financial institutions,* Working Paper No. 196, Cambridge, UK: ESRC Centre for Business Research.

Archer, S., Karim, Rifaat A. and Al-Deehani, T. (1998), 'Financial contracting, governance structures and the accounting regulation of Islamic banks: an analysis of agency theory and transaction cost economics', *Journal of Management and Governance*, **2**, 149–70.

Ball C. and Stoll H. (1998), 'Regulatory capital of financial institutions: a comparative analysis', *Financial Markets Institutions & Instruments*, **7**(3), 1–57.

Baltensperger, E. (1980), 'Alternative approaches to the theory of the banking firm', *Journal of Monetary Economics*, **6**, 1–37.

Basel Committee on Banking Supervision (1997), *Core Principles for Effective Banking Supervision*, Basel: Bank for International Settlements.

Basel Committee on Banking Supervision (1999), *Core Principle Methodology*, Basel: Bank for International Settlements.

Central Bank of Malaysia (2004), Governor's speech in the IFSB Summit, Islamic Financial Services Industry and The Global Regulatory Environment, *Approaches to Regulation of Islamic Financial Services Industry*, London.

Chapra, M. Umer and Khan, T. (2000), *Regulation and supervision of Islamic banks,* Jeddah, Saudi Arabia: Islamic Development Bank – Islamic Research and Training Institute. Occasional Paper # 3.

Cook, J., Deakin, S. and Hughes, A. (2001), *Mutuality and corporate governance: the evolution of UK building societies following deregulation*, Working Paper No. 205. Cambridge, UK: ESCR Centre for Business Research.

Dar, Humayon A. and Presley, John R. (2000), 'Lack of profit loss sharing in Islamic banking: management and control imbalances', *International Journal of Islamic Financial Services*, (2).

El-Hawary, D., Grais, W. and Iqbal, Z. (2004), *Regulating Islamic financial institutions: the nature of the regulated*, World Bank Policy Research Working Paper 3227, Washington, DC: World Bank.

Elhiraika, Adam B. (2004), *Islamic financial system and saving: an empirical assessment*, Islamic Development Bank – IRTI. Paper submitted to the International Seminar on 'The prospects of Arab economic cooperation to boost saving and investment', Alexandria, Egypt, June 16–18.

Errico, L. and Farahbaksh, M. (1998), *Islamic banking: issue in prudential regulation and supervision,* IMF Working Paper – WP/98/30, Washington, DC: International Monetary Fund.

FSA (2004), Mansion House speech – Speech by Callum McCarthy, www.fsa.gov.uk/Pages/Library/Communication/Speeches/2004/SP195.shtml: FSA Communication documents.

Haron, S. and Ahmad, N. (2000), 'The effects of conventional interest rates and rate of profit on funds deposited with Islamic banking system in Malaysia', *International Journal of Islamic Financial Services*, **1**(4).

IFSB – Islamic Financial Services Board (2005), Capital Adequacy Standard for institutions (other than insurance institutions) offering only Islamic financial services, www.ifsb.org: Islamic Financial Services Board.

Karim, Rifaat A. (1996), 'The impact of the Basel capital adequacy ratio regulation on the financial and marketing strategies of Islamic banks', *International Journal of Bank Marketing*, **14**(7), 32–44.

Karim, Rifaat A. (2001), 'International accounting harmonization, banking regulation, and Islamic banks', *International Journal of Accounting*, **36**, 169–93.

Khan, T. and Ahmed, H. (2001), *Risk management: an analysis of issues in Islamic financial industry*, Occasional Paper No. 5. Jeddah, Saudi Arabia: Islamic Development Bank – Islamic Research and Training Institute.

Khan, Muhammad S. (1986), *Islamic interest-free banking: a theoretical analysis*, IMF Staff Papers, Vol. 33, pp. 1–27

Lewis, Mervyn L. and Algaoud, L.M. (2001), *Islamic Banking*, Cheltenham, UK and Northampton, MA, USA: Edward Elgar.

Martens, A. (2001), *La finance islamique: fondements, théorie et réalité*, Cahier 20, Montréal: Université de Montréal – Centre de recherche et développement en économique.

Merton, Robert C. (1995), 'Financial innovation and the management and regulation of financial institutions', *Journal of Banking and Finance*, **19** (3–4), 461–81.

Sundararajan, V. and Errico, L. (2002), *Islamic financial institutions and products in the global financial system: key issues in risk management and challenges ahead*, IMF Working Paper WP/02/192, Washington, DC: International Monetary Fund

Yasseri, A. (2002), 'Islamic banking contracts as enforced in Iran', in M. Iqbal and David T. Llewellyn (eds), *Islamic Banking and Finance. New Perspectives on Profit-sharing and Risk*, Cheltenham, UK and Northampton, MA, USA: Edward Elgar.

Zaher, Tarek S. and Hassan, Kabir M. (2001), 'A comparative literature survey of Islamic finance and banking', *Financial Markets, Institutions & Instruments*, **10** (4), 155–99.

8. Investing with values: ethical investment versus Islamic investment

Celia de Anca

ETHICAL INVESTMENT/SOCIALLY RESPONSIBLE INVESTMENT (SRI)

Background

Ethical investment can be found with other denominations, including sustainable investment and probably the most popular term socially responsible investment (SRI). Some experts place more emphasis on negative elements in the ethical funds, and a stronger focus on the positive criteria in SRI. Recently, investors have tended to include corporate governance along with social and environment issues, and thus the term ESG (environment, social and governance) investment has also become frequent. However, generally speaking all denominations refer to a particular investment in which, in addition to financial criteria, social, ethical and environmental criteria are also considered.

According to the Social Investment Forum, socially responsible investment can be defined as 'An investment strategy that takes into account a company's ethical, social and environmental performance as well as its financial performance when selecting and managing investment portfolios' (Social Investment Forum, 2006).

SRI can be traced back to its origins in the Quaker and Methodist religious movements of the nineteenth century. Religious investors have traditionally shied away from being involved in investing in enterprises that produced weapons, or which were in the alcohol, tobacco or gambling industries.

In more recent times, in the USA in the 1970s, as a way to oppose the Vietnam War, ethical investment began to take shape. In 1971 the first modern ethical fund was born, the Pax World Fund, founded by a group of university students opposed to financing the war industry with their savings. In this fund all corporations related to the war industry were excluded. That same year the environmental organization *Greenpeace* was established. In the 1980s the ethical movement was linked to the fight against the apartheid regime of South Africa and aimed at boycotting USA corporations involved in the racist regime.

In Europe we can find the first ethical initiatives in the UK in the 1970s linked to the Anglican Church, although only in 1984 did ethical investment acquire legal status. The first ethical fund, the Friends Provident Stewardship, of Quaker origin, was launched in 1984. This first fund excluded corporations related to the South African apartheid regime, and corporations related to arms, alcohol and tobacco.

The organization EIRIS created to screen UK corporations was established in 1983. In the same period the Social Investment Forum was established in the USA and the UK, with the objective of promoting SRI investment.

SRI Investment Criteria

SRI investment has a dual purpose:

1. To change a company's attitudes and improve corporate responsibility in regards to societal concerns.
2. To support corporations that favor social justice and the environment and apply sustainable and development criteria in their strategies.

Social investment initiatives can be found in a variety of financial instruments, including mutual funds, pension funds as well as different private and institutional savings schemes.

Generally the different instruments can be classified according to three strategies:

1. *Screening*: The practice of including or excluding publicly traded securities from investment portfolios or mutual funds based on social and/or environmental criteria.
2. *Shareholder advocacy*: Actions socially aware investors take in their role as owners of corporations, including dialoguing with companies on issues of concern, as well as filing and voting proxy resolutions. An example of advocacy is a famous case with the French corporation ELF. This company accepted the elaboration of environmental criteria in its annual reports, as well as appointing an Environment Director, following a campaign promoted by the Investment Fund Friends IVORY and SIME, a fund manager that owned 0.05 per cent of the company at the time (*The Ethical Investor*, 2000).

3. *Community Investing:* This is a flow of capital from investors to communities that are under-served by traditional financial services. It provides access to credit, equity, capital, and basic banking products.

Screened funds have been the most widespread SRI strategy over the last decade. In general screening criteria can be classified as negative and/ or positive. The negative/positive criteria vary according to the different investors, which is why there is a large variety of funds based on what is important for each investor.

Negative criteria

The investor excludes from the investment portfolio all corporations that operate in a series of activities that the investor intends to avoid. The most general negative criteria include nuclear energy, arms, pornography, alcohol and tobacco. Also some investors might consider excluding corporations that operate in genetic manipulation, intensive farming, water pollution, and so on.

The negative criteria evolve with time, for example twenty years ago tobacco and alcohol were at the top of the list. Today the most negatively perceived activities include corporations that harm the environment or that are involved in the arms industry and third world debt.

Positive criteria

In addition to not investing in corporations whose activities are perceived as negative, most of SRI funds also try to foster positive criteria, in order to favor corporations that signal positive changes that affect society in a positive manner, or favor human rights.

Positive criteria might include: a higher transparency in company reporting, environmental initiatives, improvement in employees' equal rights, or corporations involved in services and products that can improve living conditions, such as new sustainable energy technologies.

SRI Supervision

The majority of investment funds have a panel or committee in charge of defining a set of criteria and preparing a list of acceptable corporations. The fund manager then selects companies from the accepted list in accordance with financial criteria. Alternatively, some funds have a first list based on financial criteria to which the ethical committee applies the SRI criteria and identifies acceptable securities.

In many cases, once the set of SRI criteria are defined, the fund subcontracts a specialized organization that screens corporations according to the defined criteria. These organizations are found in different countries: EIRIS (Ethical Investment Research Services), in the UK, IMUG (Institut fur market Unwelt Gesellschaft) in Germany and Austria, ARESE in France, Avanzi in Italy, Fundación Ecología y Desarrollo in Spain, Caring Company in Sweden, Ethibel in Belgium, and KLD (Kinder Lydenberg) or Domini in the USA.

There are also international networks, like the SIRI group (Sustainable Investment Research International Group) or Eurosif (the European Social Investment Forum). SIRI was created in the year 2000, and in 2003 it became the SIRI Company to provide professional SRI financial services. The SIRI Company has a total of 100 researchers spread throughout relevant countries that monitor a total of 4000 corporations all over the world according to SRI criteria including environmental, civil and women's rights, corporate governance issues, animal rights, corruption and anti-nuclear issues. Eurosif is a pan-European group created in 2001 to address sustainability through financial markets. Current member affiliates of Eurosif include pension funds, financial service providers, academic institutes, research associations and NGOs. In 2006 the United Nations Environment Program Finance Initiative and the UN Global Compact launched the Principles for Responsible Investment (PRI) initiative to foster environmental, social and corporate governance (ESG) issues. In its first year PRI has attracted over 180 institutional signatories globally.

The USA was the first to produce an SRI index in 1990 with the Domini Social Index 400 established by KLD, a pioneering agency for ethical investment that monitors 400 corporations. In 1999 the Dow Jones Company together with the Sustainable Asset Management launched a series of five ethical indexes: the Dow Jones Sustainable Group Indexes.

In the UK the *Financial Times*, together with the London Stock Exchange, launched in July 2001 a series of four reference indexes under the generic name of FTSE4good index series.

During the last decade the SRI movement has been progressively extended to the general public and it has been consistently growing in the financial markets. The general attitude is moving away from the negative criteria and using positive criteria to foster positive attitudes in the corporate world towards the environment, employees and societal considerations.

SRI Global Market Share

There is no widespread global definition of what constitutes a global social investment, and therefore it is very difficult to compare figures from country to country. However, there are a growing number of financial agents across the globe with an interest in different social and ethical practices that vary from screening practices in western markets to a range of smaller tools for community investment in Asia. According to the Social Investment Forum there are social investment products available in more than 21 countries across the world.

Although there are different criteria to define what constitutes an ethical fund, and which take into account the differences in the world's financial markets, there are at least 600 SRI funds worldwide.

USA

The Social Investment Forum 2005 report has identified $2.29 trillion in total assets under management in the USA using one or more investment strategies (screening, shareholder advocacy and community investment). Assets in screened mutual funds reached $179 billion in 201 mutual funds (Social Investment Forum, 2006).

Europe

According to Eurosif the broad European SRI market was estimated in 2006 at €1 trillion, representing as much as 10–15 per cent of the total European funds under management, including €105 billion in screened institutional and retail assets (*European SIRI Study,* 2006). The European market is dominated by institutional investment (94 per cent) with only 6 per cent of retail investment. The SIRI Company report on retail funds estimated 375 green, social and ethical funds operating in Europe in 2005 with a total amount of €24.1 billion (UK, Sweden France and Belgium accounting for 63.7 per cent of available funds) (SIRI Company, 2005).

Canada

According to Canada's Social Investment Organization (SIO) the value of SIRI assets under management reached 504 billion Canadian dollars in 2006, dominated largely by several pension funds, mostly in the public sector. Retail SRI funds amounted to 18.1 billion Canadian dollars in 2006 (EIRIS, 2007).

Asia-Pacific

In Australia the SRI portfolio reached US$11.98 billion in 2006. In New Zealand the SRI investment was estimated in 2006 at US$37.2 million. Japan, one of the most developed SRI markets in the region, reached US$2.5 billion in 2006 (EIRIS, 2007).

Emerging markets

The International Financial Corporation (IFC) estimates that SRI assets in emerging markets reached US$2.7 billion in 2005, with South African and Brazilian markets playing a key role. Brazil is leading the development of responsible investment in Latin America. Bovespa (the Sao Paulo Stock exchange) launched a responsible investment index (called the Bovespa Corporate Sustainable Index ISE) tracking the financial, corporate governance, environmental and social performance of listed companies. In May 2004 the Stock Exchange in Johannesburg also launched a responsible investment index (Social Investment Forum, 2006).

SRI Profitability and Future Trends

SRI investment aims to balance financial criteria with ethical consideration and therefore aims to achieve the maximum financial profitability within the limits marked by the sustainability criteria. Some aspects are worth taking into consideration:

1. If the fund is global it allows for greater profitability since it can take advantage of the best performing securities in the global market.
2. Traditionally larger corporations have acquired a bad reputation and were thus excluded from the SRI portfolio. However recently positive signs in these corporations have made them acceptable in SRI investment, thus also improving profit margins for the funds.
3. Ethical and financial analyses must be done separately for each of the different selection criteria.
4. Traditionally, SRI investment was seen as giving less return than conventional investments, since SRI had significant limitations and a large number of SMEs in its portfolios. However this perception is not always real. For example, during the decade of the technological boom, SRI investment performed much better than traditional investment, although when the dot.com bubble burst SRI investments were also more heavily affected.

Analysts in general consider that in theory SRI investment does not offer any additional financial advantage, although neither is it financially harmful. In the long term, there are certain advantages due to the fidelity of the investor, and an improved performance by the corporations in question, because of sustainability criteria.

ISLAMIC INVESTMENT

Background

Islamic finance is a mode of finance based on *Shari'ah* principles. In essence the Muslim believer's view of economics is based on man's obligation to organize his affairs in accordance to the will of God.

Shari'ah is basically about economic justice and is not against making money. It does, however, emphasize ethical arguments as more important than the non-ethical profit return in the economic process. Islam recognizes private property as well as the legitimate profit resulting from economic transactions. Capital as well as labor and land are considered as constituent elements of the economic process, and as such it is legitimate for capital to obtain a profit as long as is a justifiable reward, the goal not being equality but the avoidance of gross inequality.

The Islamic financial mode based on partnership goes back to the time of Muhammad. However the current financial system of most Islamic countries originated in the nineteenth century, in the period of European colonialism, and the expansion of European-based trade. Therefore the first banks established in most Arab and Muslim countries were based on the model of their European competitors (Wilson, 1997a). In the 1950s, a group of Islamic researchers in Pakistan began to explore the possibility of using Islamic traditional forms to finance modern economic transactions. In 1958, a small rural co-operative bank was established in West Pakistan. In this first Islamic financial initiative, the landlords from the area deposited their savings in the bank and obtained funds in exchange on the basis of a *mudarib* contract. In 1963, Ahmed el Naggar created an Islamic bank in the Egyptian delta. The initiative was successful and, on its nationalization in 1972, it had managed to acquire more than 10,000 depositors.

The origins of the Islamic banking movement were thus first developed in the 1950s and '60s; however, its full development occurred in the mid-'70s after the oil crises of 1973, coinciding with the emergence of Islamic movements.

In the mid-1970s, a number of Muslims in Muslim countries as well as in the West were reluctant to hand over their funds to banks and financial institutions that invest in companies engaged in unethical and socially harmful activities. The demand of a growing number of Muslims to deposit their money in Islamic-based instruments fostered the emergence of an Islamic Banking Industry during the 1970s in Muslim and non-Muslim countries. It is in this period that the first major Islamic banks were created, including the Dubai Islamic Bank established in 1975, the

Kuwait Financial House established in 1977, the Bahrain Islamic Bank established in 1981 and the Qatar Islamic Bank established in 1983.

During the 1970s and 1980s the Islamic banking industry was based on basic instruments of deposits and finance which avoided interest. Thus most of the financial instruments were driven by the concept of *mudaraba* (equivalent of trust financing) or *murabaha* (cost plus financing). During the 1990s, Islamic financial institutions became increasingly more innovative, and developed more complex instruments and structures to meet the demands of modern day business. In recent years, driven by the financial liquidity of oil and an increased demand for such products, the industry has witnessed a large expansion both in terms of its size, as well as in the innovation of new financial products.

If ethical investment played a pivotal role in the ethical movement, as stated in the first part of the chapter, banking has been the driving force in the Islamic counterpart. Conventional banking based on ethical principles such as *Triodos Bank* appeared after the ethical investment industry was already well developed. In contrast, Islamic investment products were developed when the Islamic banking industry was well established.

The first Islamic investment funds appeared in the market in the 1980s. The Amana Income Fund was launched in the USA in 1986 by members of the North American Islamic Trust (NAIT). The fund still exists today, managed by Saturna Capital Corp, a small asset company based in Washington (al-Rifai, 1999). The same year Kleinwort Bensons' Islamic Fund was launched in London. This fund was closed three years later due to insufficient subscriptions.

Investment Criteria

Islamic Investment Funds can be defined as a 'joint pool wherein the investors contribute their surplus money for the purpose of its investment to earn halal profits in strict conformity with the precepts of Islamic *Shari'ah* (Usmani and Justice, 2000). Their validity in terms of *Shari'ah* will always be subject to:

- the profits from the investment carrying a pro-rata profit earned by the fund and never a fixed return tied up with their face value;
- the investment being done in a business acceptable to *Shari'ah*.

Islamic Investment Funds might include equity funds, *ijara* funds, commodity funds and *murabaha* funds and so on; the most developed are the equity funds.

In principle, placing funds in interest-yielding funds, or in certificates of deposits, will not be tolerated from a *Shari'ah* point of view since such instruments are mainly based on interest. Equity investment, as shown in the definition, can be acceptable if the company itself is acceptable under *Shari'ah* norms.

Experts will agree that if a company neither borrows money or charges interest, nor keeps its surplus in an interest-bearing account, its shares will be accepted from a *Shari'ah* point of view. Some scholars state that it is only allowed from a *Shari'ah* point of view to deal with those companies even though they recognize that such companies are very rare in contemporary stock markets. A large number of experts do not, however, endorse that view, and accept a certain degree of non-conforming practice.

The Dow Jones Islamic Index Group (http://indexes.dowjones.com/djimi/imhome.html) states that the criteria applied by the Dow Jones Islamic Index group when accepting the inclusion of a company are divided into two categories:

1. The primary business of the company must be *halal* (permissible), therefore business involving, among other forbidden practices, conventional banking, alcohol, weapons, pork or gambling are not acceptable.
2. Financial screens then are applied:

    ●   Total debt divided by trailing 12-month average market capitalization is 33 per cent or more.
    ●   Cash plus interest-bearing securities divided by trailing 12-month average market capitalization is 33 per cent or more.
    ●   Accounts receivables divided by 12-month average market capitalization is 33 per cent or more.

However we can find diversity in the financial criteria used to screen out stocks. As an example Yasaar's Limited, the advisor company of indexes such as the FTSE-SGX Asia Shari'ah 100 index, prefers to use as its financial ratio the total asset to total debt as opposed to market capitalization to debt or assets which is deemed to be more volatile (*Islamic Banker*, 2006b).

Diversity can be also found in the acceptance of the company's activity. All experts agree on the unacceptability of companies whose primary activity is the production of alcohol or pork. However certain cases are open to debate, for example for some scholars, companies can be acceptable if the non-conforming practice does not represent the main business of the company. For example, an airline company selling alcohol during flights can be acceptable since the selling of alcohol is not its main activity.

Moreover some indexes and investment funds often prohibit other areas, in addition to alcohol, pork or gambling which are common to all Islamic funds. For example, the *Shari'ah* board of the DJIM, Turkey, recommends the stocks of tobacco companies and arms manufacturers to be screened out on the grounds that the products are either harmful to health or destructive (*Islamic Banker*, 2006a).

Supervision and Specialized Bodies

The early funds of the 1980s did not attain the desired success, due to a lack of trust in their Islamic standards or sometimes due to disappointing returns for the investors. Since the approval of Islamic funds by the Islamic *Fiqh* Academy in Jeddah in 1995 (one of the largest legal bodies in the Muslim world), a new generation of funds was launched, this time with greater success. Today the Islamic investment equity funds market is one of the fastest growing sectors within the Islamic financial system. Other Islamic financial regulatory bodies such as the AAOIFI (Accounting and Auditing Organization for Islamic Financial Institutions) and the Islamic Financial Services Board (IFSB) help in giving transparency and general credibility to the industry.

Other challenges the industry faced during its early stages included the need for benchmarks to promote the sharing of information. The launch of the International Islamic Indexes series, by FTSE and Dow Jones, has helped promote the industry in the last decade. The Dow Jones Islamic Market Index was launched in February 1999 as part of the Dow Jones Global Index Series (DJGI). The DJGI, which includes stocks, analyses companies in 47 countries covering 10 economic sectors and 122 industrial groups. Out of this general index a *Shari'ah* supervisory board applies the above-mentioned criteria, on which the *Shari'ah* universe is formed. In a similar process in 1999 the FTSE established its FTSE Global Islamic Index series. Out of a general universe a screen is applied to form the *Shari'ah*-accepted universe.

Further development of these indexes has given rise to ventures like the February 2006 launch of the FTSE-SGX Asia Shari'ah 100 index. This index constitutes a partnership among the Singapore Exchange (SGX), the London-based FTSE and the *Shari'ah* compliance company Yasaar Limited. This fund is 50 per cent Japan-weighted with the other half comprising stocks from Hong Kong, Singapore, Taiwan and South Korea, all the stocks having been screened for *Shari'ah* compliance by Yasaar Limited.

Also Dow Jones launched the Dow Jones Islamic Market (DJIM) Turkey index in September 2005. This index is used by various funds in Turkey such as the *DJIM Turkiye a Tip Borsa Yatirim Fonu* launched by the Istanbul based Bizim Menkul Degerler (BMD) Securities Inc.

These international indexes, as well as some regional ones such as the RHB Index, help asset management companies as well as the general Muslim investor. Small investors do not have the means to analyse the Islamic acceptability of companies around the world and therefore prefer to place their capital in funds already established by fund management groups, which screen the accepted companies to be included in their portfolio.

Global Market

Estimates of the Islamic financial industry suggests that there are $300 billion of assets managed according to Islamic principles and more than 280 institutions ranging from commercial companies to investment banks and investment funds. Other estimates go as high as $500 bn (*Financial Times*, 2007). Although Islamic banking still represents only 1 per cent of global banking assets some observers estimate a potential growth of 12–15 per cent per annum

In terms of the number of Islamic Equity Funds, Failaka estimates that there are near 300 funds worldwide (*Failaka*, 2008), including balanced funds, with a cumulative total of $16 billion of managed assets.

Most of these equity funds were launched after 1995, and now offer a large variety of products, including (*Islamic Banker*, 2006a):

- Global funds (including al-Ahli Global Trading Equity, Global Equity fund, Al-Safwa International equity)
- Regional funds (including Al-Ahli Asia Pacific Trading Equity Funds, Al-Fanar Europe Limited)
- Country equity funds (including: Amana Income Fund, AIF Saudi Company Shares, most Malaysian funds)
- Sector funds (including Al-Fanar Technology Ltd, al-Ahli Healthcare Trading Equity Fund)
- Hedge funds (including Al-Fanar US Equity Hedge Funds)
- Index funds (including Al-Baraka Dow Jones Islamic Market Index Fund)
- Ladies' funds (Al-Johara Ladies Fund)
- Children's funds (Al-Rajh Children's funds)

Fund managers include some of the most reputed international asset management companies such as Wellington Management Co. USA, UBS Switzerland, Citibank USA, HSBC UK, Merrill Lynch USA, BNP Paribas France and National Commercial Saudi Arabia.

Asia represents nearly half of all *Shari'ah*-compliant funds, mostly in Malaysia by Malaysian-domiciled funds. Islamic funds dealing strictly in GCC countries represent 12 per cent of the total *Shari'ah*-compliant universe.

Profitability and Future Trends

Failaka research shows Islam-compliant funds occasionally outperform their conventional peers, occasionally underperform these rivals, and often match the broader market's overall performance. Much of the disparities between Islamic funds and conventional funds in 2006 were due to key industry sectors such as banking and technology (Failaka Advisors, 2007). 2006 was a very strong year for the banking sector, particularly investment banking, and since Islamic funds exclude bank stocks these gains did not benefit the industry. There was a reversal of this trend, however, during 2007 and particularly at the beginning of 2008. These funds are also very sensitive to the market fluctuations of the technology sector. It is often said that many Islamic funds are tech-heavy. This is partly because, due to capital structure, many technology firms emphasize equity over debt, and are less likely to deal with prohibited industries.

With the continuous interest in the Islamic financial system, there are positive signs that more funds will be launched. In 2006 Deutsche Bank established five new DWS Noor funds (Failaka Advisors, 2007). Other western majors have just joined the fray or are thinking of launching similar Islamic equity products. However, and despite these successes, this market has seen a record of poor marketing as the emphasis is on products and not on addressing the needs of investors, and as a result quite a number of funds have closed down over the last few years. Nevertheless, positive signs indicate an improvement in the marketing side of the industry.

Islamic finance and investment has important challenges ahead, but it is in the twenty-first century a fully consolidated industry that will probably take a significant share of the international markets in the future. This type of finance will be managed by non-governmental initiatives attracting a large part of the Muslim capital around the world. It is therefore essential for the business community to understand the Islamic financial transactions and to learn how to operate with them over the coming decades.

ISLAMIC INVESTMENT VS ETHICAL (SRI) INVESTMENT: THE UK MARKET

Islamic investments funds (IIF) are similar in many ways to socially responsible investment funds (SRI funds), as the previous sections suggest. However, in order to be able to draw some conclusions with regard to similarities and differences, we need to compare both types of funds in terms of portfolio, performance or client base.

A comparison of existing IIFs (around 300 globally) with SRI funds (around 600) can be misleading since regional and market variables can have a considerable effect on results. Asia is home to nearly half of all *Shari'ah*-compliant funds, mostly Malaysian-domiciled funds, followed by GCC countries, which have 12 per cent of the total *Shari'ah*-compliant universe. In Asian and GCC markets, however, SRI funds are rare. By contrast the US and Europe lead the SRI funds market with more than 200 mutual funds in the US and nearly 400 funds operating in Europe. Islamic funds are also present in these markets.

Hence it would be more accurate to concentrate on one particular market in which both funds operate, such as the UK, to obtain more reliable results. An analysis of the UK market can give some idea of the similarities and differences in terms of:

1. the performance of the investment, showing how IIFs perform *vis-à-vis* SRI funds;
2. the destination of funds, and thus how portfolios compare;
3. the origin of funding, and thus the client base;
4. managers and standards.

The UK market also permits the use the FTSE index series, and compares two similar indexes in Islamic and SIRI investments: the FTSE Shari'ah All World Index from the FTSE Global Islamic Index Series (GIIS) and the FTSE4good Global Index from the FTSE4Good Index Series. (www.ftse.com).

Both indexes invest in the global market, in large and mid-sized companies.

Islamic Investment Performance *vis-à-vis* Socially Responsible Investment

The first interesting observation comes from comparing the total return index calculations for the performance of both indexes (see Figure 8.1). We can see that both have performed quite similarly over the past five years except for some significant changes in 2007 and 2008 in which the *Shari'ah*-based index outperformed the SRI equivalent. Different reasons can explain this outperformance, including the differences in portfolio, and in particular the higher component of oil industries in the *Shari'ah*-based index, as well as the weight component of banking and investment in the SRI index.

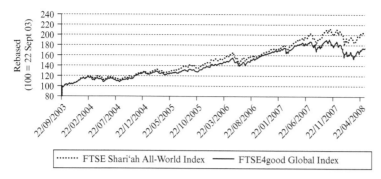

Source: FTSE Southern Europe www.ftse.com.

Figure 8.1   Performance chart since Shari'ah *inception (total return USD)*

IIF vs SRI portfolio

A close analysis of the portfolio of both types of indexes as shown in Figure 8.2 will help the performance analysis:

1. ***Financials:*** Islamic investment funds avoid interest-based finance, and thus the financial sector weight is very limited in the FTSE Shari'ah All World Index. This is not the case of the SRI investment (although outside the indexes, some of the strictest green funds also exclude banks from their portfolio because of their contribution to third world debt).
2. ***Oil and gas, basic and industrial materials:*** SRI investments tend to be very concerned about the impact of these industries on the environment and invest only with careful screening in the sector as shown in the FTSE4good index. Islamic investment by contrast tend to be less concerned about the potential harm of these sectors as shown in their weight in the FTSE Shari'ah All World Index.
3. Both Islamic and SRI funds do, however, invest heavily in technologies, telecommunications and consumer services, since they are less likely to be involved in interest charges or harmful manufacturing (alcohol, and so on).

Client Base

According to the IFSL Research report on Islamic Finance in 2008 (www. IFSL.org.uk/research), nine managers of Islamic equity funds can be found in the UK and ten managers of Islamic funds, half of which represent global equities, the rest being regional or with a specific focus.

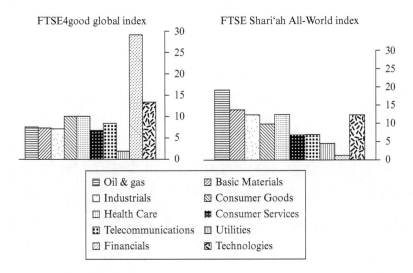

Source: www.ftse.com.

Figure 8.2   SRI investment and Islamic investment

Most of the Islamic funds registered in the UK tend to operate off-shore and focus on larger investments of over $5000, and some exceptionally large investments which require a minimum of $100,000. Such funds include the Al Fanar Asia Ltd or the Taib Crescent Global Fund. Some even require a minimum of $1,000,000, like the Emirates Dynamic Liquid Fund. Recently, however, some Islamic funds are now offered on-shore and are open to the retail market in the UK. These include the SW Islamic Equity Fund or the Parsoli Global Islamic Equity Fund. These funds tend to have minimum investments of around $2000.

SIRI investment, on the other hand, tends to rely on a base of small investors, as well as investment from NGOs, charities and public institutions. EIRIS reports 79 ethical and green funds open to the general public with a client base of 720,312 investors in the UK market. Most SIRI funds require a relatively low minimum investment of around $1000, such as the Aberdeen Ethical World Fund (£500 lump sum, £50 per month) or the Jupiter Ecology Fund (£500) (www.uksif.org/).

Supervisory Bodies and Managers

Most ethical funds and Islamic funds in the UK market have their own committee to define the investment criteria and supervise the investment

(*Shari'ah* boards in the case of Islamic investment or ethical committees in the case of SRI investment). Alternatively both types of funds will seek external advisors (*Shari'ah* advisory companies or professional SRI organizations). They differ, however, in how these bodies function. The *Shari'ah* advisors comprise Islamic scholars that work on the legality of a certain financial operation according to *Shari'ah* law. The ethical committees, by contrast, will include different professionals, academics, NGO activists or business people, that will agree on a set of SRI principles according to the fund's client base, and work with asset managers to make sure these criteria are met. Their work will not be based on whether or not financial products adhere to a set of laws, although a certain degree of law is involved since the criteria for setting higher principles are based on the international legal principles of human rights, international environmental legal principles and other international norms. SRI boards focus increasingly on positive criteria and on how to foster certain companies to become best performers in the sector (best in class), rather than exclude non-conforming companies.

Both Islamic funds as well as SRI funds tend to be managed by professional asset management companies and investment banks, some of which manage both types of funds such as the HSBC Investments or UBS.

Concluding Remarks

Important differences thus exist between Islamic investment and SRI investment, as is shown by the UK case, however there are also some significant similarities. There are in both cases minority movements with great development potential. Both investment schemes try to channel the savings of individuals that wish their money to be invested according to their principles and values. Both investment systems operate in a similar manner with negative criteria to exclude activities perceived as harmful for the society, and with positive criteria to foster activities and attitudes perceived as positive for society. The movement in both cultures illustrates a similar trend that consists of a growing awareness of individuals with more responsible business behavior, investing following the values of the investor.

INVESTMENT WITH VALUES, BUT WHICH VALUES?

Values are rather difficult to define, since they are understood differently by different people and different cultures. In its research work, EIRIS has established more than 40 areas of activity, selecting more than 350 social indicators. These indicators can include executive salaries, gambling, environmental criteria or third world debt. The intention of organizations such as EIRIS is not to define what ethical behavior is but rather to foster greater disclosure by corporations of operations and activities, to allow the individual investors to decide what they consider ethical and thus worth the effort of investing their money. Perhaps an exception can be made with the environmental criteria since the latest research and work have managed to define some concrete scientific parameters and thus more adjusted indicators.

Ethical criteria vary largely following the different cultures, for example EIRIS conducted a survey among the UK public which revealed that 80 per cent of the people surveyed included the criteria of experimenting with animals as one of the most important ethical considerations. By contrast in a similar survey in the USA, animal experimenting is not considered very relevant.

Japan, for example, does not consider anti-social behavior in criteria such as nuclear power, weaponry, tobacco, alcohol or gambling, all of which are highly relevant in European SRI funds. In Japan the most relevant popular criteria are in areas oriented to environment and human rights.

There is also criticism of some of the SRI attitudes. For example some of the more strict SRI investors wish to exclude all corporations involved in activities in third countries renowned for human rights abuse. Tesco, for example, was excluded from the FTSE4good for its involvement in Indonesia. This type of behavior raises the question of the potential harm of the withdrawal of multinationals from certain third world countries that can intensify already terrible poverty.

We can also find a degree of diversity in Islamic funds. Most have clear standards regarding alcohol, gambling or pornography, but there are, however, some differences regarding issues such as weapons and/or the acceptable level of non-permissible debt in a particular company. They also increasingly foster positive criteria in the companies in which they invest.

For some players in the industry, Islamic investment is merely another diverse part of the SRI movement and thus these funds are sometimes included in the general SIRI funds universe. For example, the 2005 Social Investment Forum reports that some US Islamic funds were included in the general list (Social Investment Forum, 2006).

Investment with values, be they ethical, sustainable, responsible or Islamic, should be considered only as one response to the social demand for more ethical business behavior. It constitutes only a simple financial mode for individual investors who feel they want an active role in the business life of their societies, and to invest their savings with maximum profit but in accordance with their personal principles and values. The success of the movement will lie in its diversity, not in defining what an ethical investment is, in absolute terms, but in offering the tools to allow for an individual choice according to an individual ethic within a large diversity of criteria.

INVESTMENT WITH VALUES: CONVERGENCE OF CULTURAL DIVERSITY?

There are signs of convergence in the attitudes of Islamic and Western behavior at the beginning of the twenty-first century. There is a popular demand emerging in both cultures for a more ethical and human concern in the business behavior of their societies. A movement has taken shape in both cultures aiming to include business attitudes as part of their value systems.

Financial scandals such as Enron or World.com have created a global concern that demands a higher degree of responsibility from corporations in terms of societal needs. The demand for a higher business responsibility emerges within the value system of each culture, be it Western or Islamic. There is popular demand for the integration of business life into a value system based on the values of each culture; values that represent a religion or a specific ethic principle. But both ask for further development of the free individual in a harmonious and cohesive society.

In today's society the global economy dominates all aspects of social life. The financial markets have been the first to be globalized, representing a free movement of giant financial flows and economic interests, many of which are beyond the control of any government. Our society is probably moving away from one dominated by political ideologies, to one dominated by financial interests. It is therefore no coincidence that anti-globalization movements raise their voices mainly against international financial markets and the multinationals.

The current globalization process will inevitably give rise to the integration of Islamic and Western societies. This integration will be difficult and will require enormous efforts to achieve a larger frame where each culture can transcend its own tradition in order to form a higher human culture.

However, before reaching a higher level of integration each culture will have to find its own development path. Islamic culture will have to find ways to maintain common identity while allowing for the multiplicity of its people. The West on the other hand will have to find a higher social cohesion while maintaining its achieved individual freedoms. In the present climate of chaos and confusion, many radical movements take advantage to use people for their own political and dogmatic ends. It is in this globalized context of confusion and dogmatic views that Islamic and SRI investment represent an optimistic path towards a greater understanding. The majority of the Islamic and SRI investment followers do not intend to impose dogmatism or dominate, they only aim to have the personal freedom to choose, and to be able to live their financial lives according to their principles, and help foster more sustainable corporate behavior.

The similarities that can be found in the Islamic and SRI investment schemes are a positive illustration of how it is possible to harmonize individual religious and ethical principles against a highly diverse backdrop.

BIBLIOGRAPHY

Abdul, Latif A. and R. Janahi (2005), 'Potential use of Salam Financing in Malaysia', in I. Munawar and Kh. Tariqullah (eds), *Financial Engineering and Islamic Contracts*, NY: Palgrave Macmillan, pp. 123–44.

Abuamria, F.MJ. (2007), *El mecanismo de funcionamiento de los bancos islámicos y su tamaño en los mercados financieros. Un estudio comparativo internacional de su eficiencia,* Granada: Fundación Euro-Arabe.

Ahmad, K. (2005), 'Globalization: Islamic Perspectives, Challenges and Prospects', in Iqbal Munawar and Ah. Ausaf (eds), *Poverty in Muslim Countries and the New International Economic Order*, NY: Palgrave Macmillan, pp. 15–27.

al-Hallaq, S.(2005), 'The Role of Islamic Banks in Economic Growth: the Case of Jordan', in I. Munawar and Ah. Ausaf (eds), *Islamic Finance and Economic Development,* NY: Palgrave Macmillan, pp. 202–14.

al-Rifai, T. (1999), 'Islamic Equity Funds, a Brief Industry Analysis', Failaka intl. http://www.failaka.com.

Chouldhury, M.A. (1992), *Money in Islam. A study in Islamic political economy*, UK: Macmillan.

de Anca, C. (2003), *Economía islámica y economía ética. Convergencias en la diversidad cultural: Fondos islámicos de inversión y fondos de inversión éticos en el mercado de Londres*, Madrid: UAM ediciones.

EIRIS (2007), *The State of Responsible Business: Global corporate responses to environment, social and governance (ESG) challenges*, London: EIRIS, September, www.eiris.org.

Esposito, J. (2002), *What Everyone Needs to Know about Islam*, Oxford: Oxford University Press.

European SIRI Study (2006), www.eurosif.org.

Failaka Advisors (2007), '2006 Islamic Funds Report', Dubai.

Failaka Advisors (2008), '2007 Failaka Islamic Funds Report' (www.failaka. com.)

Financial Times (2007), 'Backwater sector moves into global mainstream. Islamic Finance', *Financial Times Special Report*, Wednesday, May 23, 1.

Gillian, T. (2006), 'Koran bans creation of money but Islamic transactions have much in common with West', *Financial Times*, 2 June, 6.

Gimigliano, G. and G. Rotondo (eds) (2006), *La Banca Islamica e la Disciplina Bancaria Europea*, Milan: Giuffrè.

Islamic Banker (2006a), 'Brown Sees Britain Gateway to Islamic Finance', *Islamic Banker*, May/June, London: Mushtak Parker Associates, 2–4.

Islamic Banker (2006b), 'Licensing and ETF challenge for FTS-SGX', *Islamic Banker*, 120–21, January/February, London: Mushtak Parker Associates, pp. 16–17.

Islamic Banker (2007), 'Financial Stability Test Boost for MIFC Banks', *Islamic Banker*, May/June, London: Mushtak Parker Associates, pp. 8–11.

Mariani, A.M., M. NorGhani and S. Fatin (2005), 'Efficiency of Islamic Banks in Malaysia', in I. Munawar and Ah. Ausaf (eds), *Islamic Finance and Economic Development*, NY: Palgrave Macmillan, pp. 94–104.

Munawar, I. and Kh. Tariqullah (eds) (2005), *Financial Engineering and Islamic Contracts*, NY: Palgrave Macmillan.

Saqib, R. (2007) 'Islamic Private Equity, *MENA* Region', Islamica, December, Dubai: Tradewind Business Media Co. Ltd., pp. 34–41.

SIRI Company (2005), 'Green and Ethical Funds in Europe', Milan: SIRI Company, October. http://www.siricompany.com/.

Social Investment Forum (2006), *2005 Report on Socially Responsible Investing Trends in the United States*, Washington: Social Investment Forum, http://www.socialinvest.org.

The Ethical Investor (2000), London, Sept/Oct, 1.

Usmani, T. and M. Justice (2000), *Writings on Islamic Modes of Finance*, www.failaka.com/research.php.

Wilson, R. (1997a), *Islamic Finance*, London: Financial Times Financial Publishing.

Wilson, R. (1997b), *Economics, Ethics and Religion. Jewish, Christian and Muslim Economic Thought*, UK: Macmillan.

Wilson, R. (2005), 'The Implications of Globalization for Islamic Finance', in I. Munawar and Ah. Ausaf (eds), *Poverty in Muslim Countries and the New International Economic Order*, NY: Palgrave Macmillan, pp. 27–44.

Internet Links

The Institute of Islamic Banking and Insurance http://www.islamic.banking.com/
The Islamic Chambers of Commerce http://www.islamic-comerce.org
Harvard Islamic Finance Information Page http://www.hifip.harvard.edu/
International Institute of Islamic Business & Finance (IIIBF) http://islamic-finance.net/
Islamic Development Bank http://www.isdb.org/
Siri Research http://www.avanzi-SIRI.org // http://www.siricompany.com
Social Investment Forum www.socialinvest.org/
KLD Research & Analytics, Inc http://www.kld.com
Ethical Investment Research Services EIRIS http://www.eiris.org
Failaka Advisors www.failaka.com

9. Islamic banking and the 'duty of accommodation'

Gabriella Gimigliano

The European Treaty does not lay down any provisions on the relationship between economic activities and religious freedom. On the contrary, it has been assumed that the First Amendment of the US Constitution contains a convincing argument for the duty of the accommodation of Islamic banking as domestic banks. However, the above conclusion is not confirmed when the matter is examined carefully.

THE US DEBATE

Although the authorization of an Islamic bank as a domestic bank (under either State or federal law) seems to be a long way off, since 2002 the Department of US Treasury has shown an increasing need to improve its understanding and awareness of Islamic financial products.

The US government considers Islamic finance as part of advancing economic growth in the emerging markets and, at the same time, is trying to prevent terrorists from damaging lawful and legitimate institutions, such as conventional banks, Islamic banks and money transfer services bodies.[1] Conventional and Islamic financing operations have a different structure but follow – according to John Taylor, Under Secretary of the US Treasury – the same economic principles, thereby both of them will benefit not only from transparency and rules of good governance, but also from an internationally-accepted regulatory framework (Taylor 2002, 2004).

The trend toward the chartering of an Islamic bank as a domestic bank can be based on three matters (of facts and of law), according to Thomas Baxter, General Council and Executive Vice-President of the Federal Reserve Bank of New York: (a) the growing Muslim population on US territory, able to influence the West in market economies; (b) an increasing awareness of socially responsible finance, after the Enron scandal; (c) the free exercise of religion clause – if it represents one of the core values in Western countries, law makers will need to ascertain whether some practices can be changed to accommodate Muslims who try to practise their religion freely.

Among the above-mentioned matters, the last may lead to more doubts. Indeed, Baxter has inferred from the First Amendment of the US Constitution, stating 'Congress shall make no law respecting an establishment of religion, or prohibiting the free exercise thereof', the so-called duty of accommodation: 'a corollary (. . .) is that the secular law should adapt, as much as possible, to accommodate differing religious practices' (Baxter, 2005b). Baxter recalls Justice Warren Burger's observations in order to reach the following conclusion: the First Amendment affirmatively 'mandates accommodation, not merely tolerance, of all religions, and forbids hostility towards any'. Thereby, the 'duty of accommodation' implies that the constitutional precept is able to drive legislators' initiatives and shape substantive choices in the financial context.

We do believe that when Justice Burger's observations are assessed in their own context, for example the *Lynch v. Donnelly* case, and are compared to the other constructions of the free exercise of religion clause, by the Supreme Court, the same principle will no longer be able to drive the enforcement of banking regulations. Therefore, the approach of looking beyond the labels and paying attention to economic effects represents the only clues either to authorizing an Islamic bank as a domestic bank or to making Islamic transactions permissible. But, this outgrowth has nothing in common with the 'duty of accommodation' and, as consequence, is able to draw a parallel between the attitude of European and US regulators to the matter in question. The former has always followed until now a strictly neutral approach every time it was called to rule on economic activities.

ISLAMIC BANKING AND THE FIRST AMENDMENT OF THE US CONSTITUTION

The First Amendment of the US Constitution guarantees the liberty of religion and it is made up of two clauses: the free exercise and the establishment clauses. Even though they play complementary roles, the first clause clearly safeguards individual freedom, while the latter deals with the government's actions, and its incorporation is therefore more controversial. So the major theories on the liberty of religion have been presented and discussed first in the context of the Establishment Clause.

The free exercise clause of the First Amendment may lead to the accommodation of Islamic beliefs and thereby the Islamic banking model. In fact, the Western banking model as laid down in domestic banking regulations requires conduct that the Muslim faith prohibits and, therefore, may be assessed as a burden to religious observance. However, in the Smith case, the Supreme Court held that a law will be compliant with the First Amendment until there is a 'valid and neutral law of general applicability on the ground that the law proscribes (or prescribes) conduct that his religion prescribes (or proscribes)'.[2] So the free exercise clause finds its limit in a neutral law of general applicability which is presumed to safeguard a 'compelling government interest of a higher order', unless the legal provision lacks rational scrutiny and the interest can be served in a less restrictive way (Chemerinsky 2005, p. 1477). The rules on deposit-holder guarantees, disclosure requirements and capital adequacy represent the most relevant regulatory obstacles to the Islamic banking model and no less restrictive a way has been found to pursue the same objective in public policy (Rutledge 2005).

A couple of observations on the Establishment Clause come to mind. The accommodation approach, which seems to be held by Baxter in order to justify a statutory action, is just one among others. There are three major theories to both clauses: the accommodation approach, the strict separation approach and the neutrality theory. All of them try to avoid making those holding a faith and those who do not subscribe to any religion feel unwelcomed, but a different criterion might shift the outer limit of government action backwards and onwards.

The accommodation approach provides that the Court should construe the Establishment Clause in such a way as to recognize the relevant function of religion and 'accommodate its presence in the government' (Chemerinsky 2005, p. 1490). The advocates of such a view hold that religion must be welcomed, protected and encouraged as must other beliefs and associations, in order to create a nation which is pluralistic rather than secular. However, as their opponents have sustained, the 'grey area' of this approach concerns the outer limits of the concept of 'coercion' and its strict definition. As this theory infers that the government complies with the constitutional clause until it expressly establishes a church or prescribes religious participation, the Establishment Clause might not be able to take into account the less obvious ways of advancing a religion or a particular belief.

According to the strict separation approach, religious and civil authorities belong to two different contexts and no contact is allowed between them. In fact, this theory states a permanent separation; therefore, it might become an obstacle to the liberty of religion, in itself preventing government from providing any form of assistance, including the fire, police and public health services.

Finally, the neutrality theory provides that government is not able to use religion as a criterion for action and inaction. This theory is based on the symbolic 'endorsement' test, which is considered as 'a way of assessing the likely perceptions of and reactions to government conduct' (Chemerinsky 2005, p.1489). Therefore, neither religion nor secularism may drive the government choices. The controversial issue deals with the standpoint from which the endorsement test should be applied. Who is the 'reasonable observer'? Some judges have identified such a figure as the well-educated and informed person, some others in a *quisque de populo*. However, the different standpoint may influence the extent to which control over the government has been exercised

Furthermore, Baxter has recalled the 'duty of accommodation' as stated in *Lynch v. Donnelly*, where the city's inclusion of a crib in a Christmas display was challenged. This display was set in a park owned by a non-profit making organization in the heart of the shopping centre and was composed of many figures and decorations traditionally associated with the Christmas event.[3] The Court reversed the District judgement and stated the city was constitutionally entitled to include the crib in the public Christmas display because the real objective of the First Amendment was 'to prevent any national ecclesiastical establishment, which should give to an hierarchy the exclusive patronage of the national government'.

However, the Court mentioned the accommodation approach and referred to a 'pluralistic' society but applied the symbolic endorsement test, which is typical of the neutrality theory. The inclusion of the crib in the public Christmas display was a decision compliant with the First Amendment because the display: (a) 'showed a significant historical religious event long celebrated in the Western World' for *essentially* secular purposes;[4] and (b) did not imply the endorsement of a religion because there is no sign of contact between religious and civil authorities and no expenditure of maintenance had been necessary during the past 40 years.[5] Furthermore, the accommodative approach seems to find an inner limit: in *Lynch v. Donnelly*, where the Court holds that only a law conferring 'an indirect, remote and incidental benefit upon a religion' is constitutionally valid,[6] therefore compliance with the First Amendment would be questionable for any statute laid down in order to remove the legislative burdens to authorizing an Islamic bank as a domestic bank, unless the legislative initiative is founded on a secular purpose and effects.

THE US WAY FORWARD: GOING BEYOND STATUTORY LABELS

The so-called accommodative approach to Islamic banking is based on a functional premise, but is far from being rooted in the First Amendment.

It simply represents a way of construing the statutory provisions taking into account the substance rather than the form of banking and financial operations.

The effect-based approach was followed by the Office of Comptroller of the Currency (OCC) in 1997 and in 1999, which issued two key interpretative letters dealing with some financial products designed to be *Shari'ah* compliant: *ijara* and *murabaha*.

The *ijara* product is a residential net lease home finance product, with which a customer–lessee will contact a seller to buy a single family residence and will offer a down payment for this purchase. However, before funding the remainder of the price, the lessee will make a net lease agreement and, at the same time, a purchase agreement with a bank. Hence, while the bank will supply the remainder of the purchase price to acquire the property from the seller on commitment of the customer, the customer–lessee will provide monthly lease-payments until the whole price, comprising principal, interest, insurance and property taxes, is paid off (Vogel and Hayes 1998, pp. 143–5).

Murabaha products are financing facilities: the bank will enter into a purchase agreement with the seller and into *murabaha* agreement with the customer. After acquiring ownership of the real estate, commercial inventory or commercial equipment (raw materials, commodities, finished goods, or commercial equipment to fit out Islamic mosques, community centres and schools) on behalf of the customer, who has to select and inspect the goods to buy, the bank will resell the property to him or her at the purchase price plus a mark-up on an instalment basis. The resale price includes the cost of shipping, handling, insurance; the mark-up is based on a recognized index (such as LIBOR, the London Interbank Offered Rate).[7]

As a federal branch of a foreign bank filed the request for an interpretative letter, the OCC replied to the following questions: (1) whether the activities engaged in by the branch under *ijara* and *murabaha* agreements were incidental activities within the meaning of 'business of banking' enshrined under 12 U.S.C. §24 (Seventh); (2) whether the above-mentioned agreements complied with section 29 of the National Bank Act, setting out several strict restrictions on a bank's ability to purchase, hold and conveyance real estate.

Section 12 U.S.C. lays down that a national bank shall have power to exercise 'all such incidental powers as shall be necessary to carry on the business of banking'. According to the Congress, 'incidental powers' may be performed 'discounting and negotiating promissory notes, drafts, bills of exchange, and other evidences of debt; by receiving deposits; by buying and selling exchange, coin, and bullion; by loaning money on personal security; and by obtaining, issuing, and circulating notes according to the provisions of title 62 of the Revised Statutes' (Macey, Miller and Carnell 2001, p. 123).[8]

The OCC holds that *murabaha* financing facilities amount to conventional financing transactions because the bank has no liability to the customer for any failure on the part of the seller and requires the customer: (a) to pay a downpayment not less than 25 percent of the purchase price (to be paid by the customer for the goods before the bank will agree to purchase the goods); (b) to ensure the goods or the equipment; (c) to indemnify the bank from all actions, claims or costs relating to goods to be purchased.

The balance due under the *murabaha* agreement will be secured by a first mortgage in favour of the bank, therefore if the customer defaults on the payment schedule, the bank will be able to sell the real estate and try to recover the difference between the amount of the downpayment plus the amount realized on the sale and the amount the customer agreed to pay under a breach of contract action.

In the same way, when the bank enters into a net-lease–purchase agreement, it will act neither as a real estate broker nor an agent: in fact, the customer will be required to find the property he or she wishes to buy and to negotiate the terms of the purchase contract with the seller. Moreover, the net-lease–purchase will compel the customer–lessee to maintain the property, paying charges, costs and expenses which an ordinary purchaser would pay for, and will allow the bank–lessor to make neither representation nor warranties regarding the property or its suitability.

If a customer defaults, both legal models set out that the bank will provide notice of sale, giving the customer the opportunity to cure the default within a defined time; instead, the bank will either sell the property or hold it as OREO (other real estate owned), selling the property in compliance with section 12 USC § 29.

The OCC considered the activities performed by the branch as banking business and ruled out that *ijara* and *murabaha* agreements were in breach of section 29, holding the transactions were 'functionally equivalent to' or a 'logical outgrowth of' secured loans,[9] because in conventional real estate loans and in *murabaha* transactions and in net-lease–purchase agreements the bank shall bear the same degree of risk: should the client not meet his or her own obligations, the bank will be forced to foreclose on the property.[10]

Furthermore, the OCC replied affirmatively to the second question posed by the foreign branch – the compliance of both types of transactions with Section 29 of the National Bank Act. Section 29 NBA provides strict restrictions on bank ownership; such restrictions attempt to '(1) keep the capital of banks flowing into the daily channels of commerce; (2) deter banks from embarking on hazardous real estate speculations; and (3) prevent banks from accumulating and holding large masses of real estate in perpetuity'. As before, the OCC holds that the bank, even though it has legal entitlement to real estate both under *ijara* and *murabaha* agreements,[11] does not take possession of the property in any time during the transactions. Indeed, the bank does not operate the property, pay taxes, insurance or other charges. Therefore, the OCC draws the conclusion that the rationale of section 29 has not been infringed.

But the 'functional interchangeability' approach has been applied to draw the outer limits of the business of banking apart from the *Shari'ah* compliant products: the Courts have kept 'leasing' within the meaning of the lending activities and, more generally, of the 'incidental' banking activities, paying attention to the types of risk ordinarily present in both of them.[12]

THE EU FRAMEWORK AND EXPERIENCE

The US and EU regulators are both driven by a secular functional-oriented approach to the authorization of Islamic banking, so that the 'functional interchangeability' approach can build bridges between the US and the European legal frameworks. The latter has provided a functional construction both of the notion of 'undertaking' and the definition of the 'banking business'. This conclusion may be inferred both from the European jurisdictions and the up-to-date developments of the concept of 'credit institutions' under the European Banking Code (Directive 2006/48 EC, OJEC 2006 L 177, 1).

As a general rule, the European Courts have provided the so-called *effet utile* doctrine which sounds as: 'a corollary to the teleological method of interpretation adopted by the ECJ judges in order to apprehend the meaning of Community law in light of its purpose. Accordingly, once the purpose or end of a legal provision is clearly identified, the detailed terms shall be interpreted in order to produce the desired effect' (Charpentier 1998).[13]

With regard to the definition of 'business' or 'undertaking' contained in the competition provisions, the Courts have performed a functional construction focusing more on the subject matter the entity in question is concerned with than on its legal status; for this reason the concept of undertaking/business does not correspond to the legal personality one as provided under company law. Indeed, the competition rules have been enforced according to a substantially-based approach and, therefore, in the Commission's and in the Courts' proceedings the concept of 'undertaking' encompassed every entity engaged in an economic activity, assuming that an activity is considered as economic 'if it faces actual or potential competition by private companies' (Gyselen 2000).

Furthermore, the functional approach was enforced in the financial intermediaries' prudential regime when the Directive 28/2000 EC (Official Journal of the European Communities of the 27 October 2000, L 275/37) was enacted amending the notion of credit institution, as provided under the European Banking Code. As a consequence, both traditional banks and electronic money institutions are regulated as credit institutions under the prudential supervision directive.

The rationale behind this is to preserve the stability of financial markets submitting activities posing risks of the same nature to the same prudential supervision regulation and monetary control. Indeed, in the *Report on Electronic Money* (1998), the European Central Bank pointed out that 'since electronic value loaded on prepaid cards and stored in computers is similar in economic terms to bank deposits, there is no reason why the same concerns should not arise to a certain extent with regard to electronic money if it comes to be used in large quantities'.[14]

CONCLUDING REMARKS

In conclusion, the US Constitution and the First Amendment are far from providing any arguments in favour of a duty of accommodation of Islamic banking, while on the other hand, the US jurisdictional experience seems to prefer a secular approach to economic activities. Within the European legal framework, where there is no legal prescription on the matter, the freedom of service drives us to assume that the nature of the economic activity in itself does not represent an argument against the banking authorization but neither does it play in favour of the authorization.

Whether and when an Islamic bank is authorized as a domestic bank is a question hardly answerable. However, it is foreseeable that the enforcement of the same functional-based approach, namely the assessment of the aims and the risks of the activities performed, might driven the US and EU regulators to the same conclusion in the near or remote future.

NOTES

1. Even before 2002, the *New York Times* had published more than one article on Islamic banking, stressing the strong interest in Islamic financing products by conventional banks and American Muslims. It depends either on the profitability of having access to a minority and niche markets (Brown 1994) or on the higher degree of conservatism among American Muslims.

2. Employment Division, Department of Human Resources of *Oregon v. Smith* (497 U.S. 872 1990). 'The Court today interprets the Clause to permit the government to prohibit without justification conduct mandated by an individual's religious belief, so long as that prohibition is generally applicable'.
    The only exception is made when it involves not only the liberty of religion but also other constitutional protections, such as freedom of speech and the freedom of press.
3. The display contained, among the other things, a Santa Claus house, reindeer pulling Santa Claus' sleigh, candy-striped poles, a teddy bear, hundreds of coloured lights, and a large banner reading 'Season greetings'.
4. 'Were the test that the government must have "exclusively secular" objectives, much of the conduct and legislation this Court has approved in the past would have been invalidated' (*Lynch, Mayor of Pawtucket v. Donnelly*, p. 8).
5. 'This case does not involve a direct subsidy to church-sponsored schools or colleges, or other religious institutions, and hence no inquiry into potential political divisiveness is even called' (*Lynch, Mayor of Pawtucket v. Donnelly*, p. 9)
6. *Lynch, Mayor of Pawtucket v. Donnelly*, pp. 8–9. See also, *Thorton v. Caldor* (472 U.S. 703 1985): the Supreme Court held that 'the statute goes beyond an incidental or remote effect of advancing religion. The statute has a primary effect that impermissibly advances a particular religious practice'.
7. There is no standard form of *murabaha* agreement and the detailed form and content will be agreed by the bank and its customer.
8. 'As a matter of logic, the clause would seem to establish two zones of permissible activities for national banks: first, the "business of banking" strictly construed; and second, other activities that, while not part of the "business of banking", are nevertheless necessary to carry on the business of banking. This second category is evidently broader than the first one; how much broader is a matter of debate'.
9. The construction of a loan as the 'bank's direct or indirect advance of funds to or on behalf of a borrower based on an obligation of the borrower to repay the funds or repayable from a specific property pledged by or on behalf of the borrower' (Interpretative Letter #867, p. 6).
10. Interpretative Letter #806, December 1997; Interpretative Letter #867, November 1999.
11. 'Legal title' refers to 'one which is complete and perfect so far as regards the apparent right of ownership and possession, but which carries no beneficial interest in the property, another person being equitable entitled thereto' (*Black's Law Dictionary* 1990, p. 897).
12. 'A lease ceases to be a secured loan when the lessor assumes material burdens other than those of a lender of money and is subject to significant risks not ordinarily incident to a secured loan', see *M & M Leasing Corp. v. Seattle First National Bank*, 563 F.2d 1377 (9th Circ. 1977).
13. Moreover, in Adidas case law the Court stated that 'where a provision of Community law is open to several interpretations, only one of which can ensure that the provision retains its effectiveness, preference must be given to that interpretation'. Judgement of the Court 14 October 1999, C-223/98, § 24.
14. The Directive 2000/46 EC has stated that an 'electronic money' is a 'monetary value as represented by a claim on the issuer which is (i) stored on an electronic device; (ii) issued on receipt of funds of amounts not less than the monetary value issued; (iii) accepted as means of payment by undertakings other than the issuer'.

BIBLIOGRAPHY

Baxter, Thomas Jr. (2005a), *Welcome speech to the seminar on legal issues in the Islamic financial services industries*, March 1.

Baxter, Thomas Jr. (2005b), *Regulation of Islamic financial services in the United States*, March 2.

Black's Law Dictionary (1990), Andover: Thomson Reuters.

Boss, S. (2001), 'Loans, interest rates and a religious principle', *New York Times*, July 5.

Brown, K. (1994), 'Islamic banking: faith and creativity', *New York Times*, April 8.

Charpentier, L. (1998), *The European Court of Justice and the rhetoric of affirmative action*, European University Institute, Working Paper RSC, 98/30.

Chemerinsky, E. (2005), *Constitutional Law*, Second edition, New York: Aspen Publishers.

Chinoy, S. (1995), 'Interest-free banking: the legal aspects of Islamic financial transactions', *Journal of International Banking Law*, **10** (12), 517–24.

European Central Bank (1998), *Report on Electronic Money*, Frankfurt.

Gyselen, L. (2000), 'Case law', *Common Market Law Review*, **37** (2), 425–48.

Louri, V. (2002), '"Undertaking" as a jurisdictional element for the application of EC competition rules', *Legal Issues of Economic Integration*, **29** (2), 143–76.

Macey, Jonathan R., Miller, Geoffrey P. and Carnell, Richard S. (2001), *Banking Law and Regulation*, New York: Aspen Publishers.

McCoy, P. (2000), *Banking Law Manual*, New York: Lexis Publisher.

Rutledge, J. (2005), *Remarks at the 2005 Arab Bankers Association of North America (ABANA) Conference on Islamic Finance: players, product and innovations in New York City*, www.arabbankers.org/shared/custompage.jsp.

Taylor, John B. (2002), *Introductory remarks*, United States Treasury at the Islamic Finance 101 Seminar held at the US Treasury Department, Washington DC, www.stanford.edu.

Taylor, John B. (2004), *Understanding and supporting Islamic finance: product differentiation and international standards*, Forum on Islamic Finance Harvard University, www.treas.gov/press/releases/js1543.htm.

Tesauro, P. (2005), *Diritto comunitario*, Padova: Cedam.

Vogel, Frank E. and Hayes, S. (1998), *Islamic Law and Finance*, Boston: Kluwer.

Wilson, R. (1995), 'Islamic banking and its impact on the international financial scene', *Journal of International Banking Law*, **10** (10), 437–45.

Wilson R. (1997), 'The issue of interest and the Islamic financing alternatives', *Journal of International Banking Law*, **13** (1), 23–9.

10. The remuneration of sight accounts and the feasible competition between Islamic and Western systems

Gennaro Rotondo

This chapter will attempt to outline the methods of interaction and integration between the Islamic and the European banking models from the standpoint of banking rates on sight accounts by looking into two issues: (1) the rationale of the EC Court of Justice's judgment, of October 5 2004, C-244/04 (Rotondo 2006), about French law on sight account remuneration; and (2) a common practice in European systems not to remunerate it, as in the Italian experience.

Also, the structure of current accounts in the Islamic framework is not so far from the current account model in Western banking regulations, but the former bears neither charges nor interest. Current accounts (*al-hisab al-jari*) and saving accounts are (*hisab al-tawfir*) sight accounts. In Islamic current accounts, customers can withdraw money and write cheques within the limits either of the balance or of the funds granted, but customers may not have access to international credit card networks.

THE REMUNERATION OF SIGHT ACCOUNTS: A 'LIKELY' COEXISTENCE OF ISLAMIC AND WESTERN FINANCE MODELS

Remuneration of sight accounts still conserves value in monetary and competition policy. Apart from the monetary function which the European Central Bank takes over, the interest rate represents an attractive factor for choosing a particular current account provider, even if most of the time clients pay banks' interest rates back as account administration fees.

Nevertheless, consumers continue to keep their savings in bank accounts, thanks especially to the wide range of banking services. This may confirm the asymmetric relationship between interest rates and the propensity to deposit, but also underlines far from rational elements (in economics terms) that are able to influence savers' choices. Therefore, consumer choice-making may easily be conditioned also by the ethical purposes pursued through Islamic banking activities (Piccinelli 2006; Ragusa Maggiore 1994, p. 847).[1]

Therefore, the interest rate shows no more relevant influence on savers' choices than in the past and this situation may allow Islamic financial intermediaries to perform some competitive activities in the European financial markets.

But in contrast, the fact that such financial frameworks prevent the national financial intermediaries, the harmonized financial intermediaries and the European subsidiaries from paying out borrowing (interest) rates on sight accounts – as in the case of the French banking regulations, reported hereafter – will create a more suitable market for Islamic financial intermediaries. Hence, regulations like the French one will, in the end, improve competition. This seems, somehow, to contradict the rationale of European Court of Justice's judgment, which reinforces the strict enforcement of the freedom establishment clause.

THE PROHIBITION OF INTEREST-BEARING SIGHT ACCOUNTS IN THE FRENCH LEGAL SYSTEM

The first issue concerns the existence, also in a European legal system (the French one), of a provision which forbids banks to pay out borrowing rates on sight accounts.

In France, a general decision of the Credit National Council of May 8 1969 prohibited paying out borrowing (interest) rates on sight accounts. This decision was taken pursuant to art. 1756-bis of the Tax Code, embodying the prohibition of interest-bearing deposits, when the funds deposited were less than a fixed amount as established by either the Banking Regulation Committee or the Minister of Economics and Finance. The Monetary and Financial Code, under art. L. 312–13, provided that 'Notwithstanding any provisions to the contrary, it shall be prohibited for any credit establishment which receives funds from the public for sight accounts or accounts for less than five years, by any means whatever, to pay remuneration on those funds exceeding that fixed by [regulation of the Committee for Banking and Financial Regulation] or the minister responsible for the economy'. The Committee, enforcing the 1969 decision and art. L. 312–13 of the Monetary and Financial Code, forbade the remuneration on sight accounts (art. 2 , rule n. 86–13, May 14, 1986).[2] The prohibition was applied to 'sight' accounts held in euros and opened by persons resident in France, whatever their nationality. Furthermore, the Banking Regulation Committee also applied the same rule to the deposit-taking activities carried out in France by European Credit Institutions.

Finally, art. 46 of Law n. 2003–706 (published in the O.J. of August 2 2003) deleted the words in brackets from art. L. 312–13 but, at the same time, subsequent art. 47 confirmed the permanent validity of the Committee's regulations quoted above. Hence, no substantial change was brought to the relevant legal framework (General Advocate Conclusions, case C-442/02, Caixa-Bank France, paragraph 6).

According to the Court of Justice Judgement, the national legislation prohibiting European credit institutions from marketing contracts on interest-bearing accounts was in breach of art. 43 of the EC Treaty if it hindered the subsidiaries of foreign companies from competing on deposit-taking activity with the national banks and their extensive branch network. The domestic judge had to verify whether there were different forms of banking account comparable with sight accounts, not covered by the prohibition and which would help foreign subsidiaries in competing with French credit institutions. Therefore, the Court stated that 'art. 43 EC precludes legislation of a Member State which prohibits a credit institution which is a subsidiary of a company from another Member State from remunerating sight accounts in euros opened by residents of the former Member State' (Judgement of European Court of Justice, October 5 2004, paragraph 25).

BORROWING INTEREST RATES ON SIGHT ACCOUNTS IN THE ITALIAN BANKING SYSTEM

The second issue that confirms the possibility of competition between Islamic and western financial systems, is the wide praxis not to remunerate sight accounts, such as as in the Italian system.

The Italian legal framework has never prohibited interest-bearing sight accounts, but during the 1960s and 1970s a debate on the matter arose. This debate stresses the distance between the Italian banking system and the origins shared with the Islamic banking model. In fact, the explanation of this trend could be found in the Banking Law enacted in 1396 (hereinafter, Banking Law), according to which 'banking business' was a 'funzione di interesse pubblico' (art. 1, Banking Law): the legal framework set out the 'banking business' as an activity run in the public interest and such a choice was coherent with the active intervention of the State in the economic structure (Rispoli 1981, p. 83; Vitale 1987, p. 63; Costi 2007, p. 23). This theory is well stated in art. 32 of the Banking Law, under which the control of interest rates in lending operations was set out as a specific tool to influence the level of liquid assets in the whole economic system (Porzio 1976).

If borrowing interest rates were no longer paid out on sight accounts, the account holders would think more seriously about storing such substantial funds in sight accounts and would invest their savings in some other more profitable banking products, for example, trust deposits (Mottura 1966, p. 155; Manes 1975, p. 1031).[3]

Under the Banking Law, the distinction between the deposits performing only the monetary function and those for investment became more evident because their extremely different returns prevented funds with a different economic nature from blending. In this way, it would have a positive effect in two directions, both to improve the lending and monetary function of the banking system and to increase the level of liquid assets (Fontana 1975, p. 1228; Vitale 1987, p. 39). According to the same theory, it should not be assumed that bank account holders would suffer a loss on the deposited funds: the prejudice was set by means of more favourable contractual conditions and the free use of current accounts (Fontana 1975, p. 1227). Therefore, under the Banking Law, the idea of remuneration on sight accounts took shape as one of the means of economic and monetary policy (Fontana 1975, p. 1225; Manes 1975, p. 1030; Vitale 1987, p. 25).

Thereafter, it became clear that consumers' propensity for saving was rarely influenced by the interest rates for borrowing. Instead, consumers' choice (low–medium income savers) was directed towards deposits as they were risk-averse customers, deeply influenced by their traditional culture and possessing a low level of knowledge of economics. For all these reasons, consumers' choices were rarely made according to criteria of a rationale based on a knowledge of economics (Mottura 1966, p. 31).

In addition to this, customers used to choose sight deposits because of their fiduciary relationship with the bank and the simple structure of the contract (Mottura 1966, p. 32): all circumstances which allowed borrowing (interest) rates to become less relevant than they should have been. Psychological components prevailed over the profit-making aspect.

CONCLUSIONS: THE WAY AHEAD

Islamic banks will be able to act competitively and efficiently within the European framework if they solve the essential problem of liquid assets. It is known that one of the most important problems for Islamic banks is the lack of liquid assets, especially short-term assets. It depends on the prohibition of access to the inter-banking market. But in some States, the problem has been solved by providing new types of bonds and forms of short-term investment fund complying with Islamic precepts (Piccinelli 2006). But the French regulations on sight accounts are far from being a help in solving such an issue, and access to liquid assets has been addressed by the EU Court of Justice to confirm the general anticompetitive attitude of French proscriptions.

In this way, Islamic banks and European financial intermediaries may coexist in the European framework only if the market is more efficient, and European lawmakers should cease to enforce their regulations for protecting their national banking market.[4]

It is less likely that Islamic and European experiences can join to become a single banking model (Piccinelli 2006; Ragusa Maggiore 1994). On the other hand, if regulations keep their identities safe, also setting up different supervisory authorities,[5] they will be able to work as distinct but well-matched models, improving competition on a 'globalized' financial market.

NOTES

1. Ragusa Maggiore (1994, p. 847) has shown that the ethical foundations of Islamic banks may be efficient in a Western context too: under the Islamic framework, *Qur'an* proscriptions and businessmen acting with a clear conscience are enough to administer the market. Profit is not forbidden but it must come about through ethical control.
2. The rule was confirmed with the decree from the French Minister for Economics and Finance.
3. From the standpoint of enterprises, if the interest rates on sight accounts were not paid, banks would have some economic advantages: expenses on borrowing interest rates would be vastly reduced. In addition to this, funds stored for longer periods in sight accounts would be addressed somewhere else, increasing the speed of current account banking and making the monetary system function stronger.
4. See, Caixa-Bank France case law, mentioned above. But, it can be found in more than one example of Italian antitrust case law (mergers on the banking market).
5. Since Islamic banks collect funds from the public and provide the typical banking services, it is normal that Islamic banks will be under the supervision of a monetary authority. The activity of supervision should pay attention to the liquid asset profile, although some authors have held that short-term investment tools can be developed in compliance with *Shari'ah* principles and the problem of liquid assets solved.

REFERENCES

Costi, R. (2007), *L'ordinamento bancario*, Bologna: Il Mulino.

Fontana, F. (1975), 'Alcune osservazioni sull'opportunità di remunerare i depositi a vista', *Bancaria*, 1225–32.

Manes, P. (1975), 'Considerazioni sull'opportunità o meno di remunerare i depositi a vista', *Bancaria*, 1029–33.

Mottura, P. (1966), *I saggi di interesse dei depositi bancari*, Milan: Giuffrè.

Piccinelli Gian, M. (2006), 'Operazioni di provvista e di gestione del risparmio: il modello del cliente-socio', in G. Gimigliano and G. Rotondo (eds), *La banca islamica e la disciplina bancaria europea*, Milan: Giuffrè.

Porzio, M. (1976), *Il Governo del credito*, Naples: Jovene.

Ragusa Maggiore, G. (1994), 'La danza degli interessi', *Diritto fallimentare*, I, 845–8.

Rispoli, M. (1981), 'Il controllo sull'attività creditizia. Dalla tutela del risparmio al dirigismo economico', in M. Porzio (ed.), *La legge bancaria. Note e documenti sulla 'storia segreta'*, Bologna: Il Mulino.

Rotondo, G. (2006), 'Divieto di remunerazione dei fondi a vista e libertà di stabilimento nel settore bancario', *Diritto della banca e del mercato finanziario*, II, 683–704.

Vitale, P. (1987), *Pubblico e privato nell'ordinamento bancario*, Milan: Giuffrè.

PART IV

Response from the European countries:
English, French, German and Italian
experiences

11. The French licensing authority faced with the globalisation of Islamic finance: a flexible position

Christophe Arnaud[1]

Under Islamic principles, *Shari'ah* law (prescribed in the *Qur'an*) defines the framework within which Muslims should conduct their lives. The over-arching principle of Islamic finance and banking products is that all forms of interest are forbidden. The Islamic financial model works on the basis of risk sharing. The customer and the bank share the risk of any invest-ment on agreed terms, and divide any profits or losses between them. In addition, investments should only support practices that are not forbid-den.[2] Moreover, an Islamic credit institution[3] is not permitted to lend to other banks at interest.

Islamic banking assets have been growing at a rate of just under 20 per cent a year since 2000 and are currently worth about US$5000bn globally.

The United Kingdom, where the Muslim population is three times less than in France, is home to five licensed Islamic banks, the only licensed ones in the European Union, and lists £5.5bn in *sukuk*, or Islamic bonds, on its stock exchange. Since 2003 the United Kingdom has been reform-ing laws to ensure that *Shari'ah*-compliant investments are not prone to higher levies than their conventional equivalents.

Up to 2008 in France, and although some financial institutions seem to be willing now to enter into a licensing process for this purpose, the devel-opment of Islamic finance has concerned mainly investment banking and not retail banking, but this situation could evolve: even though France has a Muslim population of about 6m, only a handful of French banks, such as BNP Paribas and Société Générale currently offer wholesale Islamic services. These types of structures are called 'Islamic windows'. These windows have contributed significantly to the development of Islamic finance, although the French Islamic windows do not provide retail prod-ucts at all. However, France is taking a significant step towards estab-lishing Paris as a western centre for Islamic finance. Generally speaking,

France's goals are to attract global funds, and, particularly, to make France more competitive in the area of Islamic finance since France, being an international finance centre, has to handle the phenomenon of forum shopping within Europe and the rest of the world.

In this chapter, we will focus[4] on: (a) the French Committee of Credit Institutions and Investment Firms' (CECEI) position; (b) the specific issues related to Islamic finance that the licensing authority has to cope with.

THE FRENCH LICENSING REGULATORY FRAMEWORK AND THE DEVELOPMENT OF ISLAMIC FINANCE IN FRANCE

CECEI is the foreign banks' gateway to the French territory. It is the competent authority for delivering authorisation to new banks, whatever the origin of the funds and also for authorising shareholder changes and mergers of existing banks, and for broadening the scope of banks' activities when the initial authorisation has circumscribed the field of activities.

The CECEI and Parisian Financial Markets' Positions

CECEI pays close attention to the developments in the banking sector, both in terms of its structures and of its activities, and to the smooth operation of the Paris financial market. It is fully aware of the importance of foreign capital and of the need for domestic players to diversify their sources of financing and expand their activities abroad. They are also aware of the importance of innovation, both for investment banking and retail banking. In this area, they also make sure that banking services are able to satisfy the needs of all of the population.

At this stage, two main observations can be pointed out.

First, French banking authorities are in favour of opening the Paris banking and financial centre to foreign investments. The French banking sector is very open to foreign investments: at end-2007, the number of commercial banks under foreign control was greater than that under French control. However, this predominance of foreign-owned banks does not hold true in terms of market shares, because foreign-owned banks have not sought to develop retail and network banking activities, but have instead adopted a niche strategy, focusing on specific categories of clients and special financing and market activities. Moreover, a large number of banks from the Middle East, the Gulf and Islamic countries are already established in France; some of them have been in France for the past 30 years[5]. For instance, at end-2007, six Lebanese banks, four Iranian banks, two Pakistani banks, two Qatari banks, one Egyptian bank, one bank from Abu Dhabi, one Kuwaiti bank and one Jordanian bank were established in France. So far, none of these institutions has formally asked the French authorities to examine the possibility of offering Islamic products in France. Furthermore, CECEI has not received, in the framework of Europe-wide mutual recognition procedures, any notifications of requests made relative to the right of establishment and the freedom to provide services from other European banking authorities in favour of so-called Islamic banks that they would have authorised. The underlying questions one may have concern the size of the actual demand for such products in France. There seems to be a discrepancy between the volume – clearly substantial at the international level – of funds, in particular from Gulf countries, that may be invested in so-called Islamic projects on the one hand, and the emergence of concrete projects in the banking sector, in particular in retail banking. We have already been informed of a number of establishment projects, which clearly shows that the issue is topical. But none of these projects have, so far, fully developed and therefore no cases have yet been submitted.

Second, CECEI, in particular, does not discriminate between the different projects that it examines on the basis of the national origin of the funds. It makes its judgements within the remit of its missions as defined by the Monetary and Financial Code, only on the basis of identified criteria which pertain to the quality of shareholders and managers, the existence of an environment conducive to the smooth exercise of its oversight role, financial soundness, the bank's capacity to comply with prudential ratios, the strength of its governance and internal control and anti-money-laundering systems.

CECEI's Approach to Authorisation

First of all, it should be emphasised that CECEI cannot deliver 'Islamic banking' authorisations or licenses under the non-discriminatory principle. The authorisation by the CECEI of credit institutions claiming to be Islamic should be subject to the same principles, rules and standards that apply to any institution seeking to establish itself in France. As we will see, the Islamic side does not affect most of the criteria used, which would involve examining:

1. The individual quality of the fund providers.
2. The integrity, competence and experience of the bank managers.
3. The acceptability of the ownership structure. There is no obstacle, in principle, to third-country shareholders of banks in the European

Economic Area as long as they are not in financial difficulty and are subject to a banking authority that can ensure effective supervision on a consolidated basis and with whom they are in close co-operation. It is more complicated when the shareholder is not a bank (for example financial holding companies, business services or industrial companies); however, this problem is not confined to Gulf State companies.

4. The company's ability to carry out its development objectives under conditions compatible with customer security and the smooth functioning of the banking sector: CECEI is very vigilant in this respect as regards internal control requirements and the organisation envisaged complying with Regulation 97-02 in this field. Risk management must be ensured by the control system employed and, within this framework, particular attention must be paid to countering money laundering and the financing of terrorism. The only specific concerns raised on this subject by Islamic finance are the systematic replacement of single banking 'occidental' operations by structured products to fit with *Shari'ah* principles and, in due consequence, a change in the number of operations to follow. But, the supervision of each operation is not by itself an issue;

5. Internal control notably covers compliance: the financial institution's bodies must therefore ensure that the products offered to customers respect all of the provisions concerning banking and financial products in French law. In this respect, it is worth mentioning the relationship between the role of the *Shari'ah* committee or *Shari'ah* scholar board that a bank may set up and the bank's governing body and internal control. Indeed, the existence of a *Shari'ah* committee, responsible for ensuring that all of the financial products offered to customers comply with Islamic finance principles, is entirely up to the institution's internal decision-making, in the same way as certain management companies offering socially responsible investment products ensure that the investments they carry out comply with standards relative to socially responsible investment. However, the role of the *Shari'ah* committee must be limited to that of vetting and certifying products and should not extend beyond this to interfere with the bank's governance and internal operating modes. In this respect, UK experience shows that the FSA has imposed a principle of strict separation between the role of the *Shari'ah* committee and bank governance;

6. The bank's capacity to respect prudential rules in a consistent manner: CECEI will work in close co-operation with the Commission bancaire, the French banking supervision body, to ensure that the legal/financial engineering of Islamic financial products is correctly interpreted in the accounting system and measured in terms of risk and that the

required minimum capital to cover these products is sufficient. In this respect, the prudential weighting of certain loans, notably housing loans, will probably have to be specified.

To summarise, analysis is likely to privilege the economic and financial reality over the legal form of transactions. The operation will be analysed and supervised not by assumption of their legal components, but, as far as possible, by examining their final economic effects.

SPECIFIC ISSUES RELATED TO ISLAMIC FINANCE

Although there are many risks which are common to Islamic and conventional credit institutions, several risks are specific to Islamic credit institutions and/or products.

Shari'ah Forum Shopping

There is a diversity of opinion as to whether particular practices or products are *Shari'ah* compliant. This means that some products and services may be approved as being *Shari'ah* compliant by some *Shari'ah* scholars but not by others. Moreover, the approval of Islamic credit institutions' products and services will depend on the competent jurisdiction which can become a source a complication for regulators. Indeed, even if a regulator pays attention only to their national law, the Islamic product has to comply with the *Shari'ah* and, hence, indirectly, the regulator has to pay attention to it since it will apply its proper national rules (but according to the classification given by the *Shari'ah* committee). Fortunately, common *Shari'ah* standards are being developed by organisations such as the Islamic Financial Services Board (IFSB) and the Accounting and Auditing Organization for Islamic Financial Institutions (AAOIFI).

Issues Concerning *Shari'ah* Scholars

It is common for individual scholars to hold positions on the *Shari'ah* scholar boards of a number of Islamic credit institutions. This raises concerns over the ability of *Shari'ah* scholar boards to provide enough rigorous challenge and oversight of firms' products and services. Another issue is where the *Shari'ah* scholar board of a firm is responsible for the yearly *Shari'ah* audit as well as approving products for *Shari'ah* compliance. In conventional credit institutions, the banking authorities would want to see these issues carefully managed. Indeed, a banking authority such as CECEI will use the common criteria governing all credit institutions but from information given by the *Shari'ah* scholar board on Islamic products or services. Moreover, there is a global shortage of experienced professionals within the Islamic sector. More education and training should be provided in France such as university degrees and professional training courses.

Specific Issues on Retail Islamic Products

Retail banking seems to open more issues than investment banking, in which Islamic products are just a case of structured products among others. Henceforth, preliminary work has to be done during the licensing process by asking the institutions and their counsels to explain how they will undertake the transposition of their products into French law through contractual agreements.

1. Considering there are no accounting rules in France concerning loans extended by customers to their banks, the '*qard*' could raise difficulties. As a result, the *qard* must be considered as redeemable funds from the public, like a deposit, and should therefore be eligible for the deposit guarantee fund. The bank is obliged to repay the customer the total amount of the *qard* on demand.
2. Another example is the *mudaraba* where the customer provides funds that are invested by the bank in projects permissible by Islamic law, whereby any profits accrued or losses incurred are shared between the parties on a pre-agreed basis. In this case, *mudarabas* cannot be considered as deposits, or even as redeemable funds, since they are advances from the customer to the bank for investment purposes, inasmuch as the latter could be considered as similar to investment funds that do not benefit from protection from the deposit guarantee fund.
3. Housing loans are structured as leasing agreements through the '*ijara*' process, but all the customers' protections included in the Consumer Code have to apply to these contractual arrangements.

These questions could easily be solved but have to be addressed when studying the licensing file and connected to the accounting issues to be dealt with by the Banking Commission.

CONCLUDING REMARKS

In conclusion, three ideas shall be stressed about the development of Islamic finance in France:

(a) Islamic finance should not need any exceptional consideration under French law; the only point is that the structure of the proposed products needs to be examined thoroughly on a case-by-case basis to avoid any misunderstanding about the way in which they proceed;

(b) the main goal of the authorities is to ensure that institutions and customers using Islamic financing schemes are protected by the same level of strength and legal soundness as those using conventional schemes;

(c) the specific issues that arise could be dealt with in the existing framework even if, as for any other licensed credit institution, specific conditions are required which need to be noted in the licence.

NOTES

1. The opinions or analysis presented in this chapter are the sole responsibility of their author, and not Banque de France or Comité des établissements de crédit et des entreprises d'investissement (CECEI). They should not be considered as prejudging any decision to be taken by the CECEI. Concerning the general policy of CECEI, the readers can consult CECEI's website (www.cecei.org, in English at: http://www.banque-france.fr/gb/supervi/agrement/agrement.htm), and especially its annual report.
2. Trades in alcohol, betting and pornography are not allowed.
3. The term 'Islamic credit institution' will be used equally in the following discussion to refer to credit institution on the one hand and investment firm on the other hand.
4. Fiscal issues are not addressed in this chapter. They are the same in France as in the UK, and the fiscal department of the ministry of finance is thinking about the most efficient way to solve them.
5. A branch of the Qatar National Bank has been authorised in France since 1977.

12. German banking supervision and its relationship to Islamic banks

Johannes Engels

TASKS OF GERMAN BANKING SUPERVISION

Following the adoption of the Law on Integrated Financial Services Supervision (Gesetz über die integrierte Finanzaufsicht – FinDAG), the Federal Financial Supervisory Authority (Bundesanstalt für Finanzdienstleistungsaufsicht – BaFin) was established on 1 May 2002. The functions of the former offices for banking supervision (Bundesaufsichtsamt für das Kreditwesen – BAKred), insurance supervision (Bundesaufsichtsamt für das Versicherungswesen – BAV) and securities supervision (Bundesaufsichtsamt für den Wertpapierhandel – BAWe) have been combined in a single state regulator that supervises banks, financial services institutions and insurance undertakings across the entire financial market and comprises all the key functions of consumer protection and solvency supervision. This Federal Financial Supervisory Authority makes a valuable contribution to the stability of Germany as a financial centre and improves its competitiveness (German Federal Financial Supervisory Authority 2003).

The BaFin is a federal institution governed by public law that belongs to the portfolio of the Federal Ministry of Finance and as such has a legal personality. Its two offices are located in Bonn and Frankfurt/Main, where approximately 1500 persons are employed. The BaFin supervises about 2000 banks, 650 financial services institutions and around 630 insurance undertakings (BaFin Report 2008).

The decision to set up the BaFin was made basically in light of the fundamental changes on the financial markets which required a legislative response that would ensure the future stability of the German financial system.

So, the single regulator was set up mainly for the following reasons: an increasing number of clients of banks, financial services institutions and insurance companies are demanding integrated financial products. The providers of such products have adapted themselves to these demands and developed cross-sectoral products and strategies. The former distinctions between banking and financial services on the one hand and insurance business on the other are gradually disappearing: insurance companies have entered the traditional banking business by offering integrated financial services, for instance within the scope of asset management, whereas at the same time banks have developed new lines of products and, with these, are now dealing in core businesses once exclusively reserved for insurers. Consequently, suppliers are competing for the same clients with similar or even identical products. Furthermore, competition is intensified by the use of electronic distribution channels on the internet and by the savings potential involved. The client, in turn, is mainly interested in the product, this means it is of minor importance to him whether it is offered by a bank or an insurance company.

As a result, there is now a growing tendency among banks, financial services institutions and insurance undertakings to form cross-sectoral groups for whom it is easier to place broad product ranges effectively in the market. In the past, banks and insurance companies maintained only loose connections whereas today, powerful financial conglomerates have emerged in Germany which operate at a global level. The trend towards integrated bank-assurance groups is expected to continue.

In view of these developments, the former separation of supervisory functions into the BAKred, BAV and BAWe had become obsolete: over the last few years, a growing number of states have established modern integrated supervisory structures. Comprehensive powers and a full-scale overview of the market enable the German regulator to carry out supervision effectively and thus to contribute to the stability of Germany as a financial centre. This helps to avoid imbalances in competition which can easily occur as a result of regulatory differences in a fragmented supervisory system.

The structure of the BaFin takes account of the sectoral differences: separate organizational units were created for banking supervision, insurance supervision and securities trading supervision/asset management. Cross-sectoral tasks necessitated by the developments in the financial markets are carried out by several cross-sectoral departments which are organizationally separated from the traditional supervisory functions. The tasks of these departments include the supervision of financial conglomerates, coordination of the work in international supervisory forums and the fight against money laundering across all sectors. The latter has been of particular importance ever since the terrorist attacks in New York (German Federal Financial Supervisory Authority 2003).

The BaFin, as a single regulator, is since that merger better able than any other supervisory structure to develop equal rules for equal risks and thus to ensure equality of regulatory treatment and a level playing field. In addition, since May 2002 this structure of German supervision has helped to strengthen Germany's role as a financial centre and its ability to compete on an international scale (German Federal Financial Supervisory Authority 2003).

The banking supervision has three main supervisory objectives, the paramount one being to ensure the functioning of the entire financial industry in Germany. From this objective, two others can be inferred: to safeguard the solvency of banks, financial services institutions and insurance undertakings – which in the past was mainly a task of the BAKred and the BAV – and to protect clients and investors (Pricewaterhouse-Coopers – Deutsche Revision 1998).

Essentially, the BaFin comprises three supervisory directorates which now perform the supervisory tasks of the three formerly separate supervisory offices. They do not, however, deal with cross-sectoral issues; those have been assigned to three cross-sectoral departments. The directorates are each headed by a First Director.

THE DIRECTORATE FOR BANKING SUPERVISION

There is a first directorate in the pillar of banking supervision. It has been assigned all regulatory powers in the framework of solvency-oriented supervision of banks. Banking supervision aims at securing the functioning of the banking industry in order to keep the economy stable, while at the same time it is intended to provide maximum protection for clients' capital deposited with banks. Banking supervision is essentially based on the German Banking Act (KWG) as well as on specific legislation such as the Mortgage Bank Act (Hypothekenbankgesetz) and the Building Societies Act (Bausparkassengesetz). Apart from this, Deutsche Bundesbank continues to be involved in the ongoing supervision of banks in accordance with section 7 of the Banking Act (Panowitz and Jung 1988, p. 40).

The tasks of the directorate for banking supervision are manifold, given that banks have to meet many legal requirements before they are allowed to provide banking services. For example, they must comply with the capital adequacy requirements and have an appropriate organizational structure as well as at least two professionally qualified and reliable managers.

The BaFin monitors compliance with these requirements to make sure that banking services are provided only by undertakings that are solvent and can be expected to manage the business properly. The persons employed in the directorate for banking supervision monitor banks on an ongoing basis in order to verify their compliance with the capital adequacy requirements and if they maintain sufficient liquid funds. As regards the important lending business of banks, the BaFin checks if banks comply with statutory risk limits (this means large exposure limits) and if their bad debt provisions are in line with their risk exposure.

Growing complexity of banking business compels banks to take suitable measures for the purpose of controlling and monitoring the manifold risks involved in such transactions. As a result, the focus of supervision is on the banks' internal risk-controlling and -management systems. Furthermore, in line with this risk-oriented supervisory approach the banking supervisor has to be regularly informed about the economic situation of the respective institution, its business strategies and lines of business, as well as its project pipeline, and must evaluate these projects from a banking supervisory point of view.

The main sources of information available to the banking supervisory staff include a multitude of notifications and, in particular, the audit reports of annual accounts prepared by auditors or audit associations. Moreover, exceptional audits provide the BaFin with a better insight into a bank's economic situation. If clients' deposits entrusted to the bank are at risk the BaFin may take measures to avert these dangers, which may even go as far as withdrawing the authorization to provide banking services. Moreover, the supervisory authority may dismiss unqualified managers.

The directorate for banking supervision consists of four departments and comprises 28 sections (German Federal Financial Supervisory Authority 2007).

THE PROCESS OF SUPERVISION

Federal Financial Supervisory Authority's Sources of Information

Besides the annual accounts that are submitted, the main sources of information for the Federal Financial Supervisory Authority are the auditors' reports on the annual accounts. The auditors' reports for all larger banks are always requested, as are those for problem banks, while the others are requested on an alternating basis. The evaluation of the auditors' reports is generally carried out by the Deutsche Bundesbank; that is a valuable service to the Federal Financial Supervisory Authority (Panowitz and Jung 1988, p. 42).

The second most important source of information is provided by special audits, which in most cases are carried out on behalf of the BaFin by a private auditing company. In only a few cases the statutory auditing associations are also commissioned with special audits. In the case of special audits, Federal Financial Supervisory Authority jargon distinguishes between 'occasioned audits', which means audits that are ordered for particular reasons, and so-called 'routine audits'.

Another important source of information is constituted by the announcements or reports that banks are required to submit to the BaFin on a variety of matters either regularly or for particular reasons. One example of the regular reports is the monthly balance sheet statistics, in which banks have to supply relevant economic data. Others are the monthly reports concerning principles or the reports about large loans which have to be made four times a year. The evaluation of these reports is carried out primarily by the Deutsche Bundesbank (Panowitz and Jung 1988, p. 44).

Measures and Sanctions

Given cases of deficiencies in business organization, insufficient liquidity or inadequate equity capital and in cases of a risk to the security of bank deposits, the BaFin has at its disposal an extensive range of measures and sanctions that it can implement, but not all of which are of practical relevance to the banking sector.

The 'simple letter' is considered first as the least drastic measure for cases of minor deficiencies, while the 'serious letter' is considered for more serious deficiencies. The serious letter usually contains notice that in case of repetition of the deficiency the BaFin will consider implementing bank supervisory measures. In terms of their legal status, simple and serious letters are not formal legal measures.

The next most stringent measure is a warning, which can be made to a member of a managing board personally. The warning may be compared to a yellow card in football; it is to notify the board member in question that in case of repetition or continuation of the offence he or she can expect a demand for dismissal. A warning is only legally possible when the law has been contravened.

The most drastic measure in the practice of supervising banks is the demand for dismissal, by which the bank is required to remove the board member in question from office in accordance with the procedural regulations of the German Banking Act. A demand for dismissal is possible if a board member's reliability is no longer given, or, if following serious deficiencies, it is determined that the person is no longer professionally suitable, or if the board member continues his or her illegal conduct in spite of being warned.

If a member of the board of directors does not agree with a warning or a demand of dismissal, he or she can make an objection. The law section has to decide about the objection. If this is not successful, he or she has the possibility to go the Administration Court. In most cases BaFin wins at the court; but other decisions are possible (German Federal Financial Supervisory Authority 2007).

Besides these measures, the Federal Financial Supervisory Authority can impose sanctions in case of risk to the security of bank deposits. It can prohibit granting loans, issue instructions to institutions' management or temporarily ban the institution from accepting bank deposits and from making loans, which means provisionally shutting down the bank (a so-called moratorium). It can also impose operations bans or appoint supervisory personnel to the bank. The most severe measure is to revoke the bank's license. As far as co-operative and savings banks are concerned, measures of this kind are not common.

ISLAMIC BANKING SERVICES IN GERMANY

Development

With a Muslim population of more than 2 million people, considerable direct investments in and extensive trade relations with the Muslim world, Germany might be an interesting location for an Islamic bank. So far, however, there is neither an Islamic bank operating nor has an application for a full banking license been made (Naggar 1984, p. 415). During the last 15 years, the BAKred/BaFin has had only some preliminary talks with a few representatives of interested parties. These parties were, on the one hand, groups of Muslims living in Germany who wanted to set up an Islamic bank in order to provide interest-free banking services for their community (a kind of 'self help approach' with references to cooperative banking), and, on the other hand, Islamic financial institutions established and operating in the Muslim world who wanted to set up a branch or a subsidiary in Germany (as a part of their internationalization strategy).

Up to mid-2009, there has been no application establishing credit institutions which carry out exclusively Islamic banking products, for the following reasons:

1. BAKred/BaFin has some doubts about the commercial viability of an Islamic bank targeting its services to a rather small number of potential customers in Germany.
2. There seem to be some conflicts between the German Banking Act and crucial Islamic banking techniques. For example: the German Banking Act prescribes that the aggregate book value of investments

in shares and claims resulting from capital contributions as a silent partner and in profit participation rights (plus some other types of investment) may not exceed the liable equity capital of the bank.

3. There are serious concerns regarding the safety of deposits: if the profit and loss sharing principle is applied to 'deposits' in investment accounts with Islamic banks, there is no guarantee for the full repayment of the deposited amount. Meanwhile, there was a paragraph added to the German Banking Act according EC Directive. It compels credit institutions which do not participate in any deposit protection scheme to clearly inform their customers about this fact (Nienhaus 1995, p. 1).

4. The German respective European accounting, reporting, auditing and monitoring techniques were developed and adapted to types of financial institutions from which Islamic banks deviate substantially. If, for example, *murabaha* transactions are legally trading transactions and thus off-balance-sheet items for a conventional bank, they are the core of trade financing of Islamic banks and must be on balance for a correct assessment of their financial position and exposure.

The last argument is the most serious one because this one has far-reaching European implications. It was often argued in recent years that the completion of the European single market, the mutual recognition of licenses and the home land supervision would facilitate the entry of Islamic banks into the German or any other EU market since an interested party could open a bank in the county with the weakest banking regulations and the most generous supervisory authority. This bank would get a 'European Passport', that means the right to open branches or subsidiaries in other EU member states without further licensing procedure. But what looked like a relief at first sight might turn out to become an added and serious difficulty; since the implications of the 'European Passport' can affect all EU member states, all EU banking supervisory authorities closely cooperate and coordinate their licensing procedures in particular with regards to financial institutions of new types. Thus, the reservations of the German BaFin and of all other supervisory authorities throughout Europe must be taken into account in all European countries. In effect, not the limpest but the strictest authority may determine the conditions for the entry of an Islamic bank into the EU market.

The conclusion is that the argument of the inconsistency of Islamic banking techniques with conventional bank control and supervision methods has a high relevance for strategic considerations of Islamic banks as well as for the licensing decisions of supervisory authorities throughout the European Union. It is hard to imagine that European authorities will take the initiative to develop an accounting and reporting system for Islamic banks that fits into the conventional environment.

Islamic Financial Institutions and Banking Transactions according to German and European Banking Law

1. German Banking Law restricts the use of the term 'bank' in the firm name to credit institutions1(§ 39 KWG) holding a license in accordance with § 32 KWG. The definition is given in § 1 (1) KWG: 'Credit institutions are enterprises engaged in banking transactions'. Nine types of banking transactions are listed in the Law; this list is not final but can be extended by the Federal Minster of Finance (after consultation with the German Federal Bank) 'if, in the accepted view of the business community, this is justified having regard to the supervisory aims of this Law' (§ 1 (1) KWG). The listed banking transactions are:

   - the deposit business,
   - the credit business,
   - the discount business,
   - the securities business,
   - the safe-custody business,
   - the investment fund business,
   - the revolving credit business,
   - the guarantee business,
   - the giro business.

   The Law does not explicitly declare whether an enterprise has to perform all these transactions and whether it must not be engaged in any other type of transactions for qualifying as a bank (Nienhaus 1995, p. 1). But it follows from the legal practice and from the commentaries:

   - that it is sufficient to perform only some or even just one of the named banking transactions for qualifying as a bank and
   - that a financial institution can be a bank even if it is also engaged in transactions which are neither enumerated in the law nor are typical of banks (that means other than, for example, currency exchange or leasing of assets). There were even examples in Germany where the non-banking transactions were quantitatively more important than the banking transactions, namely co-operative banks in rural areas with large commodity transactions.

2. The EC has defined a credit institution in Article 1 of Directive 77/780/
    EEC – to which Article 1 of Directive 2000/12/EC refers – as an enter-
    prise which is engaged both in deposit and credit business. At the first
    view, this seems to be stricter than the German definition:

    - the (implicit) list of 'banking transactions' is shorter and com-
      prises (explicitly) only the deposit and credit business;
    - the EC Directive requires that both types of business are per-
      formed.

A financial institution which qualifies as a credit institution under
EC law also qualifies as a credit institution, namely a bank, under the
German Banking Law (where either the deposit or the credit business
alone is sufficient). But the article is – at least on first sight – not true:
a financial institution being a bank according to the German law but
not engaged in the deposit and credit business is not a credit institution according to article 1 of the EC Directive 2000/12/EEC. This
may have serious implications for Islamic financial institutions: if the
European law has priority over the national law not for established
credit institutions but for the licensing of new banks, then the differences may prevent the establishment of an Islamic bank not only in
Germany (where it might have been licensed in the past as long as only
the German law was applicable) but in all EC countries (Nienhaus
1995, p. 1).

Deposit business

Deposit business means the receipt of monies from others as deposits, irrespective of the payment of interest [§ 1 (1) KWG]. Islamic banks receive
monies from others for two types of accounts: current accounts and
investment accounts. The question is whether payments to these accounts
constitute deposits. No legal definition of 'deposits' is given in the banking
law, but one can see deposits as a kind of loan from the depositors to the
bank. In a loan contract, the borrower has to return what he or she has
borrowed. In analogy this means that the bank has to return (on call or on
a specified date) the full amount of money paid in by a depositor.

Current accounts with Islamic banks are deposits in this sense: the
money a customer holds on a current account does not participate in
the profit or loss of the bank and is payable on the customer's demand.
Investment accounts participate in the profit and loss of the bank. In cases
of loss the Islamic bank is not obliged to return the principal amount paid
in to the investment account in full. Thus, an essential feature of a deposit
(the full return of the deposited money) is missing.

The conclusion is that not all but parts of the monies received by Islamic bank constitute deposits and that, consequently, Islamic banks can perform the deposit business (Nienhaus 1995, p. 2).

Credit business

The German Banking Law defines the credit business as 'the granting of money loans and acceptance credits' (§ 1 (1) 2 KWG).

In a loan contract, the borrower is obliged to repay fully the amount received from the lender. Islamic banks can grant money loans, but since the bank can claim the full repayment of the amount granted to the borrower irrespective of his profits or losses, these loans must be free of interest or any other advantage for the bank. Therefore, commercially oriented Islamic banks will not grant free loans at all, or only in minimal amounts. But even if the amounts were greater, it is doubtful whether the granting of free loans without any (direct) return for the bank should be considered as credit business.

According to the opinion of the BaFin, the professional disbursement of cash against cheque is a credit business. If this is done against a service charge which is a fixed amount and not a percentage of the amount disbursed, Islamic banks could offer such a service performing this type of credit business.

Acceptance credit – where a bank signs a draft or promissory note as drawee – means that a bank transfers its creditworthiness to a customer. The bank charges a fee for this service. Conceptually, Islamic banks have no problems in offering acceptance credits if the service fees are calculated irrespective of the amount and term of the draft, but it is doubtful whether this would be an economically viable method. Some doubts remain as to whether Islamic financial institutions can perform the credit business in this specific form. But since they can and do perform other banking transactions, they can be credit institutions as defined by § 1 (1) KWG.

If Islamic banks cannot perform the credit business based on money loans (and if the disbursement of checks and the granting of acceptance credits against service charges) are commercially not viable or insignificant, then the definition of credit business in the EC directives becomes essential. While the German law defines the credit business as 'money loans and acceptance credits', the EC Directive 77/780/EEC speaks only of 'granting credits on [the bank's] own account' with no further specification. The EC Directive 2000/12/EC explicitly refers to this definition. In an annexed list of that directive with transactions which will be mutually recognized within the EC when credit or finance institutions open branches in other member countries, the term 'credits' is not used, but 'lendings' (Nienhaus 1995, p. 4).

In an attached footnote, lendings are in particular consumer credits, mortgage loans, factoring with and without recourse, and trade financing (including purchase of export receivables without recourse) (Nienhaus 1995, p. 5)

Two types of transactions of Islamic financial institutions are candidates for being considered as lending, that is credits, namely *murabaha* – mark-up transactions – and *musharaka* – profit- and loss-sharing (PLS) financings.

The final aim of many forms of lending is not to provide liquidity for arbitrary use by the borrower but to enable him or her to purchase certain goods. Mortgage loans or (some forms of) consumer credits are examples where the bank provides money only for the purchase of well-defined goods (which may serve also as collateral for the credit). *Murabaha* transactions serve exactly the same purposes. The legal difference is that the client and the bank are not engaged in a purely financial transaction but in a sale transaction; the economic purposes and effects, however, are the same as in most conventional forms of lending. Further, in many forms of lending the financial transaction is only formally but not in substance separated from the sale transaction; that is the financial transaction would not be performed without the specified sale transaction (for which the bank provides the financial means). If it is accepted that in many conventional lending cases the financing and the sale contract constitute an economic unit, then the differences between some forms of conventional lending and *murabaha* transactions vanish.

In other cases the purpose of lending is not the purchase of goods but the provision of liquidity, for example for the payment of wages of workers. Sale transactions are not applicable in such cases where no goods but liquidity is needed. Not only conventional banks but also Islamic finial institutions can provide liquidity, but instead of lending contracts with fixed interest they will conclude financing contracts of the *musharaka* type with profit- and loss-sharing arrangements (Piazolo 1997, p. 122).

Summing up: the term 'credit' in the EC directive must not be interpreted as 'money loans' (and acceptance credits) only; it has a broader meaning and includes different forms of lending.

Islamic financial institutions can take recourse to two financing techniques – namely *murabaha* and *musharaka* – which are not identical with but in all relevant aspects so similar to some conventional lending techniques that they should be considered as lending. Thus, Islamic financial institutions can perform the lending business and can be defined as credit institutions in the sense of the EC directives.

Other banking transactions
Islamic financial institutions can perform at least three more banking transactions listed in § 1 KWG.

- Securities business: Islamic financial institutions can purchase and sell securities for the accounts of others provided these securities are interest-free. Examples are shares of joint-stock companies or Participation Term Certificates which were developed in Pakistan as an alternative to interest-bearing bonds and debentures.
- Safe-custody business: Islamic financial institutions can engage in the custody and administration of (interest-free) securities for the accounts of others.
- Giro business: Islamic financial institutions offer transfers and clearings against service charges especially to clients holding current accounts.

In total, Islamic banks can perform at least four of the nine banking transactions listed in § 1 KWG. Therefore, they could be credit institutions according to German Banking Law as well as to European law, and – once they have been licensed – could use the term 'bank' in their firm name (Piazolo 1997, p. 122).

Investments

Real assets and shares and Islamic models of financing § 12 (1) KWG prescribes: 'The aggregate book value of the investments of a credit institution in real estate, buildings, equipment and fittings, ships, shares in credit institutions and in other enterprises, as well as claims resulting from capital contributions as silent partner and in profit participation rights . . . may not exceed the liable equity capital'.

Islamic banking would be impossible if the purchase of commodities for the purpose of *murabaha* financing were to be classified as 'investments in equipment and fittings', and the provision of capital on a PLS basis as in *musharaka* financing were to be classified as 'investment in shares' or 'claims resulting from capital contributions' within the meaning of § 12 (1) KWG. Commentaries point out that the purchase of real assets for the purpose of leasing (with the bank as lessor) do not fall under this paragraph (Nienhaus 1995, p. 6).

Murabaha financing should not be affected: the equipment and fittings to which § 12 (1) KWG is related are those used by the bank itself and not commodities purchased on behalf of a client. Further, commodities purchased by the bank for a *murabaha* financing are not 'investments' because they are not kept by the bank but sold immediately, that is as soon as possible to the client on whose behalf the bank purchased them. Therefore, Islamic banks can apply that instrument, which is utilized for most financing activities, including under German banking law.

Musharaka financing could be affected if the capital provided had to be classified as 'shares' or 'capital contributions'. First, it must be noted that 'share' does not only mean 'shares of joint stock companies' but any participation in capital for a company in a legal form which is determined by the applicable company law (that is, the law of joint stock companies, of private or public limited companies, and so on). Similarly, for capital contributions as silent partner and in profit participation rights, specific rules of the company law must be observed. The common denominator of all the different forms of 'investments in shares' and 'capital contributions' of § 12 (1) KWG is that the bank provides capital which is equity instead of borrowed capital and which is provided for a longer or even indefinite period of time and not for the short or medium term. In contrast to this, capital provided by a *musharaka* financing is borrowed capital for a limited and specified period of time. *Musharaka* financing does not increase, for example, the shareholders' equity of a joint stock company, and capital provided under a *musharaka* contract to private companies is legally like a profit participating loan and not like a silent partnership (Nienhaus 1995, p.7).

In total, § 12 (1) KWG should not preclude the application of Islamic modes of financing in Germany (Nienhaus 1995, p. 8).

Losses of conventional and Islamic banks   Finally, it should be noted that the rules and regulations of central banks for conventional financial institutions are neither designed to guarantee the depositors an 'adequate' return nor should they give full protection against risks which people have taken consciously when they entrust their money to such financial institutions as investment trusts. Losses against which customers shall be protected are only those which would result from the non-fulfillment of contractual obligations by the financial institutions (Piazolo 1997, Section 125).

Ignoring the case of illiquidity, the customer's money is endangered by losses which exhaust the equity capital of the institution (and lead to failure). With respect to the calculation (and occurrence) of losses which erode the shareholders' equity, some fundamental differences between conventional and Islamic banks must be observed.

1. Ignoring administrative expenses in the broadest sense (staff salaries, office rental, and so on) the profit/loss of a conventional bank

is – roughly speaking – the difference between total income on the one hand and interest payments and valuation adjustments for assets on the other hand. For German banks, the interest payment normally amount to approximately 80 per cent of total income.

2. An Islamic bank has no fixed interest payments: the profit/loss is just the difference between total income and value adjustments. The shares paid to holders of investment accounts do not diminish the profits of the bank (or cause losses) as the interest payments do in a conventional bank; they are a part of gross profits, and paying returns on investment accounts is part of the distribution of gross profits.

3. Compared to conventional banks, Islamic banks have nearly no fixed costs, namely only administrative expenses, but no interest payments. Their gross profits exceed the gross profits of conventional banks by an amount that corresponds to the interest payments of conventional banks (Nienhaus 1995, p. 9).

4. If there is no need for write-offs on assets, then a decreasing income from the employment of funds alone cannot cause losses in Islamic banks (as it could – at least in principle – in conventional banks).

5. It is possible that a balance sheet of an Islamic bank still shows a profit while the balance sheet of a conventional bank in the same situation shows a loss. A balance sheet of an Islamic bank shows a loss only if the value adjustments exceed the total income of the bank from *murabaha* and *musharaka* financing and other transactions (minus administrative expenses) while losses may occur in conventional banks if the value adjustments exceed approximately 20 per cent of the total income (that is the 'normal' difference between income and interest cost). In extreme cases, a conventional bank may go bankrupt (because the losses exceed the liable equity capital) while the balance sheet of an Islamic bank in exactly the same situation would still show a modest profit (Piazolo 1997, Section 125).

As long as the balance sheet of an Islamic bank does not show losses (and if the financial result of the balance sheet is the basis for the distribution of profit or loss shares to the holders of investment accounts), the nominal value of money paid into investment accounts will not decrease. The main risk for holders of investment accounts is not that they will lose part of the money they have transferred to the bank but that their return will be less than it could have been if the funds were employed somewhere else. What is uncertain and exposed to risk is not the principal amount but the income earned from it (Nienhaus 1995, p. 11).

CONCLUSION

Islamic financial institutions differ from conventional banks in various legal and economic respects. But despite these differences, they can be considered as credit institutions and should be eligible to get a banking license from the BaFin which shall be recognized in all other EC member states because it is in conformity with the respective coordination directives of the EC. Once this is accepted and once an application for an Islamic banking license has been made, the European banking supervisory authorities will have to think about adoption of their regulations. Credit institutions of a new type require innovative ideas for the design of adequate and fair regulatory instruments (Nienhaus 1995, p. 12).

REFERENCES

German Federal Financial Supervisory Authority (2003), *Annual Report 2002*, Bonn/Frankfurt (M).
German Federal Financial Supervisory Authority (2007), *Annual Report 2006*, Bonn/Frankfurt (M).
Naggar, A. (1984), *Islamische Banken in Theorie und Praxis*, ÖBA – Zeitschrift für das gesamte Bank- und börsenwesen, 12, Wien.
Nienhaus, V. (1995), Presentation held on 18 May 1995 at Federal Banking Supervisory Office, Berlin.
Panowitz, R. and Jung, H (1988), *Banking Act – German English Commentary*, Frankfurt (M): Luchterhand Verlag.
Piazolo, M. (1997), 'Islamic Banking – ein Wachstumsmarkt auch für westlche Banken', *Zeitschrift für das gesamte Kreditwesen*, **50**(3). 122–6.
PricewaterhouseCoopers – Deutsche Revision (1988), *Banking in Germany*, Frankfurt (M).

13. Islamic banking and prudential supervision in Italy

Luigi Donato and Maria Alessandra Freni

INTRODUCTION

This chapter analyses the operations of Islamic financial institutions from the perspective of a conventional financial supervisor, as the Bank of Italy is, in order to establish whether and to what extent they could participate in our national market. Before entering into the details of this issue some preliminary considerations are needed. On the one hand there is a limit to the analysis stemming from the fact that to date Italy has had no direct, practical experience with Islamic financial institutions. As a result the analysis and the conclusions necessarily suffer from some degree of abstractness. This limitation can be overcome, at least in part, by drawing on the experience of other national markets with a regulatory framework similar to Italy's. Supervision is no longer conceived as a set of strictly domestic arrangements but as part of a broader system in which the basic rules are European or international. What happens within this global supervisory system can certainly help us in understanding phenomena, such as Islamic finance, that are not concretely present at the national level.

On the other hand there is a secure point of reference that consists of the standards and basic supervisory rules that cannot be altered at the national level because, as noted, they are founded at the EU level or higher. The regulatory framework governing financial activities in Italy and Europe rests upon objective rules whose purpose is to ensure the prudent management of intermediaries and the stability of the system as a whole, absolutely without prejudice to entrepreneurial independence and a level playing field for intermediaries.

In any event, the entry of Islamic finance cannot be dealt with by imagining the creation of a special regulatory regime (adoption of *ad hoc* rules), either for or against. Against this background the issue must be dealt with in terms of integration with, rather than separation from, conventional finance. Any setting of the two financial systems in opposition to one another would be not only anti-historical but also irrational, in that it would be a source of conflict, of impediment to economic integration, and of instability. The work of the Islamic Financial Services Board – especially the rules on capital requirements – testifies the effort being made by Islamic finance to operate on the basis of standards, internationally accepted and comparable to those that apply to conventional financial institutions (IFSB 2005).[1]

The United Kingdom experience, which proves how the setting-up of an Islamic bank is possible in a background characterized by the enforcement of supervisory rules based on EU directives, might be the starting point to verify the compatibility of such a bank with the Italian regulatory system (FSA-UK 2007).[2]

However, it must be noted that the operations of Islamic financial institutions may also involve the application of laws that are not subject to EU or international harmonization, such as private law and commercial law. This may produce differences in the operating conditions granted to Islamic financial institutions in different EU countries.

Finally it must also be considered that Islamic finance is a complex phenomenon embracing various sectors of intermediation. In the countries in which they are active, Islamic financial institutions in banking, insurance and financial services offer a well-ramified set of products ranging from micro-credit to the issue of complex bond-like securities, from small deposits to personalized portfolio management for prime customers. Even without considering insurance products and matters related to trading in financial instruments, it is plain to see that Islamic financial intermediation departs from the classical commercial banking model specifically in the area of fund-raising and lending. The religious ban on the payment or charging of interest means that Islamic banks must resort to modes of fund-raising and lending alternative to the deposit and loan contracts that conventional banks ordinarily use. It follows that one must examine the phenomenon from a broader perspective than that used to study conventional banking, considering Islamic financial institutions as operating primarily along lines that can be likened to those of investment banking, asset management or collective investment schemes.

The economic function of Islamic finance nevertheless remains financing economic activity by employing surplus funds in investments that reward the most meritorious initiatives. The risks are those typical of financial intermediation and imply the necessity of applying forms of prudential supervision over intermediaries and over activities, to safeguard their proper management and prevent any crisis from having systemic repercussions (Iqbal 2003; El-Hawary, Grais and Iqbal 2004).

THE MAIN FEATURES OF ISLAMIC FINANCE

The special feature of Islamic finance is the effort to reconcile the practices and rules of finance with the observance of religious precepts. Some of these precepts, in particular the precepts of *riba* (ban on interest) and *gharar* (condemnation of speculation), have enormous impact by comparison with conventional finance, marking fundamental differences in contracts with customers and in the composition of financial institutions' assets and liabilities. The Muslim religion espouses a concept of economy based on solidarity, in which the compensation for the lending of money must be commensurate with the profit realized by the borrower (Piccinelli 2003). This explains why Islamic finance relies on contracts that are participatory in nature (Errico and Farahbaksh 1998). This characteristic is essential to understanding the possibilities of including Islamic finance within the European market.

Islamic financial institutions guarantee to the various stakeholders (shareholders, managers, savers, investors and borrowers) that the business done complies with Islamic law and that the funds raised or lent will not be used for activities that violate Muslim principles (such as the production or sale of pork or alcohol, or prostitution).

The economic precepts of Islam are rooted far back in history. The development of Islamic finance, however, is relatively recent, which helps explain the novelty of its expansion in non-Muslim countries. The first practical experiences date to the 1960s with the foundation of an Islamic bank (Mit-Ghamr) in Egypt. In 1973 the Islamic Development Bank (IDB) was founded to finance the most underdeveloped Islamic economies and to devise innovative instruments of finance.

Geographically, Islamic finance is common in those areas where Islam is the most influent religion (Middle East, Gulf area, South East Asia, North Africa, as well as Sudan and South Africa). It is now expanding – following the trails of immigration flows – also in non-Islamic countries (Europe, United States and Canada). In these latter countries, *Shari'ah*-compliant financial products may be offered by conventional banks through specialized structures known as 'Islamic windows' (*The Banker* 2007).

Islamic finance involves all the sectors of intermediation, and Islamic institutions offer a range of products comparable to those of conventional intermediaries.

According to the latest figures, more that 500 financial institutions provide *Shari'ah*-compliant products worldwide; in particular there are 292 commercial banks (both fully Islamic and those offering Islamic windows or selling Islamic financial products), 115 investment banks and financial companies and 118 insurance companies. The total *Shari'ah*-compliant assets accounting to the first top-500 Islamic financial institutions grew by 30 per cent in the period 2006–2007 to reach $500,482 million. Forty-seven countries have Islamic financial institutions or institutions offering *Shari'ah*-compliant financial products and services (*The Banker* 2007). It was estimated that within the next decade Islamic banks will come to hold a significant share (as much as 40 or 50 per cent) of Muslims' deposits (OICV-IOSCO 2004).

The statistics and likely future developments suggest that the issue of Islamic finance also needs very careful consideration in countries not currently hosting Islamic intermediaries. This is the frame in which to set the prospects for the demand for Islamic financial products in Italy.

Islam is Italy's second religion, counting about 1.2 million believers, including about 60,000 who have Italian nationality (Brugnoni 2008).[3] The Muslim immigrants come mainly from North Africa,[4] a fact that is significant considering that the areas in which Islamic finance is most widely diffused are the Gulf and the Far East. The fact that the banking practices and customs of their home countries are on the European pattern suggests that Italy's Muslim immigrants, once integrated into the economic and social structure, could well be much readier than in other European countries to use the conventional banking circuit and less inclined to demand special Islamic financial services.

For the most part the Muslims resident in Italy are in the lower income brackets; or, at most, they may be owners of small enterprises. For most of them, the main financial need is to send remittances back home, and this is still served chiefly by informal instruments (*hawala*) (Criscuolo, Donato and Mascelloni 2003).

In short, from an economic standpoint we can say that so far there is no significant manifest demand for Islamic financial services in Italy. As matters now stand, the most plausible thesis is that the conventional banks' range of investment and lending products not in direct conflict with Islamic precepts is adequate, without the constitution of Islamic intermediaries. And this appears to be the strategy of the Italian banks, which are offering products designed for immigrants and in cooperation with the various immigrant communities. The road to their financial integration, that is, is already open.

ISLAMIC FINANCE TRANSACTIONS

As already mentioned, contracts in Islamic financial operations are 'participatory' in nature. They can be divided into two large groups: 'directly' and 'indirectly' participatory. The former, also known as profit- and loss-sharing agreements (PLSs), are based on the joint exposure of both lenders and borrowers to profits and losses derived from the enterprise or the deal; the latter are called lease and sale-based agreements (LSBs), as they deal with the leasing and selling of goods (Piccinelli 1996; El-Hawary, Grais and Iqbal 2004; Vogel 2006).

There are two main types of contracts, within the category of directly participatory ones (PLSs): *mudaraba* and *musharaka*. *Mudaraba* is a transaction whereby a person or financial institution lends money to another, which the latter will invest in some business, enterprise or project, and then return to the former when the contract expires, together with a percentage of profits previously arranged. However, the person borrowing this money does not have any obligation to return it, should the enterprise go bankrupt or the project fail. Therefore, risk is borne entirely by the money lender. *Mudaraba* is similar to limited partnership and joint venture.[5] *Musharaka* involves that both lenders (usually financial institutions) and entrepreneurs enter into partnership, contribute capital and agree to bear risks and enjoy returns of an enterprise or project, in proportion to the amount of capital invested. Both parties will bear losses. *Musharaka* is similar in nature to a partnership deed, and can also be used to carry out complex venture capital and project finance operations.

In indirectly participatory contracts (LSBs) profit depends on either the price goods are sold or purchased at, or their rental cost. Sale-based contracts are widely used, since they can satisfy a wide number of financial needs, ranging from commercial to consumer credit. *Murabaha* is the most common means of short-term finance. Under this contract, a bank undertakes to buy an asset requested by a client, and then sells it back for a higher price (mark-up), previously arranged in the contract, which includes the bank's fee. Finally, there are also other fairly common forms of financing, comparable to leasing (*ijara wa iqtina*) and operational leasing (*ijara*).

Fund-raising is carried out in the near totality of cases on the grounds of provisions set in directly participatory contracts, *mudaraba* in particular. Through unrestricted investment accounts, clients endow banks with funds, which can be freely invested on any activities falling within the scope of the banking business. Banks' only obligation is the *bona fide* management of such funds, which must be returned when the contract expires only if profits have been made, together with a percentage of these profits, previously arranged in the contract. Unrestricted investment accounts can be compared to participatory investment and collective investment schemes.

Islamic banks offer current-account deposits as well. Here, banks are not bound to reimburse the sums, but clients are allowed to withdraw the entire amount, or part of it, at any time. Although no remuneration is envisaged here, at the end of each period customers have a right to small donations (often in kind) and to credit accommodation. This contract is therefore comparable to conventional banks' current-account deposits, wherein economic benefits for customers are given by high liquidity, the use of the payment system, and the certainty that funds deposited in the bank will always be available for withdrawal.

All things considered, this analysis of contracts shows that, with regard to risk sharing, Islamic banks appear to be burdened by not so much pressure as conventional ones; conversely, Islamic financial intermediaries' clients seem to enjoy fewer guarantees.

BUSINESS MODELS AND PRUDENTIAL REGULATIONS

The practical functioning of Islamic banks and the risks inherent in their activities can be described using two theoretical models. One is a basic 'conceptual model' describing the basic characteristics of Islamic banking, which in the light of the state of development of Islamic finance can be considered to be of primarily theoretical relevance. The other describes the operational features of the banks in a more highly evolved, diversified business environment; this is the 'prevailing operational model' actually adopted, in most cases, for the exercise of Islamic banking (Errico and Farahbaksh, 1998, p. 9; Archer, 2004; El-Hawary, Grais and Iqbal, 2004, p. 10; Dalla Pellegrina 2004, p. 505; Montanaro 2004, p. 11).

The basic conceptual model postulates that Islamic financial institutions are characterized by the predominance, on both the asset and the liability side, of directly participatory contracts (PLSs) based on *mudaraba*. The two-tier *mudaraba* is said to work as follows: on the one hand investors finance the bank through *mudaraba* transactions (as a rule, open *mudaraba*); and the bank in turn uses the funds so raised to finance firms, under contracts that are themselves patterned after the *mudaraba*. In some cases this traditional model is compatible with somewhat different schemes that envisage, on the asset side, joint ventures (*musharaka*) and that allow, on the liability side, a small portion of sight deposits.

In a word, the Islamic financial institutions that operate according to the basic conceptual model display the typical characteristics of investment banks.

The prevailing operational model is more complex, more highly diversified on the fund-raising side and especially on the lending/investment side. Assets include not only *mudaraba* and *musharaka* but also indirectly participatory contracts (LSBs). On the liability side, though essentially the *mudaraba* scheme prevails, fund-raising also allows a significant portion of sight deposits and short-term funds or funds available to customers on short notice.[6]

The Islamic banks operating on this basis can be likened to commercial or universal banks both in their economic function and in their allocation of risks between the bank and the depositors/investors. This second model is the one that supervisory authorities actually face, when Islamic banks apply to operate cross-border. As noted, this is a complex, highly evolved model that involves a number of different types of financial risk, largely similar to those faced by traditional financial institutions, and it is clear that appropriate prudential regulations are needed.

The Islamic Financial Services Board has performed a detailed analysis of the financial risks inherent in the main types of Islamic financial transactions and, on this basis, set capital requirements with which Islamic financial institutions must comply in order to ensure prudent management. The requirements are largely patterned on the standards of the Basel Committee on Banking Supervision, in particular the standard approach under the New Capital Accord (IFSB, 2005).

The risks to which Islamic banks are exposed are those typical of intermediation: credit risk, counterparty risk, market risk and liquidity risk. The risk of default – failure to repay the money lent – owing possibly, among other causes, to fraud on the part of the borrower, characterizes profit- and loss-sharing contracts, so that in addition to adequate capital coverage Islamic banks must also have particularly effective risk management systems for the selection of borrowers and for monitoring the activities financed (Chapra and Khan 2000; IFSB 2005; FSA-UK 2007).

Market risk is found mainly in transactions based on leasing or sale. The prevalence of such contracts among the assets of Islamic banks could result in an excess of fixed investment, with adverse consequences on liquidity. Liquidity is a problem of some importance for Islamic banks, because it was not until very recently that the countries where they mainly operate began to develop a significant interbank market for short and very short-term funds. And in Western countries Islamic precepts impede these institutions' access to finance in central bank money.

Finally, on the fund-raising side, there is the special type of risk that experts of Islamic finance call 'displaced commercial risk'. This consists in the practice, in some cases followed by Islamic banks spontaneously, in others required by the national supervisory authorities in order to avoid withdrawal of funds and ensure the stability of the banks, of crediting to investors/depositors the 'expected' profit, subtracting this from the share of profit that would otherwise go to the bank. This practice, especially in protracted periods of low profits, could progressively erode the bank's capital.

Without going into the merits of the standards set by the Islamic Financial Services Board – which in any case represent possible capital adequacy and risk management rules for Islamic financial systems and cannot imply derogation to the capital requirements of Italian or European law – one can note that their adoption decisively negates the old thesis that Islamic banks need no capital adequacy regulation. Such theses derived from the basic conceptual model, on the postulate that the predominant or exclusive presence of *mudaraba*-type transactions on both the asset and the liability side meant that the risk of failure of the businesses financed was taken consciously and on an informed basis by investors behaving as shareholders rather than as depositors with conventional banks. Unlike ordinary depositors, as 'quasi-shareholders', the persons entrusting their savings to the Islamic banks were reputed to exercise stricter control over management, reducing the necessity to limit risk-taking via compulsory solvency ratios (Dalla Pellegrina 2004).

Instead, the Islamic Financial Services Board refers to the more highly evolved model of Islamic banking, with assets differentiated by type of contract and risk and forms of fund-raising allowing for short-term or even short-notice withdrawal. The model underlying the proposed capital rules for Islamic banks also affirms the 'passive role' of Islamic depositors. In other words, it recognizes their inability, typical of uninformed investors, to exercise effective control over managers and considers the risk that they may react to poor management and low return on their investment by withdrawing their funds, which would threaten the stability of the bank or even, if the bank is large and an active participant in the payment network, of the entire banking system (Montanaro, 2004; Sundararajan and Errico 2002; Sundararajan 2004).

THE PROSPECTS FOR ISLAMIC FINANCE IN ITALY

The success and spread of a product or of an institutional-operational model for the financial industry must not be allowed to depend on the rules. It is not the regulator's or supervisor's job to determine the economic needs of the market, the products and services that firms and households need. Selection of the enterprises that offer financial services and products is up to the market. Market participants, for their part, must observe the rules, whose objective in the financial sector is to ensure stability, transparency, investor protection, and hence a level playing field among financial institutions.

It will therefore be the market itself that determines whether or not Islamic banks will enter the Italian financial system and stay there. Their presence will be weighed by the same general rules applicable to all intermediaries operating in Italy and that guarantee financial stability and a level playing field. The offer of Islamic products must also comply with standards of contractual and market transparency and with investor protection legislation.

In general, Islamic financial institutions may enjoy two sources of attraction for customers: the awareness that they are investing their savings without violating religious precepts and higher yields in return for forgoing the right to immediate restitution of the money lent. In theory, this second feature could attract funds from non-Muslim investors as well.

The problem of protecting savers for whom profit is not the crux of their investment choices has already been pondered by the supervisory authorities in relation to initiatives of ethical banking and the offer of ethical saving and investment products. The solution was to recognize the legitimacy of motivations different from the mere search for the highest return, but to concede no derogation from the rules on financial intermediation that would result in disparities in guaranteeing the interests that it is the supervisors' duty to safeguard: the stability of intermediaries and investor protection.

Allowing lower prudential standards for Islamic banks than those required of conventional banks would not only discriminate against Islamic customers in terms of safeguards for their economic interests but also give those institutions an unfair competitive advantage over their conventional counterparts, the price of whose products incorporates the cost of complying with the supervisory requirements (FSA-UK, 2007).

As for the second potential point of attraction for Islamic banks, we have seen that in general the relationship between savers and the bank cannot be simply reduced to the 'deposit' scheme of conventional banking. Rather it is more comparable to other kinds of fund-raising and, especially, to collective asset management. But especially when we are dealing with persons long since integrated into the economic and social life of non-Muslim countries and used to conceiving the relationship with their bank the way Europeans do, we must wonder how far this aspect, which sets Islamic banking sharply apart from conventional banking, can be truly perceived by the saver and hence accepted in the event of a negative investment outcome. For that matter, the experience indicates that Italian investors themselves are hardly inclined to accept negative financial events, and not only when the responsibility lies with the issuers or sellers of financial products.

Actually, the Islamic financial institutions themselves and some super-visory authorities implicitly recognize that savers have a 'right' to the expected profit. It is therefore important, in order among other things to contain 'displaced commercial risk', that in application of the Consolidated Law on Banking and the Consolidated Law on Finance customers be given all due information and fully transparent contractual conditions.

THE CONSTITUTION OF AN ISLAMIC FINANCIAL INSTITUTION IN ITALY

The Italian financial legislation, like the European framework from which it derives, consists in a consistent, complete set of rules under which a variety of forms of intermediation, including Islamic finance, can be con-ducted. In addition to banks the Italian and European financial system comprises other types of financial institution that could serve as a point of reference for operators interested in marketing Islamic financial products in Italy: for instance, SGRs (*società di gestione del risparmio* – asset man-agement companies), which under the Consolidated Law on Finance may provide individual portfolio management services or institute collective investment funds, and SICAVs (*società di investimento a capitale variabile* – open-end investment companies). Despite the many significant analogies between asset management and the type of intermediation exercised by Islamic banks, however, in their home countries the latter as 'banks' are not required to keep customers' managed assets separate from their own capital, as asset management companies must do in the Italian system (Article 22 of the Consolidated Financial Law).

Transposing the Islamic banking model to Europe as a non-bank inter-mediary may be feasible, therefore, perhaps even easy, but it would not seem to be the exhaustive answer to the question of the possibility of con-stituting an Islamic bank in Italy. If anything, it is a reasonable alternative to such constitution (Castaldi 2003).

The opening of an Islamic bank in Italy is possible provided that the ordinary rules and controls applying to the constitution of a new bank or the establishment of a foreign bank branch are complied with.

The minimum capital required for a new bank is €6.3 million. The appli-cation must be submitted to the Bank of Italy, accompanied by the act of incorporation, the bylaws and documentation attesting to the existence of this capital, the integrity of the shareholders, and the competence and integrity of the management.

In addition, the applicant must present a business plan in which the founders demonstrate the future capacity of the bank to take part in the market and to operate in sound and prudent fashion. In considering the application, the Bank of Italy weighs the business plan, the origin of the initial capital, the quality of the shareholders, their financial capacity and their ability to sustain the bank in the delicate start-up phase, the administrative organization, and the internal control system (Banking Law, article 14; Bank of Italy, Supervisory Instructions for Banks, Title I, Chapter 1).

For an Islamic bank, to avoid opaque governance, there must be explicit definition of the role and responsibilities of the *Shari'ah* board, which must not in any case be empowered to exercise any of the functions that are performed by the management and control bodies of ordinary banks (FSA-UK 2007).[7]

To be authorized, a bank must also join a deposit guarantee scheme. Membership in the Interbank Deposit Guarantee Fund should not be excessively burdensome for an Islamic bank, as both regular and extraordinary contributions are proportional to the volume of deposits guaranteed, which for these banks is likely to be small in relation to their overall business, if not entirely absent.

One key strategic theme for Islamic banks is certainly the Italian law on corporate purpose. There is, in fact, a sort of paradox in the fact that the authorization envisaged in Article 14 of the Italian Banking Law concerns the exercise of conventional banking business, while the very definition of Islamic banking seems to preclude it.

In current law, however, the scope of the authorization to engage in banking is not strictly limited, in practice, to the mere traditional notion of banking as the taking of deposits and lending. Unquestionably, there are intermediaries in Italy which, though authorized as banks, do not perform both of these typical banking functions at once or in significant volume; for instance, they may specialize in investment services. Even if it could appear as a paradox, often for these banks there is not a perfect consistency between the scope of authorization (banking business) and the activities actually carried out (financial services). In fact, in Italy authorization allows a bank to engage in a vast range of activities that are financial in the broad sense; they may include a certain percentage of banking business in the strict sense, but they do not necessarily have to. Though it may sound paradoxical, authorization and effective carrying out of activities are often disconnected.

Truth of the matter is that in Italy the concept of 'bank' accepted for supervisory purposes is broader than the one proposed by traditional theories dealing with banking intermediation. In our legal system, both concepts of 'bank' and 'banking activity' coexist, though neither defines the other. Banking activities are made up of savings collection and credit granting, whereas banks are those bodies carrying out such activities (and allowed to carry out others as well). 'Banks' are not identified as the bodies that carry out that activities, but as the intermediaries 'authorized' to carry out banking business and/or other financial activities, if not reserved by the law to the exclusive exercise by other intermediation groups (such as insurances, reserved to insurance companies, and collective management funds, reserved to SGRs and SICAVs), otherwise there would be no legal difference between so-called *de facto* banks, that is, unauthorized bodies which unlawfully collect reimbursable funds and grant credit, and *de jure* ones – as they also are the intermediaries authorized to carry out banking activities.

Article 10, paragraph 3 of the Italian Banking Law, when dealing with banks carrying out financial activities, in addition to banking ones, might seem to consider illegitimate all those banks whose activities are not significantly, or even predominantly, traditional. However, such provision may easily be interpreted as a set of operational faculties, and not as the preordained constraint on the carrying out of a predominant activity. Authorizations to banks, as envisaged here, allow them to carry out a wide range of financial activities which may include a certain amount of banking activities (in the strict sense of the word).

Furthermore, an absolute coincidence between the concepts of 'bank' and 'banking activity', based on the hypothesis that the authorization is no longer in force, should be excluded; as a matter of fact, the Italian Banking Law, article 14, paragraph 2 *bis*, and the Bank of Italy's Supervisory Instructions (Bank of Italy, Supervisory Instructions for Banks, Title I, Ch. 1, sec. VI, par. 5) generally mention the hypothesis that an 'activity' has not been carried out. Such provisions aim either at preventing authorizations from being frozen for too long and used only when initial circumstances have changed; or making sure that authorizations are not requested in order to hand them over to others afterwards. It is then fundamental that authorized bodies begin to operate quickly; after all, it would not be possible to put supervision into effect and carry out interventions on inoperative banks. For example, it appears difficult to assume an administrative compulsory winding-up, based on the existence of certain requirements (such as administrative irregularities and extremely serious breach of provisions and estimated losses) which may be linked to operating enterprises; and that explains why paragraph 2 *bis* of article 14 was added to the Italian Banking Law by Legislative Decree 4 August 1999, n. 342.

The concrete notion of 'bank' on which supervisory activity rests thus refers to a universal intermediary free to choose its particular entrepreneurial vocation. There is no banking supervisory rule setting a minimum amount of deposit-taking or lending in order to be a 'bank'. In any case, any such threshold limits would require prior classification of all transactions on the asset and on the liability side in order to define them as 'banking' or not, the sort of archaic regulatory approach that has long since been abandoned.

Of course, a banking charter might seem to be oversized for the type of business planned. But from the standpoint of prudential supervision this choice certainly does not conflict with the principle of sound and prudent management. Let us mention the recent inclusion within banking law of the institution of loan consortiums, that is institutions whose main business is collective loan guarantees (Law 326/2003). This activity can be performed by financial intermediaries or 'consortium' guarantee banks. And the latter, which must engage primarily in the collective guarantee of loans to their members, can engage in ordinary banking only residually. Surely this weakens the narrow definition of the bank as an enterprise that engages in banking business.

The financial industry scenario seems consistent with a no-longer traditional concept of banking. The legislative framework for financial institutions allows banking and financial intermediaries to easily shift from one institutional form to the other; a non-bank financial intermediary may become a bank and *vice versa*, by modifying the corporate purpose according to market needs. After all, the 1993 Banking Law has definitely done away with the institutional and operational specialization constraints, which characterized the previous legislation: the law no longer makes a distinction between commercial banks (*aziende di credito*) and investment ones (*istituti di credito*), and a wide range of operational schemes is now available, including 'universal banks', 'specialized banks' and banking groups, within which different financial companies (investment companies, asset management companies, leasing companies) may operate on a variable scale (Castaldi 1997).

In fact, the broad notion of 'bank' that is now enshrined, in practice, in Italian legislation can be highly significant for Islamic banks, whose specific operating characteristics are such that even without engaging in traditional banking business on a large scale they could be part of the Italian financial system.

As for the asset and liability composition that is likely to characterize Islamic banks in practice, let us examine the indications of the Bank of Italy on 'associazione in partecipazione' (Article 2549 of the Civil Code), set out in the *Bollettino di Vigilanza* of January 2003. In several respects the type of association in participation considered by the supervisors resembles the investment deposit (based on *mudaraba*) practised by Islamic banks. These are initiatives whereby, via association in participation (partnership) contracts, the bank as associator conventionally assigns to third parties as associates the possibility of participating in the profits deriving from banking activity, in exchange for an economically measurable contribution.

The Bank of Italy dealt with two potential problems. One is that the association in participation contract could lead to interference in the management of the bank by non-banking persons, which would result in unauthorized persons engaging in banking activity. In this regard the Bank of Italy holds that association in participation as regulated by the Civil Code does not give associates any decision-making or managerial power, and thus does not violate the terms for the exercise of banking as long as there are no additional contract clauses giving non-banking third-party associates the right to take part in management.

The second problem concerns the possibility that, through the mechanism of transfer of profits and losses, non-financial third-party associates may acquire a position of control in the form of dominant influence (Article 23(2) of the Banking Law), in violation of the national law requiring separation between banking and all non-financial business enterprises (Article 19(6) of the Banking Law). To obviate the risk that association in participation could be used to circumvent the limits to the acquisition of equity by non-financial persons, the Bank of Italy recalled the need for such initiatives to be submitted in advance to the Bank of Italy for an assessment of all the elements relevant to banking supervision.

The recent reform of company law (Capolino and Donato 2004) has enriched the variety of business opportunities available and can offer Islamic banks ways to couch contracts in terms compatible with the *Shari'ah*. The reference here is to new financial instruments which, though covered in the rules on bonds, nevertheless make the timing and amount of redemptions conditional upon the economic performance of the company (Articles 2346 and 2411(3) of the Civil Code), and to the rules on capital allocated for a specific transaction (Articles 2447-*bis et seq.* of the Civil Code), which may enjoy contributions from third parties (Article 2447-ter.1(d) of the Civil Code).

As to corporate assets, a limitation laid down in the regulations that could prove significant for Islamic financial institutions is the requirement that banks' fixed assets in equity and in real property must not exceed their supervisory capital.

To conclude, the scenario holds a wealth of possibilities for the activity of Islamic banks, and obviously poses an equally vast array of questions for the application of Civil Law and supervisory regulations.

OPENING A BRANCH OF A FOREIGN ISLAMIC BANK

There are two other ways of entering the Italian market in order to perform banking activities of an Islamic character: opening a branch of an

Islamic bank established in a non-EU country, and opening the branch of an Islamic bank already constituted in another EU Member State.

The procedure for establishing the branch of an Islamic bank located in a non-EU country is basically similar to that for constituting a new bank. The requirements are an endowment fund of €6.3 million, submission of the business plan, and experience and integrity requirements for the managers. Authorization is issued by the Bank of Italy after consulting the Ministry for Foreign Affairs. In considering the application, account is also taken of several specific factors: the existence of adequate supervisory rules in the bank's home country; the absence of impediments to information exchange with the home-country supervisors; advance permission of the latter to open the branch in Italy; the attestation of the home-country supervisors to the financial soundness and to the adequacy of the organization, administration and accounting arrangements of the bank and of any group to which it may belong; and conditions of reciprocity (Article 14(4) of the Banking Law).

The final possibility is entry into Italy as the branch of an EU Islamic bank. The procedure for establishing the branch of a Community bank is fast and simple, requiring only notification on the part of the supervisory authorities of the home EU country. The procedure reflects the 'single passport' and recognition of supervision over the parent bank, which are the foundations of the European single market in banking services. However, the established practice of supervisors is to deny permission for a newly formed bank to expand abroad. This position reflects supervisors' concern for the stability, for the sound and prudent management, of the newly formed bank. There is a natural path of expansion for any enterprise, and to expand, especially beyond national borders, a bank's capital situation and organizational and internal control arrangements must be consistent with the plan to move into foreign markets. The home country authorities, even more than the host country authorities, may therefore oppose the plan being notified where it sees a risk for sound and prudent management. But where an Islamic bank – like any other – is demonstrably sound in all technical respects in one EU member country, it can perfectly well expand into others; and the host country authorities have no power to prevent it.

CONCLUSION

There are now 79 foreign banks with branches in Italy, accounting for 8.2 per cent of all banking activity, and more than 500 other foreign intermediaries operate without permanent establishments or branches. There are also 22 subsidiaries of foreign banks, accounting for about 11 per cent of the total assets of units doing business in (Bank of Italy 2008; Saccomanni 2008).

Our analysis has found no legal impediment to authorization of a bank whose bylaws specify that it will conduct its banking business according to Islamic principles. At the same time, there is no getting around the existing rules, nor is there any possibility of an easing of the prudential and investor-protection rules *vis-à-vis* such a bank.

In practice, the Bank of Italy will not evaluate the Islamic banking model in general; rather, individual applications will be examined on a case-by-case basis and determination made according to their specific characteristics.

Prudential supervision is already conducted on the basis of general rules over a wide range of intermediaries that no longer conform to standard, predetermined legal and operational models. The past differences in the supervisory rules for banks and non-bank intermediaries have themselves been attenuated. The composition of the assets and liabilities of an Islamic bank would not therefore seem to constitute a serious problem in assessing the institution's risk and setting the capital requirements accordingly. And the organizational standards laid down by supervisors are also adequate. Finally, the means of information and instruments of intervention available to the authorities are flexible enough to apply to these new intermediaries.

This, then, is the course that Italian supervisors will follow in considering the application of an Islamic bank, from the phase of rule-making to that of authorization and that of controls. The fate of any such initiative, in any case, depends in equal measure on the skill of its promoters and on the response of the market.

NOTES

1. The IFSB has also adopted guidelines on risk management (2005), corporate governance (2006), transparency and market discipline (2007), supervisory review process (2007), and recognition of ECAIs (2008).
2. As at November 2007 three Islamic banks were licensed by the UK FSA. The Islamic Bank of Britain initiated its operations as an authorized institution in 2004; the European Islamic Investment Bank and the Bank of London and the Middle East were licensed respectively in 2006 and 2007. The first of these is retail, while the other two are wholesale. At the end of 2007 other applications for licence by Islamic banks were under consideration by the UK financial supervisory authority.
3. According to the official statistics, at January 2007 Muslims represented about 32 per cent of the 3.7 million of foreign residents in Italy and 2.3 per cent of the Italian population. To these 1.2 million official residents, another 100 000–150 000 of illegal immigrants should be added. Therefore the estimated Islamic population in Italy would account for more than 1.4 million individuals.

4. According to ISTAT (the Italian Institute of Statistics 2008) foreign residents in Italy from North Africa at January 2007 amount to ca 522 000, of which 65 000 were from Egypt, 343 000 from Morocco and 89 000 from Tunisia. In addition there are about 60 000 resident from Senegal and 375 000 from Albania, where Muslims are significantly present. Immigration from Muslim Asiatic countries (mainly Pakistan and Bangladesh) is increasing significantly.

5. With respect to the Italian law, it is comparable to *associazione in partecipazione* (article 2549 of the Civil Code) or *società in accomandita semplice* (articles 2313–2324 of the Civil Code).

6. In some cases, even for funds raised via *mudaraba* banks allow customers to withdraw their money on short notice (for instance, when a family emergency arises), but they must forgo their share of the profits.

7. The role of the *Shari'ah* Board in the governance of Islamic financial institutions is also debated by supervisors of Islamic countries.

REFERENCES

Archer, S. (2004), *Capital adequacy for institutions offering Islamic financial services: regulatory rationales and key conceptual issues*, Seminar on Comparative Supervision of Islamic and Conventional Finance, 7–8 December, Beirut, Lebanon;

Bank of Italy (2007), *Supervisory Instructions for Banks*, Circular n. 229, 13th. Updating, April.

Bank of Italy (2008), *Annual Report for 2007*, May.

Brugnoni, A. (2008), Islamic Financial Services in Italy, Islamic Finance News Guide, www.islamicfinancenews.com.

Capolino, O. and Donato L. (2004), 'Le banche e la riforma del diritto societario', *La competitività dell'industria bancaria*, Fondazione Rosselli, IX Rapporto sul sistema finanziario italiano.

Castaldi, G. (1997), *Il Testo Unico tra innovazione e continuità*, Turin.

Castaldi, G. (2003), 'Banca e finanza islamica', *Autonomia e cooperazione*, Rome: Quaderni della Camera di Commercio Italo-araba.

Chapra, M. and Khan, T. (2000), *Regulation and Supervision of Islamic Banks*, Jeddah: Islamic Research and Training Institute, Islamic Development Bank.

Criscuolo, L., Donato, L. and Mascelloni, P. (2003), 'I flussi migratori e i flussi bancari', *Immigrazione e flussi finanziari, Secondo Rapporto Bocconi*, DIA, DNA, UIC.

Dalla Pellegrina, L. (2004), *Coefficienti di capitale, efficienza e governance: banche occidentali e banche islamiche. La competitività dell'industria bancaria*, Turin: Fondazione Rosselli, IX Rapporto sul sistema finanziario italiano.

El-Hawary, D., Grais, W. and Iqbal, Z. (2004), 'Regulating Islamic Financial Institutions, The Nature of the Regulated', World Bank Policy Research Working Paper, 3227.

Errico, L. and Farahbaksh, M. (1998), 'Islamic Banking: Issues in Prudential Regulation and Supervision', IMF Working Paper 30, 1998, 6.

FSA-UK (2007), *Islamic Finance in the UK: Regulation and Challenges*, November.

IFSB (2005), *Guiding Principles of Risk Management for Institutions (other than insurance institutions) Offering only Islamic Financial Services*, December.

IFSB (2006), *Guiding Principles on Corporate Governance for Institutions Offering only Islamic Financial Services (excluding Islamic insurance (takaful) institutions and Islamic mutual funds)*, December.

IFSB (2007), *Disclosures to Promote Transparency and Market Discipline for Institutions Offering Islamic Financial Services (excluding Islamic insurance (takaful) institutions and Islamic mutual funds)*, December.

IFSB (2007), *Guidance on Key Elements in the Supervisory Review Process of Institutions Offering Islamic Financial Services (excluding Islamic insurance (takaful) institutions and Islamic mutual funds)*, December.

IFSB (2008), *Guidance Note in Connection with the Capital Adequacy Standard: Recognition of Ratings by External Credit Assessment Institutions (ECAIs) on Sharia-Compliant Financial Instruments*, March.

Iqbal M. (2003), *Islamic Banking in Theory and Practice, International Islamic Banking Conference*, Prato.

ISTAT (Italian Institute of Statistics) (2008), Annual Report 2007, May (http://www.istat.it/dati/catalogo/20080528_00/).

Montanaro E. (2004), 'La banca islamica: una sfida per le regole di Basilea', *Studi e note di Economia*, 3.

OICV-IOSCO (2004), *Islamic Capital Market: Fact Finding Report*, July.

Piccinelli, Gian M. (1996), *Le banche islamiche in un contesto non islamico. Materiali e strumenti giuridici*, Rome: Istituto per l'Oriente.

Piccinelli, Gian M. (2003), 'Etica e prassi delle banche islamiche', *Autonomia e cooperazione*, Rome: Quaderni della Camera di Commercio Italo-araba.

Saccomanni, F. (2008), *L'evoluzione del sistema finanziario italiano nel contesto europeo e internazionale*, 27 June (www.bancaditalia.it).

Sundararajan V. (2004), 'Risk measurement, risk management, and disclosure in Islamic finance', *Seminar on Comparative Supervision of Islamic and Conventional Finance*, 7–8 December 2004, Beirut, Lebanon

Sundararajan V. and Errico L. (2002), 'Islamic Financial Institutions and Products in the Global Financial system: Key Issues in Risk Management and Challenges Ahead', Washington: IMF Working Paper, 192 (02), November.

The Banker (2007), *Top 500 Islamic Institutions*, November.

Vogel, Frank E. (2006), 'Islamic finance: personal and enterprise banking', in G. Gimigliano and G. Rotondo (eds), *La banca islamica e disciplina bancaria europea*, Milan: Giuffrè.

14. Islamic banking: impression of an Italian jurist

Pietro Abbadessa

The banking model (see above, Chapter 4) is totally different from the one adopted in non-Islamic countries, but does not lack an adequate competitive force on this account. Maybe it is true that ideally the object to be pursued is the development of a dualistic banking system, in which Islamic banks may co-exist with conventional banks and compete with them. Dr Fahim Khan (1986) has shown that it can not be taken for granted that the outcome of this competition would weigh in favour of non-Islamic banks. At any rate, in order to compare these two banking models – if it is necessary to clearly distinguish one from the other – two different institutional frameworks should also exist, both at the primary level and at the regulatory level, valid for the banks operating under the Islamic and the traditional paradigm respectively. Currently, however, this condition does not exist; therefore, reasoning about Islamic banking today forces us to constrain this experience within the cultural, juridical and technical categories which belong to conventional banking. And this is no easy task.

From my juridical perspective, this chapter will try to explore to what extent, within the Italian legal system, it is possible to constitute a bank that, albeit not aiming to fully implement the programme traced by Dr Fahim Khan, internalizes, at least to some extent, the objectives characterizing Islamic banking.

With regard to this issue, Alessandro Nigro (2006) has proposed a radical theory, according to which, in its present state, the Italian banking system would not tolerate a credit institution governed by the principles of Islamic banking. The reason lies in the fact that, under Italian law, an institution can operate as a bank only if it exercises an activity which combines collecting money on deposit from the public, without having the saver run any risk, and granting credit: operational patterns both forbidden to Islamic banks. In fact, on the basis of the *riba* prohibition, banks are neither allowed to offer a fixed rate of return on deposits nor to charge interests on loans.

Surely, it would be very difficult to disagree with the premise from which this observation stems. Nevertheless, the conclusion at which Nigro arrives does not take into due consideration the circumstance that if, on the one hand, the Consolidated Law on Banking still defines banking activity in traditional terms, on the other, it has given banks the chance to exercise other financial activity in addition to banking (complying with the respective discipline) without prescribing that the second (banking) should be prevalent over the others (financial). That is precisely where the flourishing of new banks in the Italian market comes from. Sometimes they are a result of the transformation of pre-existing investment institutions which keep the denomination of bank because of the pull that it still possesses over the public, and most of them are focused in the field of financial activities other than banking, in the first instance, financial services.

On the other hand, it has been argued that the Consolidated Law on Banking would legitimate the existence of banks which exclude, *ex ante*, the exercise of banking activity or which, even though such activity is stated in their own corporate objects and programmes, do not in fact pursue it. This reconstruction is in sharp contrast with both a traditional opinion and art. 10, paragraph 3, of the Consolidated Law on Banking. This article clearly states that the above mentioned financial activities may be exercised 'in addition to the banking activity', leaving no doubt that this element can not be set aside.

The circumstances that Supervisory Instructions do not specify (so far) as being the minimum requirements in order to qualify as banking activity, are not enough to modify the conclusion reached above, therefore authorizing an expansion of the bank paradigm beyond the boundaries which the law draws. In addition, it would not be difficult to find out the possible sanctions enforceable against a bank that does not comply, in its bylaws or in its programme, with the legal provisions (withdrawal of banking licence, loss of authorization on account of failure to start the activity, extraordinary administration).

This might be the juridical framework which it is necessary to examine in order to examine the acceptability of Islamic banking within the Italian system.

On this issue, it is widely known that collecting savings without charge accompanied by an unconditioned repayment right is common in the Islamic banking context. The existence of these kinds of savings, which are not unknown in European practice, makes it possible to think that one of the essential conditions that needs to be fulfilled in order to constitute a bank (the collection of deposits without any assumption of risk by the saver), the remuneration of the deposit, is not necessary. *Vice versa*, it is not required that the bank collect money in forms that imply some risk for the saver (for example, direct collecting, obtained through the issue of the peculiar kind of securities called *ibridi* (hybrid) in the Italian system – and now after the 2003 company law reform *strumenti finanziari partecipativi* or indirect collecting, where the bank operates as a simple intermediary between the saver and the investment), which is the core feature of Islamic banking.

In both cases, we are faced with absolutely legitimate operations, widely practised in the Italian context, but which are not able to qualify an institution as a bank. In order to constitute a bank, collecting activity which does not involve the saver in any corporate risk is a prerequisite.

Therefore, in order to exist, under Italian law, an Islamic bank will have to combine the collection of reimbursable funds with credit-granting activity, using contracts that, by their specific nature, put the bank in a risk-free position, with the sole exemption of pure factual risk associated with creditor insolvency.

Keeping in mind the *riba* prohibition, the contracts which, in Italian banking practice, can be used as vehicles for this specific kind of activity are free loans (the so-called *mutuo a titolo gratuito*) and, above all, leasing contracts which, on one side, do not envisage *strictu sensu* interest payments (even though the observation smacks of formalization, the last word on the subject belongs to Islamic law scholars) and, on the other, can be brought back to the credit-granting paradigm, as Renzo Costi (2007) has demonstrated. Secondly, all the operations in which the bank operates as a simple intermediary in the circulation of goods (largely performed, in practice, by Islamic banks in order to bypass the *riba* prohibition) are surely not part of it. These operations cannot be considered to be credit-granting activities as defined by the Consolidated Law on Banking (in fact they lack the *quid proprium* of these operations that consist in a temporary increase of wealth for the credited party accompanied by a duty of reimbursement towards the crediting party) or the financial activities that banks are allowed to perform. Therefore, they are absolutely forbidden to credit institutions regulated by Italian law.

However, the restrictions imposed by Italian law on the constitution of Islamic banks could not be bypassed through the incorporation of the bank in a more tolerant European country, with the objective of operating in Italy later on under the shield of the mutual recognition principle. European law guarantees, in fact, such benefit only to enterprises whose activity consists in receiving deposits or other reimbursable funds from the public and granting credit. It follows that, if these requirements are not met (the same ones that Italian law provides for in order to be able to speak of a bank), the communitarian enterprise even qualified as a bank under the law of the country of incorporation could never be allowed to operate in Italy, given the principle of home country control.

If Italian law gives enough space for the incorporation of banks that follow Islamic principles, it should not be overlooked that, under the Supervisory Instructions in force, such a bank would be subject to relevant restrictions in the specific kind of activity that, as a consequence of the *riba* prohibition, is practised more. In particular, resources collected from the public could not be used to assume participation implying subjection to corporate risk, such as shares or other financial instruments (under different names), and that do not guarantee the reimbursement of capital. In fact, the use of these instruments is allowed under Islamic law because the return of the investment is justified in terms of risk rather then simple interest revenues, which are forbidden by the *riba* prohibition.

That having been said, at present, the only chance available for the development of Islamic banking in Italy is to concentrate operations in the financial services market, once all the minimum requirements in order to obtain and keep the banking licence are met. This option would make it possible to offer the clients the services of negotiation of financial instruments, portfolio management on an individual basis and, above all, to foster the institution of Islamic-characterized investment funds through the constitution of investment management companies (SGR).

A possible alternative would be to appeal to the new instrument of separate financial patrimony, but at present this is an unexplored track.

Under this kind of reconstruction the space available for Islamic banks is very distant from the ambitious banking model described by Dr Fahim Khan. In any case, if the regulatory system has been correctly considered, today, in Italy, Islamic banking could not be much further removed from what Italian banks born at the end of the transformation from investment companies do. They do not hesitate to squeeze banking activity in favour of indirect collecting and financial services.

BIBLIOGRAPHY

Castro, F. (1988), Voce 'Banca islamica', in *Digesto delle discipline privatistiche*, sez. civ. Turin: Utet giuridica.

Chapra, M. and Khan, T. (2000), *Regulation and supervision of Islamic banks*, Jedda: Islamic Research and Training Institute Occasional Paper 3.

Costi R. (2007), *L'ordinamento bancario*, Bologna: Il Mulino.

Dalla Pellegrina, L. (2006), *Capitalization Requirements, Efficiency and Governance. A Comparative Experiment on Islamic and Western Banks*, available at www. ssrn.com.

El-Hawary, D., Grais, W. and Iqbal, Z. (2004), *Regulating Islamic financial institutions: the nature of the regulated*, Washington DC: World Bank Policy Research Working Paper, 3227.

Errico, L. and Farahbaksh, M. (1998), *Islamic banking, issue in prudential regulation and supervision*, Washington DC: IMF Working Paper WP/98/30.

Fiennes, T. (2002), 'UK regulatory requirements for Islamic Banks', *Euromoney Seminars Islamic Financial Summit*, London.

Kahn, M. Fahim (1986), *Islamic interest-free banking. A theoretical analysis*, Washington: IMF Staff Papers, 33.

Meo, G. (2004), 'Il modello islamico di banca e l'ordinamento bancario italiano', *Diritto della banca e del mercato finanziario*, **2**, 161–71.

Montanaro, E. (2004), 'La banca islamica: una sfida per le regole di Basilea', *Studi e note di Economia*.

Nigro, A. (2006), *Intervento*, in G. Gimigliano and G. Rotondo (eds), *La Banca Islamica e la disciplina bancaria europea*, Milan: Giuffrè.

Piccinelli, Gian M. (1996), *Banche islamiche in contesto non islamico: materiali e strumenti giuridici*, Rome: Istituto per l'Oriente.

Sundararajan, V. and Errico, L. (2002), *Islamic financial institutions and products in the global financial system: key issues in risk management and challenges ahead*, Washington DC: IMF Working Paper WP/02/192.

Tacy, K. (2006), '*Islamic finance: a growing industry in the United States*', *North Carolina Banking Institute*, **10**, 355–77.

Tailor, J. (2003), 'Islamic banking – the feasibility of establishing an Islamic bank in the United States', *American Business Law Journal*, **40**, 385–416.

15. Islamic banking in the United Kingdom

Rodney Wilson

This chapter examines the experience of Islamic banking in the United Kingdom since 1980, focusing on wholesale operations, retail saving and investment products and home finance. Regulatory and legal issues are discussed, as well as institutional developments and the challenges of serving the British Muslim community of over 1.8 million people. The operations of exclusively Islamic banks are examined, notably the Al Baraka International Bank during the 1980s and early 1990s and the Islamic Bank of Britain from 2004. The activities of conventional banks offering Islamic facilities are also analysed, the focus being on the United Bank of Kuwait and its successor the Al Ahli United Bank, and more recently HSBC through its Amanah Islamic finance subsidiary and Lloyds TSB.

SHARI'AH-COMPLIANT LIQUIDITY MANAGEMENT

Initially the major Islamic finance activity involved wholesale operations, with banks in London providing overnight deposit facilities for the newly established Islamic banks in the Gulf. These Islamic banks could not hold liquid assets such as treasury bills, which paid interest, but the joint venture Arab banks in London, such as Saudi International Bank and the United Bank of Kuwait, accepted deposits on a *murabaha* mark-up basis, with the associated short term trading transaction being conducted on the London Metal Exchange (Maroun 2002, 163–75).

Although the staffs of the joint venture banks were mainly British and non-Muslims, they became increasingly well informed about *Shari'ah* requirements regarding finance, and were able to respond to the demands of their Muslim clients in an imaginative manner. There was considerable interaction between British bankers involved with Gulf clients, *Shari'ah* scholars and the British Pakistani community, notably through the Institute of Islamic Banking and Insurance (IIBI), that had been established in 1976 by Muzzam Ali, a former journalist and head of the

Press Association of Pakistan (www.islamic-banking.com). Muzzam Ali worked closely with Prince Mohammed Bin Faisal of Saudi Arabia, a leading advocate of Islamic finance, and became Vice Chairman of Dar Al Maal Al Islami in Geneva, the international Islamic finance organisation established by Prince Mohammed in 1982. The IIBI was initially located in the Kings Cross area, near to the City of London where the Arab joint venture banks operated, and in 1990 moved to more prestigious premises in Grosvenor Crescent in the West End of London.

THE AL BARAKA INTERNATIONAL BANK

The next milestone in 1982 was when the Jeddah-based Al Baraka Investment Company bought Hargrave Securities, a licensed deposit taker, and converted it into an Islamic bank. This served the British Muslim community to a limited extent, but its main client base was Arab visitors of high net worth who spent the summer months in London. Its business expanded from 1987 when it opened a branch on the Whitechapel Road in London, followed by a further branch on the Edgeware Road in 1989, and a branch in Birmingham in 1991,[1] as by then the bank had between 11,000 and 12,000 clients (Al-Omar and Haq 1996, p. 45). It offered current accounts to its customers, the minimum deposit being £150, but a balance of £500 had to be maintained to use cheque facilities, a much higher requirement than that of other United Kingdom banks. These conventional banks usually allow current accounts to be overdrawn, although then clients are liable for interest charges, which Al Baraka, being an Islamic institution, did not levy.

Al Baraka also offered investment deposits on a *mudaraba* profit sharing basis for sums exceeding £5000, with 75 per cent of the annually declared rate of profit paid to those deposits subject to three months' notice, and 90 per cent paid for time deposits of over one year. Deposits rose from £23 million in 1983 to £154 million by 1991. Initially much of Al Baraka's assets consisted of cash and deposits with other banks, which were placed on an Islamic basis, as the institution did not have the staff or resources to adequately monitor client funding. Some funds were used to finance commodity trading through an affiliate company, as Al Baraka was not a specialist in this area.

Al Baraka's major initiative was in housing finance, as it started to provide long-term Islamic mortgages to its clients from 1988 onwards. Al Baraka and its clients would sign a contract to purchase the house or flat jointly, the ownership share being determined by the financial contribution of each of the parties. Al Baraka would expect a fixed predetermined profit for the period of the mortgage, the client making either monthly or quarterly repayments over a 10–20 year period, which covered the advance plus the profit share. There was some debate if the profit share could be calculated in relation to the market rental value of the property, but this was rejected, as frequent revaluation of the property would be expensive and administratively complicated, and given the fluctuating prices in the London property market, there would be considerable risk for the bank.

Although Al Baraka provided banking services in London, its most profitable area was investment management, and in many respects it functioned more like an investment company than a bank. It lacked the critical mass to achieve a competitive cost base in an industry dominated by large institutions, and the possibility of expanding through organic growth was limited. In these circumstances when the Bank of England tightened its regulatory requirements after the demise of BCCI the bank decided that it was not worth continuing to hold its banking licence, as it would have meant a costly restructuring of the ownership and a greater injection of shareholder capital. Consequently in June 1993 Al Baraka surrendered its banking licence and closed its branches, but continued operating as an investment company from Upper Brook Street in the West End of London (*Islamic Banker*, 1997, p. 2). Depositors received a full refund, and many simply transferred their money to the investment company. This offered greater flexibility, as it was no longer regulated under the 1987 Banking Act but under financial services and company legislation.

THE UNITED BANK OF KUWAIT

By the late 1980s there was an increasing demand from the United Bank of Kuwait's Gulf clients for Islamic trade based investment, and the decision was taken in 1991 to open a specialist Islamic Banking Unit within the bank. Employees with considerable experience of Islamic finance were recruited to manage the unit, which enjoyed considerable decision-making autonomy. In addition to being a separate unit, accounts were segregated from the main bank, with Islamic liabilities on the deposit side matched by Islamic assets, mainly trade financing instruments. The unit had its own *Shari'ah* advisors, and functioned like an Islamic bank, but was able to draw on the resources and expertise of the United Bank of Kuwait as required. In 1995 the renamed Islamic Investment Banking Unit (IIBU) moved to new premises in Baker Street, and introduced its own logo and brand image to stress its distinct Islamic identity (*New Horizon* 1996a, p. 24). Its staff of 16 in London included asset and leasing managers and portfolio traders and administrators, and by the late 1990s investment business was generated from throughout the Islamic World, including South East Asia, although the Gulf remained the major focus of interest (*New Horizon* 1996b, p. 17). Assets under management exceeded $750 million by the late 1990s, just prior to the merger with Al Ahli Bank, which resulted in the bank being renamed the Al Ahli United Bank (www.ubk-plc.com).

After Al Baraka pulled out of the Islamic housing market the United Bank of Kuwait entered the market in 1997, with its Manzil home owner-ship plan based on a *murabaha* instalment structure (www.iibu.com). A double stamp duty was incurred on *murabaha* transactions, firstly when the bank purchased the property on behalf of the client, and secondly when it resold the house to the client at a mark-up. This was felt by many in the Muslim community to be discriminatory, and following effective lobbying by the Muslim Council of Britain, and a report by a committee charged with investigating the issues, the double stamp duty was abol-ished in the 2003 budget, with the change taking effect from December of that year (Norton Rose 2005). The double stamp duty also applied to the *ijara* mortgages introduced under the Manzil plan in 1999 (Jarvis and Whitfield-Jones 2003).

THE ISLAMIC BANK OF BRITAIN

The development that has attracted the greatest interest in recent years has been the establishment of the Islamic Bank of Britain (www.islamic-bank.com). It had long been felt by many in Britain's Muslim commu-nity, especially since the withdrawal of Al Baraka from the retail Islamic banking market, that the United Kingdom should have its own exclusively Islamic Bank. A group of Gulf businessmen, with its core investors based in Bahrain but with extensive business interests in the United Kingdom, indicated that they were prepared to subscribe to the initial capital of £50 million. A business plan was formulated in 2002, and a formal applica-tion made to the Financial Services Authority (FSA) for the award of a banking licence (Hanlon 2005).

The FSA was well disposed towards the application; indeed its staff charged with regulating the London operations of banks from the Muslim World were knowledgeable about Islamic banking and believed that in a multicultural and multi-faith society such as that of Britain in the twenty-first century, Islamic banking was highly desirable to extend the choice of financial product available to the Muslim community (Khan 2005). There was no objection to the new bank being designated as Islamic, as this was not felt to be a sensitive issue in the UK, unlike in some countries where there are large Christian populations such as Nigeria, where the terms Muslim and Islamic cannot be used to designate banks. In Saudi Arabia, a wholly Muslim country, the term Islamic bank also cannot be used, as the major commercial banks and many *Shari'ah* scholars object to religion being used as a marketing tool.

The major concern of the FSA was that the new Islamic bank should be financially secure by being adequately capitalised, and that the management had the capability to adhere to the same reporting requirements as any other British bank. The emphasis was on robustness of the accounting and financial reporting systems, and in proper auditing procedures being put in place. Systems of corporate governance were also scrutinised, including the responsibilities of the *Shari'ah* advisory committee, and their role in relation to the management and the shareholders of the Islamic Bank of Britain. The FSA cannot of course provide assurance of *Shari'ah* compliance, as that is deemed to be a matter for the Islamic Bank of Britain and its *Shari'ah* committee. However the FSA wishes to satisfy itself that the products offered are clearly explained to the clients, and that full information on their characteristics is provided in the interest of consumer protection.

The Islamic Bank of Britain opened its first branch on the Edgware Road in London in September 2004, less than one month after regulatory approval was given. Its operational headquarters are in Birmingham, where costs are lower, and it has opened other branches in Birmingham, Leicester, Manchester, Southall, Whitechapel and East Ham. The size of the Muslim population in the immediate locality is one factor determining the choice of branch location, the socio-economic status of the potential clients being another factor, as middle class Muslims in professional occupations with regular monthly salaries are obviously more profitable to service than poorer groups. The bank stresses the Islamic values of faith and trust, as these are fundamental, but it also emphasises value and convenience, the aim being to have standards of service and pricing at least comparable with British conventional banks.

The opening of the first branch attracted much media attention, and therefore free publicity for the bank. The bank has a well designed website to attract business, offers 24-hour online and telephone services, and has produced informative and attractive leaflets and other publicity material outlining its services. All the material at present is in English rather than Urdu or Arabic, as the costs of translation and printing have to be seen in the context of promotional benefits. Some staff members are fluent in Urdu and Arabic, but at varying levels of proficiency, and foreign language ability is not a prerequisite for appointing staff, but good English is important. Many staff members have previous banking experience, and most, but not all, are Muslim.

The Islamic Bank of Britain offers current, savings and treasury accounts, all of which are *Shari'ah* compliant. No interest payments or receipts are made with current accounts, but a chequebook and a multi-functional bankcard is provided, these initially being simply cheque guarantee cards. Savings accounts operate on a *mudaraba* basis with £1 being the minimum balance. Profits on savings accounts are calculated monthly and have been held at around 3 per cent since October 2004 (the rate on fixed term deposits of 12 months at September 2009 was 2.8 per cent). No notice is required for withdrawals from basic savings accounts, which in other words can be designated as instant access accounts. Term deposit savings accounts, which are subject to a minimum deposit of £5000, pay higher rates. In March 2005 deposits for one, three or six months earned 3.5 per cent, 3.75 per cent and 4 per cent respectively. Unique amongst Islamic banks, the Islamic Bank of Britain offers treasury deposits, with a minimum £100,000 for 1, 3 or 6 months being invested. These operate on a *murabaha* basis, with funds invested on the London Metal Exchange. This type of account in other words replicates for the retail market the type of wholesale or inter-bank deposit facilities first operated on a *Shari'ah*-compliant basis in London in the early 1980s.

The Islamic Bank of Britain offers personal finance, with amounts ranging from £1000 to £20,000 made available for 12 to 36 months. This operates through *tawarruq* with the bank buying *Shari'ah*-compliant commodities that are sold to the client on a cost plus profit basis. The client's agent, who is conveniently recommended by the bank, in turn buys the commodities and the proceeds are credited to the client's account. The client then repays the bank through deferred payments. Home purchase plans are now available, which are halal alternatives to mortgages.

ISLAMIC HOME FINANCE AND CURRENT ACCOUNTS OFFERED BY CONVENTIONAL BANKS

It is a challenge for a new entrant such as the Islamic Bank of Britain to compete in a mature market for banking services with the major conventional banks offering Islamic products, notably HSBC through its dedicated Amanah Islamic finance division (Khan 2005) and Lloyds TSB, which has entered the market through Cheltenham and Gloucester, the former building society that it bought to create a focused mortgage and retail savings subsidiary.

It was the abolition of double stamp duty, as already discussed, that encouraged new entrants into the market for Islamic home finance, notably HSBC Amanah in 2004 and Lloyds TSB from March 2005 (IFIS 2005). At the same time the Al-Ahli United Bank, the successor of the United Bank of Kuwait, reached agreement with the West Bromwich Building Society for the distribution of Islamic mortgages through its extensive branch network. A similar agreement was concluded between the London based Islamic finance subsidiary of Arab Banking Corporation, Alburaq, and the Bank of Ireland, for the distribution of Islamic mortgages through its English subsidiary, the Bristol and West Building Society (Smith 2004, p. 12)

There are a number of different structures for Islamic home finance in the United Kingdom, the original Al Baraka and the United Bank of Kuwait Manzil scheme being *murabaha*-based with fixed monthly repayments to cover the cost of the house purchase that the bank undertook, plus the mark-up profit margin. In 1999 a second Manzil scheme was introduced based on *ijara*, with the United Bank of Kuwait, and its successor the Al Ahli United Bank, purchasing the property, but with the client paying a monthly rent, as well as a monthly repayment. The rent varied, but rather than being calculated on the rental value of the property, which would have implied frequent expensive revaluations, the rent was simply benchmarked to LIBOR, the London Inter-Bank Offer Rate. As this was an interest-based rate, this was potentially controversial from an Islamic perspective, but the Bank's *Shari'ah* board approved its use as a benchmark, as LIBOR is often used in Islamic finance calculations because of its widespread acceptance in the banking community. The HSBC Amanah monthly home finance payments are also calculated in this way, as are those of the ABC Alburaq home financing facility marketed through the Bristol and West, although the later is designated as a diminishing *musharaka* scheme, as over the life of the mortgage, the client's ownership share increases as repayments are made, and the share of the bank in the equity of the house correspondingly reduces.

One factor that appears to be limiting the uptake of Islamic home finance is that the cost is higher than conventional mortgages. For Islamic financing worth £135,000 from Lloyds TSB over a period of 25 years the monthly repayments were £883 plus £21 a month for buildings insurance in March 2005. This comprised a rental payment of £693 plus a capital repayment of £190. The total monthly payment was over £100 per month more than the cost of a Lloyds TSB conventional mortgage (Cumbo 2005, p. 26). With HSBC Amanah for the same loan of £135,000 over 25 years the monthly repayments were £857, only £7 per month more than the bank's conventional mortgage, but the buildings insurance of £34 per month was obligatory with the Islamic financing as the property itself is owned by the bank, unlike with a conventional mortgage where the bank simply has a charge on the property so that it can be repossessed in the case of payments default.

A survey of 503 Muslims in ten cities throughout England undertaken by Dr Humayon Dar of Loughborough University showed that many respondents had little knowledge of *Shari'ah* compliant finance, but those who had enquired about Islamic home finance were deterred from proceeding by the higher costs (New Millennium Publishing 2004). These, however, partly reflect the limited scale of the market, and hence the higher costs per mortgage approved, as well as the costs involved in *Shari'ah* compliance, not least paying the fees and expenses of members of the *Shari'ah* committee. Of course the cost of a mortgage is not the only factor determining the level of business, as those Muslims who have signed contracts for Islamic finance have been prepared to pay a premium for *Shari'ah* compliance. Rather the issue seems to be the size of the premium, which greater competition in the market should reduce.

A further factor inhibiting the uptake of Islamic home finance is that a significant proportion of the Muslim population in the UK is in a low socio-economic position and cannot afford to buy property. This applies in areas such as East London where many of those in the Bangladeshi community are quite poor, but property prices are relatively high. One solution might be co-ownership through Islamic housing associations, with the tenant, association and bank all owning a share in the property, but at present these do not exist in the UK.

Both HSBC Amanah and Lloyds TSB offer Islamic current accounts, these being linked to the Islamic home finance being offered, as clients make their repayments through these accounts. Neither HSBC Amanah nor Lloyds TSB pay or charge interest on these accounts, but the accounts offer normal transactions facilities such as cheque books, standing orders and direct debit facilities, monthly statements and multifunctional cards that serve as cheque guarantee and debit cards. With HSBC Amanah a minimum balance of £1000 is required to maintain the account, but with Lloyds TSB there is no minimum. At present savings and investment accounts based on *mudaraba* are not offered by either bank in the UK, as the liabilities to match the Islamic mortgage assets are generated elsewhere, notably in the case of HSBC Amanah through *Shari'ah*-compliant deposits in the Gulf.

FUTURE PROSPECTS FOR ISLAMIC FINANCE IN THE UNITED KINGDOM

Although the UK has the most active and developed Islamic banking sector in the European Union, most activity until recently has been related to the role of the city of London as an international financial centre, rather than serving the retail banking needs of British Muslims. This is however likely to change in the years ahead, especially if other major UK based mortgage banks, notably Halifax Bank of Scotland (HBOS) and Royal Bank of Scotland (RBS, which owns NatWest) enter the market for Islamic mortgages. UNB Bank launched an Islamic mortgage product in 2004 aimed at the Scottish market, with the international law firm, Norton Rose, providing advice on *Shari'ah* issues, and the mortgages being based on the diminishing *musharaka* principle (IFIS 2004). HBOS and RBS have already sent representatives to several Islamic finance conferences in London, and it seems likely that the UNB Islamic mortgage aimed at the Scottish market, even though UNB is a minor player, may encourage the larger Edinburgh-based institutions such as Standard Life to bring forward their launch plans for Islamic financial products.

HSBC Amanah launched an Islamic pension fund in May 2004, where the assets held in the fund are screened for *Shari'ah* compliance, shares of companies involved in alcohol production and distribution, pork products and conventional banking being excluded, including ironically HSBC shares (Wilson 2004). The pension fund is marketed to individuals and small Muslim family businesses. This may be a more promising way forward in the UK market than Islamic mutual funds, where there has been a history of failure, from the Kleinwort Benson Islamic unit trust of the 1980s to Flemings Oasis Fund and the Halal Mutual Fund of the 1990s, all of which failed to attract sufficient investors to ensure sustainability (Wilson 2000).

The UK government is determined to create a level playing field for *Shari'ah*-compliant products. In the 2005 budget statement the same treatment was extended for *ijara* leasing mortgages and diminishing *musharaka* co-ownership mortgages as had already been applied to *murabaha* mortgages in the 2003 budget, with only a single stamp duty levy applying. The then Chancellor of the Exchequer, Gordon Brown, announced at the Muslim News Awards for Excellence in March 2005 that a consultation paper would be issued concerning equal treatment for Muslim council tenants under the 'right to buy scheme', that at present is restricted to interest-based mortgages (Parker 2005). All this bodes well for the future, as a non-discriminatory system of taxation and regulation will encourage more competition in the market for Islamic financial services, reduce prices and margins, and make Islamic products more affordable. There is much that other European Union member states can learn from the quarter of century of experience in the UK, and even if some of the lessons are cautionary, many in the Muslim community now believe that British Islamic finance is really taking off.

NOTE

1. Al Baraka satisfied the ownership and control requirements of the October 1987 Banking Act. See Bank of England (1987).

REFERENCES

Al-Omar, Fuad and Mohammed Abdel Haq (1996), *Islamic Banking: Theory, Practices and Challenges*, London: Zed Books.

Bank of England (1987), *Quarterly Bulletin*, November, 525–6.

Cumbo, J. (2005), 'Lloyds' Islamic mortgage increases buyer's choices', *Financial Times*, (Money section), London, 26 March.

Hanlon, M. (CEO Islamic Bank of Britain) (2005), 'Case study: Islamic Bank of Britain', *Euromoney 4th Annual Islamic Finance Summit*, London, 22 and 23 February.

Islamic Banker (1997), 'Why London needs an Islamic Bank', Editorial, *Islamic Banker*, London, February.

Islamic Finance Information Service (IFIS) (2004), 'Norton Rose acts on the first ever Scottish Islamic mortgage', *ISI Emerging Markets*, London, 25 November.

Islamic Finance Information Service (IFIS) (2005), 'Lloyds TSB moves into Islamic home finance', *ISI Emerging Markets*, London, 22 March.

Jarvis, S. and C. Whitfield-Jones (Jeffrey Green Russel law firm) (2003), 'Islamic home purchase finance', *Council of Mortgage Lenders Islamic Home Finance Seminar*, London, 27 March.

Khan, I. (CEO HSBC Amanah) (2005), 'Revisiting the value proposition of Islamic finance', *Euromoney 4th Annual Islamic Finance Summit*, London, 22 and 23 February.

Maroun, Youssef Shaheed (2002), 'Liquidity management and trade financing', in Simon Archer and Rifaat Abdel Karim (eds), *Islamic Finance: Innovation and Growth*, London: Euromoney Books, pp. 163–175.

New Horizon (1996a), London, December 1995/January 1966, IIBU.

New Horizon (1996b), London, July, IIBU.

New Millennium Publishing (2004), 'Demand for Islamic finance in the UK is overvalued', *Islamic Banking and Finance Magazine*, London, 24 December.

Norton Rose law firm (2005), 'Commentaries on the Finance Act of 2003 and Budget of 2005', London.

Parker, M. (2005), 'Brown offers a level playing field for Shariah compliant products', *Arab News*, Jeddah, 28 March.

Smith, D. (2004), 'Islamic banking in the UK – 2004 review', *Islamic Finance News*, Bahrain, 20 December.

Wilson, R. (2000), 'Challenges and opportunities for Islamic Banking in the west: the United Kingdom experience', *Islamic Economic Studies*, **7** (1/2), October 1999 and April 2000, 35–59.

Wilson, R. (2004), 'Screening criteria for Islamic equity funds', in Sohail Jaffer (ed.), *Islamic Asset Management: Forming the Future for Sharia Compliant Investment Strategies*, London: Euromoney Books, pp. 35–45.

16. The *riba* prohibition and payment institutions

Vittorio Santoro

The legal framework would not be exhaustive without considering the up-to-date Directive 2007/64 EC (OJEC of the 5.12.2007, L 319/1), which will be amending national banking laws not later than November 2009. Some European countries have already implemented it (for example, the United Kingdom and France), while some others, like Italy, are still at the preliminary stages.

The Directive has provided for the 'payment institution' (PI),[1] a new financial intermediary authorised to perform, as well as credit institutions and post offices, payment services throughout the European Community (Mancini and Perassi 2008). We wish to offer some comments on payment institutions discipline and the *riba* prohibition in order to assess the kind of legal obstacles Islamic intermediaries can meet.

THE PREMISE OF THE EUROPEAN DIRECTIVE 2007/64 EC

The Directive results from a public debate between European institutions, the Member States regulators and the banking associations, which has seen the launch of the Single European Payment Area (or SEPA). Such a project will attempt to create an area within Europe in which companies, citizens and other economic players can receive and make national and trans-border transfers of funds in euros under the same legal and economic conditions, regardless of their location (EPC 2007).[2]

Furthermore, the same project will deal with competition issues: the European Commission revealed a stand-still oligopolistic banking position on the European market of payment systems which makes the adoption of a single currency less efficient.[3]

Indeed, as the anti-trust analysis has stressed, both technical and legal obstacles prevent non-banking payment providers from having access to the relevant market. For this reason, while the European Payment

Council worked out uniform payment messages to be applied to every (national and trans-border) transaction performed through credit cards, direct debit and credit transfer, Directive 2007/64 EC laid down a series of disclosure duties on the providers and set out a single European licence which will submit all payment providers, other than banks and post offices, to a single prudential regime according to the home country control principle.[4]

The payment institutions are financial entities authorised to provide payment services through credit and pre-paid cards, credit transfer and direct debt (Annex of Directive 2007/64) and to run payment systems (art. 16, let. (b)).[5]

In addition, the payment institutions, like banks, will perform the monetary and credit functions: under a framework contract[6] they are permitted both to grant credit for a limited period of time (no more than twelve months) and to perform 'all the operations required for the operating of a payment account'.[7] The rules on current accounts imply that payment institutions' customers can pay in cash and withdraw the money on demand from the payment accounts as well as being allowed to send and receive funds through current accounts by the means of payment mentioned in the Appendix[8] (Santoro 2008). Are they also entitled to pay interest rates on the funds received and earn interest rates on the funds granted? In case of an affirmative reply, the *riba* prohibition would place obstacles in the way of the authorisation of Islamic legal persons. The research below provides an insight into both EC Directive 2007/64 and the Italian legislation in force.

THE INTEREST AND PI

Under the European legal framework, giving the right answer is not at all an easy task. As for passive transactions, the payment institutions' activities resemble the business of traditional banks of receiving deposits or other reimbursable funds from the public. If it were completely true, the payment institutions should pay interest on the cash received.

The Directive is unclear as to the choice to make. However, it can be inferred from the Directive that the payment institutions do not acquire the title to use the funds which still belong to the customer who has presented, received and paid them in to the account. This conclusion can be drawn from the provision under article 16, paragraph 2:

> When payment institutions engage in the provision of one or more of the payment services listed in the Annex, they may hold only payment accounts

used exclusively for payment transactions. Any funds received by payment institutions from payment services users with a view to a provision of payment services shall not constitute deposit or other repayable funds within the meaning of Article 5 of Directive 2006/48/EC, or electronic money within the meaning of Article 1(3) of Directive 2000/46/EC.

The adverb 'exclusively'[9] in the above mentioned paragraph (third line) makes the difference between the traditional bank and the payment institution: the latter will store the funds in order to perform the next future payment orders through the payment account, as well as any possible withdrawal transactions from the payment accounts. This conclusion is confirmed reading article 16, paragraph 3, let. (c) which will forbid the payment institutions from using the funds stored when they grant credit to the same or other customer.[10]

The fact is that, if the payment institutions, unlike the banks, are not entitled to use the funds stored, it sounds reasonable to assume that they will not be obliged to pay any interest to the account holders. The European Central Bank expressed the same opinion at the preliminary stage of Directive 2007/64 EC: 'It must also be ensured that payment institutions may not pay interest or provide other incentives to the account holder' (ECB 2006, § 12.5).

Regarding active transactions, the payment institutions will be authorised to grant credit. However, this kind of activity will be ancillary to the provision of payment services according to the Directive's Appendix (credit card, credit transfer, direct debit). This conclusion is confirmed by the same Directive where it provides that '(a) the credit shall be ancillary and granted exclusively in connection with the execution of a payment transaction; (b) notwithstanding national rules on providing credit by credit cards, the credit granted in connection with a payment and executed in accordance with Article 10(9) and Article 25 shall be repaid in no case exceeding twelve months' (article 16, paragraph 3).[11]

As a consequence, in the event the payment could or would no longer be performed, the payment institutions would cease to be bound by the duty to grant any financing. Moreover, the fact that the account holder has to pay back the credit within twelve months is not consistent with the *modus operandi* typical of banks, that is to say granting credit for an indefinite period of time. As a result of the considerations above, we should assume that the credit granted is a form of 'courtesy' towards the clients, for example when there is a lengthy contractual relationship.

THE ITALIAN CASE

Directive 2007/64 EC refrains from making a precise choice on both issues, giving space to national regulators. Turning to the Italian legal framework, the Directive has not been implemented yet.

We can assume that the payment institutions are in charge of providing a series of services (payment services) and, in order to fulfil its own task, a sum of money is placed on the payment account or is delivered to the payment account. Under the Italian Civil Code, the payment services contract might be considered as a contract of *mandato* in which the account holder will play the role of the *mandante*, while the payment institution will be considered as the *mandatario* who is a natural or a legal person entitled to perform one or more juridical acts (for example, arrangements or contracts) in his own name but in the interest of someone else, the so called *mandante*.

Under the Italian discipline of *mandato*, no interest is to be paid on the funds delivered to the *mandatario* for executing the order received. Some problems might arise under article 1714 of the Italian Civil Code which will compel the *mandatario* to pay an interest rate on the sum of money received in the following situations: (a) he did not obey the *mandante*'s instructions; (b) he did not deliver the sum of money to the *mandante* or from the *mandante* to a third party. Instead, it would be different if, following the rule provided by article 1714 of the Italian Civil Code, payment institutions were required to pay legal interest for the money received for the benefit of the user or otherwise provided by the user, whenever these sums of money are not given back within a reasonable length of time. Such an approach should deter payment institutions from paying back money to their customers. The intermediaries are allowed to store the money only for the time necessary to perform the transactions. In such circumstances, the payment of interest would be in direct conflict with *riba* prohibition.

However, the nature of Islamic intermediaries should prevent payment institutions from taking any speculative initiative while the supervisory authorities could address sanctions of a different nature, for example administrative sanctions, to deter this kind of conduct.

NOTES

1. Article 4, number 5), Directive 2007/64 EC stated: 'A payment institution means a legal person that has been granted authorisation in accordance with Article 10 to provide and execute payment services throughout the Community'.
2. Indeed EC Directive 2007/64 provided for a comprehensive discipline on information duties (Title III) as well as on the rights and obligations of providers and consumers of

the payment service contracts (Title IV). The same rules will be enforced also when the payment service contracts are made between providers and customers different from consumers but, in that case, they can agree not to apply some of them (precisely, most of the rules under Title IV).

3. According to the European Commission reports and decisions, the (geographic and product) market still keeps a national dimension. In fact, the range of cross-border, interoperable payment standards is still narrow, making the prices of cross-border payments much higher than the same domestic payment.

4. The payment institutions' regime is carved from the banking framework, although the prudential rules provided for payment institutions are less cumbersome because they are engaged in a more limited number of activities and, as a consequence, will generate a narrower range of risks.

5. 'Payment system means a fund transfer system with formal and standardised arrangements and common rules for the processing, clearing and/or settlement of payment transactions' (art. 4, n. 6, Directive 2007/64).

6. Art. 4, n. 12 defined a 'framework contract' as 'a payment service contract which governs the future execution of individual and successive payment transactions and which may contain the obligation and conditions for setting up a payment account'.

7. Article 4, n. 14 stated that a 'payment account' is 'an account held in the name of one or more payment service users which is used for the execution of payment transactions'.

8. The payment institutions are also entitled to perform business activities different from the provision of payment services (for example, mobile phone communications) according to the European and the national laws enforceable (article 16, let. (c) Directive 2007/64 EC).

9. The adverb 'exclusively' will limit the business of payment institutions to the operation listed in the Annex and, therefore, will be opting out of a traditional, even though obsolete, means of payment, the paper cheque. Furthermore, the Directive will not applied to payment transactions made in cash 'since a single payment market for cash already exists' (Directive 2007/64 EC, Preamble (19)).

10. 'Payment institutions may grant credit related to payment services referred to in points 4, 5 or 7 of the Annex only if the following conditions are met: '(c) such credit shall not be granted from the funds received or held for the purpose of executing a payment transaction' (article 16.3, let. (c), Directive 2007/64 EC).

11. Article 10(9) and article 25 of Directive 2007/64 EC refer to payment institutions authorised to provide payment services throughout the European Union.

REFERENCES

European Central Bank (2006), *Opinion of the European Central Bank of 26 April 2006*, OJEC of the 9 May 2006, C/109.

Mancini, M. and Perassi, M. (eds) (2008), *Il nuovo quadro normativo comunitario dei servizi di pagamento. Prime riflessioni*, Roma: Quaderni di ricerca giuridica della consulenza legale della Banca d'Italia, n. 63.

Santoro, V. (2008), 'I conti di pagamento degli istituti di pagamento', in *Scritti in onore di Marco Comporti*, Milan: Giuffrè, pp. 2411–31.

Glossary

Ijara – Bank purchases asset and leases it to customer

Ijara Muntahia Bittamleek (IMB) – Lessee has option to purchase asset

Istisna' – Agreement to sell to a customer a non-existent asset (to be manufactured and delivered at a later date)

Mudaraba – Agreement by the bank to contribute capital to a third party to be managed by a customer as labour provider (*mudarib*). Losses borne by bank. Profit shared by the bank with the *mudarib* according to pre-agreed ratio

Murabaha – Bank agrees to sell to customer on marked-up price an asset already in bank's possession

Murabaha for the Purchase Orderer (MPO) – Bank agrees to sell to customer on marked-up price an asset already acquired by the bank from the customer

Musharaka – Bank agrees to contribute capital to an enterprise on a profit- and loss-sharing basis

Riba – Usury (also includes contemporary term 'interest')

Salam – Bank agrees to purchase at a predetermined price a specified commodity to be delivered on a specified future date in a specified quantity and quality

Shari'ah – Islamic law

Sukuk – Certificates representing holders' share in an underlying asset

Parallel Istisna' and *Parallel Salam* – Separate agreements with third parties for delivery of asset/commodity corresponding to asset/commodity specified in first contract

Index